Design for a Sustainable Culture

As culture is becoming increasingly recognised as a crucial element of sustainable development, design competence has emerged as a useful tool in creating a meaningful life within a sustainable mental, cultural and physical environment.

Design for a Sustainable Culture explores the relationship between sustainability, culture and the shaping of human surroundings by examining the significance and potential of design as a tool for the creation of sustainable development. Drawing on interdisciplinary case studies and investigations from Europe, North America and India, this book discusses theoretical, methodological and educational aspects of the role of design in relation to human well-being and provides a unique perspective on the interface between design, culture and sustainability.

This book will appeal to researchers as well as postgraduate and undergraduate students in design and design literacy, crafts, architecture and environmental planning, but also scholars of sustainability from other disciplines who wish to understand the role and impact of design and culture in sustainable development.

Astrid Skjerven is Professor in design theory at The Department of Product Design, Faculty of Technology, Art and Design, Oslo and Akershus University College of Applied Sciences, Norway.

Janne Beate Reitan is Associate Professor in art and design education at The Department of Art, Design and Drama, Faculty of Technology, Art and Design, Oslo and Akershus University College of Applied Sciences, Norway.

Routledge Studies in Culture and Sustainable Development

Series Editors:
Katriina Soini
University of Jyväskylä, Finland, and Natural Resources Institute Finland
Joost Dessein
Institute for Agricultural and Fisheries Research (ILVO) and Ghent University, Belgium

Culture as an aspect of sustainability is a relatively new phenomenon but is beginning to attract attention among scholars and policy makers. This series opens up a forum for debate about the role of culture in sustainable development, treating culture and sustainability as a meta-narrative that will bring together diverse disciplines. Key questions explored in this series will include: how should culture be applied in sustainability policies; what should be sustained in culture; what should culture sustain; and what is the relationship of culture to other dimensions of sustainability?

Books in the series will have a variety of geographical foci and reflect different disciplinary approaches (for example, geography, sociology, sustainability science, environmental and political sciences, anthropology, history, archaeology and planning). The series will be addressed in particular to postgraduate students and researchers from a wide cross-section of disciplines.

Design for a Sustainable Culture

Perspectives, Practices and Education

Edited by Astrid Skjerven and Janne Beate Reitan

LONDON AND NEW YORK

First published 2017
by Routledge

2 Park Square, Milton Park, Abingdon, Oxfordshire OX14 4RN
52 Vanderbilt Avenue, New York, NY 10017

Routledge is an imprint of the Taylor & Francis Group, an informa business

First issued in paperback 2018

British Library Cataloguing in Publication Data
A catalogue record for this book is available from the British Library

Library of Congress Cataloging in Publication Data
Names: Skjerven, Astrid, 1953– editor. | Reitan, Janne Beate,
1956– editor.
Title: Design for a sustainable culture : perspectives, practices and
education / [edited by Astrid Skjerven, Janne Beate Reitan].
Description: Abingdon, Oxon ; New York, NY : Routledge, [2017] |
Series: Routledge studies in culture and sustainable development |
Includes bibliographical references.
Identifiers: LCCN 2016056785 | ISBN 9780415365758 (hbk) |
ISBN 9781315229065 (ebk)
Subjects: LCSH: Sustainable design. | Sustainable development–Social
aspects. | Material culture.
Classification: LCC NK1520 .D4653 2017 | DDC 306.4/6–dc23
LC record available at https://lccn.loc.gov/2016056785

ISBN: 978-1-138-71490-8 (hbk)
ISBN: 978-0-367-17256-5 (pbk)

Typeset in Bembo
by Wearset Ltd, Boldon, Tyne and Wear

Contents

Series introduction

Finding pathways to ecological, social and economic sustainability is the biggest global challenge of the twenty-first century and new approaches are urgently needed. Scholars and policy makers have recognised the contribution of culture in sustainability work. 'Cultural sustainability' is also being increasingly discussed in debates in various international, national and local arenas, and there are ample local actors driven initiatives. Yet, despite the growing attention, there have been only a very few attempts to consider culture in a more analytical and explicit way in scientific and political discourses of sustainability, probably as a consequence of the complex, normative and multidisciplinary character of both culture and sustainability. This difficulty should not, however, be any excuse for ignoring the cultural aspects in sustainability.

The essence of culture in, for and as sustainability is being explored trough the series in various thematic contexts, representing a wide range of practices and processes (e.g. everyday life, livelihoods and lifestyles, landscape, artistic practices, aesthetic experiences, heritage, tourism). These contexts concern urban, peri-urban or rural contexts, and regions with different socio-economic trajectories. The perspectives of the books will stretch from local to global and cover different temporal scales from past to present and future. These issues are valorised by theoretical or empirical analysis; their relationship to the ecological, social and economic dimensions of sustainability will be explored, when appropriate.

The series 'Routledge Studies in Culture and Sustainable Development' aims to analyse the diverse and multiple roles that culture plays in sustainability. It takes as one of its starting points the idea that culture serves as a 'meta-narrative' which will bring together ideas and standpoints from an extensive body of sustainability research currently scattered among different disciplines and thematic fields. Moreover, the series responds to the strengthening call for inter- and transdisciplinary approaches which is being heard in many quarters, but in few fields more strongly than that of sustainability, with its complex and systemic problems. By combining and confronting the various approaches, in both the sciences and the humanities and in dealing with social, cultural, environmental, political and aesthetic disciplines, the series offers a comprehensive contribution to the present-day sustainability sciences as well as related policies.

The books in the series take a broad approach to culture, giving space to all the possible understandings and forms of culture. Furthermore culture is not only seen as an additional aspect of sustainability – as a 'fourth pillar' – but rather as a mediator, a cross-cutting transversal framework or even as new set of guiding principles for sustainability research, policies and practices.

The idea for the series was derived from the European COST Action IS1007 'Investigating Cultural Sustainability', running between 2011 and 2015. This network was comprised of a group of around a hundred researchers from 26 European countries, and representing many different disciplines. They brought together their expertise, knowledge and experience, and based on that they built up new inter- and transdisciplinary understanding and approaches that can enhance and enrich research into culture in sustainable development, and support the work of the practitioners in education, policy and beyond.

Design brings together human beings and nature, material and meaning, production and consumption, and therefore it is essential in and for sustainability. We unconsciously and consciously design our environment, and the environment, in turn, shapes us, who we are and who we become. Sustainable design has been discussed for decades from different perspectives and at different scales, from single objects to cities and landscapes. This book adds a cultural perspective to these discussions and challenges us to become more aware of various roles of design in sustainability. It also brings forth different types of agency in sustainable design – such as design literacy, capacity to read and interpret and give meanings to our environment. The lesson learnt is that design is not something we should take as given, but something that we should take part in as active citizens.

Katriina Soini and Joost Dessein

Contributors

Astrid Skjerven is Professor in design theory at The Department of Product Design, Oslo and Akershus University College of Applied Sciences, Norway. She has a doctorate in art history from the University of Oslo. Her special fields of interest are the phenomenon of Scandinavian design seen in a global context, the impact of design on daily life and cultural sustainability. She was member of the EU COST Action IS 1007 Investigating Cultural Sustainability 2012–2015, and is a board member of the International Society on Sustainable Development Research (ISDRS). She has published articles in international scientific journals, and is co-editor of two special issues on design in the journal *Sustainable Development*. She is a member of the advisory board of the journal *FORMakademisk*.

Janne Beate Reitan is Associate Professor in art and design education at The Department of Art, Design and Drama, Faculty of Technology, Art and Design, Oslo and Akershus University College of Applied Sciences, Norway. She has a doctorate in art and design education from The Oslo School of Architecture and Design. Her special field of interest is the phenomenon of vernacular design and practical knowledge and she has published articles in books and international scientific journals. She is the founder and Editor-in-Chief of the scientific journal *FORMakademisk*.

Ezio Manzini is Honorary Professor at the Politecnico di Milano and Guest Professor at Tongji University, Shanghai. For more than two decades he has been working on design for sustainability and, most recently, on design for social innovation, and he started DESIS, the International Network on Design for Social Innovation. He has explored design potentialities in different fields, such as: design of materials, in the 1980s; strategic design, in the 1990s; and service design in the last ten years. His most recent book is *Design, When Everybody Designs: An Introduction to Design for Social Innovation* (2015).

Mugendi K. M'Rithaa is an industrial designer, educator and researcher at the Cape Peninsula University of Technology. He holds postgraduate qualifications in industrial design and higher education, as well as a doctorate in universal design. His most recent book is *Universal Design in Majority World Contexts: Sport Mega-Events as Catalysts for Social Change.*

Peter Jones has a PhD is in design and innovation management from the Union Institute's Interdisciplinary Studies programme. He is Associate Professor at Toronto's OCAD University, Canada, and is a founding faculty for two advanced MDes programmes: Strategic Foresight and Innovation and Design for Health. He leads the innovation research firm Redesign Network. He co-founded the Systemic Design Research Network and its annual Relating Systems Thinking and Design (RSD) symposium. He is author of three books, including *Design for Care: Innovating Healthcare Experience.*

Jorge Andres Caro del Castillo has an MA in product design. He is Assistant Professor at Universidad LaSalle, Mexico, and a researcher at the School of Engineering at the same institution. His principal work focuses on culture and heritage for achieving ethical design.

Petter Næss is Dr. Ing., architect and Professor in planning in urban regions at the Norwegian University of Life Sciences. He has contributed theoretically on urban sustainability, philosophy of science within the field of spatial planning, and methodology within infrastructure planning. He has published extensively on urban sustainability issues covering a wide, interdisciplinary perspective, including sustainability-relevant impacts of land use and the built environment as well as societal conditions and processes influencing urban development. A special interest field is the relationship between urban structures and transport.

Arild Berg has an MA in ceramic art and is Doctor of Art in artistic research in public space. He is Associate Professor at Oslo and Akershus University College of Applied Sciences, Norway. He is a member of the research groups Design, Culture and Sustainability, Art in Society and the Collaborative Action Research Network (CARN). His principal work focuses on how professional practitioners in art and design can do process-oriented research projects with participatory methods and qualitative approaches. The aim is to identify how new, cross-disciplinary fields of studies in art and design can contribute to innovation.

Johannes Ludwig Zachrisson Daae has an MA in human–product interaction design and a PhD in design for sustainable behaviour. He is Associate Professor at Oslo and Akershus University College of Applied Sciences, Norway. His principal work focuses on how user behaviour is affected by the way products and systems are designed and how this may be applied to reduce the environmental impact from product usage. He also works as Eco Designer for Bergfald Environmental Consultants.

Tore Gulden is Professor in industrial design at Oslo and Akershus University College of Applied Sciences, Norway. He has an MA in industrial design from the Design Academy Eindhoven, The Netherlands. His research work is primarily in the areas of game dynamics in design, concept development, emotional design, sustainable design and product longevity and their interrelation. He has been a design consultant since 1992 and has received design awards. In 2005 he became a co-founder of 2025design, whose business areas lies within environmental management, sustainable product design and strategy development.

Veronika Glitsch is a PhD candidate in culture studies at the University College of Southeast Norway. Since 2005 she has created collections under her clothing brand 'Rethink'. She specializes in redesign and up-cycling in addition to working with organic materials. She has immersed herself in pattern construction and fit to different body types. In addition to being a certified dressmaker, she has completed 11 years of higher education in fashion design and textiles. She teaches at the University College of Southeast Norway in the subject of design, redesign and tailoring.

Ingvill Gjerdrum Maus is a PhD candidate in the design literacy research team at the Department of Art, Design and Drama, Oslo and Akershus University College of Applied Sciences, Norway. She is PhD student at the PhD programme in Educational Sciences for Teacher Education, Faculty of Education and International Studies at the same institution and at the Norwegian National Research School in Teacher Education (NAFOL). Her principal work focuses on education in design for sustainability for children and youth.

Eva Lutnæs, MA and PhD in art and design education, is a senior research fellow in the design literacy research group at Oslo and Akershus University College of Applied Sciences, Norway. She is a teacher at Ener lower secondary school (Norway). Currently, her main research interests are the intersection of eco-literacy, design literacy and critical literacy, and the continuation of research to advance the assessment repertoire of teachers in art and design.

Ragnhild Tronstad has an MA in theatre studies and a PhD in media studies from the University of Oslo and is a senior advisor and researcher at the Faculty of Technology, Art and Design, Oslo and Akershus University College of Applied Sciences, Norway. She has worked as a senior researcher at the Oslo School of Architecture and Design on the research project *YOUrban: Social Media and Performativity in Urban Environments*, leading the sub-project *PLAYUR*. Her recent work focuses on the aesthetic aspects of play and gaming, and on the mediation of presence in performative and interactive arts.

Sabrina Brenner is a Dipl.-Ing. in architecture and a doctoral candidate at the University of Stuttgart where she completed the International Doctoral College 'Spatial Research Lab', curriculum 2013–2016 'Transformation of

Cities and Landscapes'. She was a researcher and lecturer at the Institute for the Foundations of Planning from 2013 to 2016 and a guest researcher at the International Centre for Aceh and Indian Ocean Studies (ICAIOS) in Indonesia. Her principal work focuses on settlement planning, precautionary adaptation to natural hazards, reconstruction and planning processes in developing countries.

Foreword

Mankind distinguishes itself from the rest of nature by the material artefacts it creates and produces in ever growing volumes. For many centuries materials and structures surrounding human settlements were 'by nature' determinants for how such structures, objects and artefacts have been designed created. This has resulted in an extremely rich cultural diversity, which increasingly has been recognised as highly valuable. In many countries now for a few decades governments have started to preserve this cultural wealth to ensure it will be available for future generations.

In the same way it has been widely recognised that in the design of new objects (of any scale, form or function) we freeze our environmental impacts for as long as the objects are being used, and if these objects are to be replaced (too soon), we add additional impacts. Design for Sustainability and Design for Circularity has been our responses to this. The focus is strongly on eco-efficiency and, more recently, also on the social dimension of sustainability. This is good and we can see a strongly growing application of such design practices.

But this is not good enough! This book highlights a very important challenge that is often overlooked. The best designs would be designs which we still want to maintain and hand over to the next generations, like we did for centuries and now do with our cultural heritage. Our challenge is to design new sustainable objects that strengthen our diverse cultural identities and that can reinforce sustainable attitudes.

One might oppose that this would be too expensive, not affordable for the mass markets. Such reasoning would be penny-wise pound-foolish. Let us look to inspiring examples. During my travels in Bhutan, one of the poorest countries, I witnessed how, even in their context, they are able to integrate their cultural heritage into sustainability policies and practices. All new building is still built in their traditional Buddhist style, as part of their Middle Path strategy, aiming for Gross National Happiness, rather than Gross National Product.

This new book on Design for Sustainable Culture comes at the right time. It's diverse content, showing the history, the approaches available and how a culture-inclusive design practices can be disseminated, will be useful and inspiring for many different audiences. As the International Sustainable Development Research Society we highly recommend it.

Prof. Dr. Walter J.V. Vermeulen
Utrecht University/Stellenbosch University
President of the International Sustainable Development Research Society

1 Introduction

Astrid Skjerven and Janne Beate Reitan

Design for a sustainable culture: methods, practices and education

The relationship between culture and nature is antagonistic. Harmony with nature has consistently been an ideal, but rarely a reality. Culture, understood as patterns of thinking, communicating and acting, has often diverged from or even *counteracted* harmony, causing damage to nature and undermining sustainability. In recent decades, our ability to shape our surroundings has increased to a degree that has resulted in profound changes to nature (Böhme, 2001). At the same time, the persistent urge for progress has sometimes prompted the rejection of cultural traditions.

Design is both a way of shaping our surroundings and an expression of the culture to which it belongs. It is a professional activity performed by highly educated practitioners, but all humans take part in shaping the environment of their daily lives, and thus design is also performed by the layperson. Therefore, knowledge of design and awareness of its potential to contribute to sustainable development is relevant to everyone.

The role of design

The term *design* has been used in various ways among the general public and within different research disciplines. It is derived from the French term *dessin* and the Italian term *disegno*, which both mean to construct something with a particular aim or intention. In this book, *design* is understood as the competence to creatively shape our surroundings using a combination of aesthetical, practical and technical means. Design is the only profession besides architecture that specialises in this combination. Traditionally, it has been read within a 'modern' tradition. It was a result of the Industrial Revolution, and was directed towards the mass-production manufacture of objects, the Modern Movement and the consumer society (Julier, 1993). This notion also maintains that the ideal goal of design is to create a meaningful life for present and future generations, thereby implicitly contributing to sustainable development. During the last three decades, along with the expansion and diversification of the design activity, understanding of the term has become blurred and its definition diluted. In 2004, the authoritative design historian Jonathan Woodham simply described it as 'an activity that concerns daily life' (Woodham, 2004), which can hardly be characterised as a definition at all.

The understanding of design adopted in this book is built on John Heskett's definition of design: 'the human capacity to shape and make our environment in ways without precedent in nature, to serve our needs and give meaning to our lives' (Heskett, 2002, p. 7). It comprises both professional and lay activity, spans from objects and services to area planning and fulfils practical, emotional and aesthetical requirements. The ability to create both cultural and physical sustainability is closely related to and dependent on the arts and aesthetics combined with other kinds of actions (Kagan, 2013). Therefore, design, which comprises all these ingredients, is an especially useful competence. Although it is a professional activity, design is also performed by everyone in the shaping of our daily surroundings and in our choice and use of material and virtual artefacts (Saito, 2007). Indeed, interactions with virtual media involve a strong materiality, which makes the two quite similar. This book has a certain emphasis on material artefacts, which also constitutes a basis for virtuality.

Sustainable design and design for sustainability have been a growing research field, particularly in the last decade (e.g. Bhamra, Lofthouse & Cooper, 2016; Chapman, 2015; Chick & Micklethwaite, 2011; Fry, 2009; Vezzoli & Manzini, 2008; Walker & Giard, 2013), since Victor Papanek (1971) started the discussion. However, unlike the present book, the connection between design, sustainability and culture is not a main theme in any of these studies. During the last four decades, designers have been engaged in using their profession in a way that contributes to sustainable development. Catch phrases like *eco design* and *green design* have flourished, and methodologies to meet these requirements have been developed. This activity has focused on the physical environment and use of eco-friendly materials. As culture has increasingly been recognised as a precondition for and main ingredient in sustainable development, the role of design has changed. The activity's ability to create aesthetically pleasing surroundings that contribute to human well-being and communication, and finding innovative solutions based on traditions has made design a core ingredient in cultural matters, whether it is culture *for, in* or *as* sustainability (Soini & Dessein, 2016). Until recently, design's significance as a tool to transform the environment and affect people's lives has been relatively unknown outside the design community. The discipline's cultural platform, humanistic intentions, multidisciplinary approach and practical goals constitute values that need to be communicated and further discussed and developed. The discourse on sustainability has hitherto been dominated by the social and environmental sciences, and design research is a fruitful complement to these disciplines.

The traditional aim of professional design activity is to shape the human environment and its artefacts in order to create a meaningful life for both existing and future generations (see Skjerven's article in this book). It is and should be further utilised to play a vital role in sustainable development. The design profession's long experience comprises various cultural traditions and can be useful in increasing cultural diversity and adapting traditions to contemporary and future requirements. On the other hand, it may also contribute to increased consumption, pollution and lack of critical reflection. The profession has been heavily criticised for this (Baudrillard, 1998; Foster, 2002). The contents of this book will hopefully shed light on its many and powerful roles by problematising its various means and effects and by presenting historic, contemporary and future solutions to create sustainable development.

There are many definitions of cultural sustainability. Our starting point is the definition provided in the United Nations World Commission on Environment and Development's (which was chaired by former Norwegian Prime Minister Gro Harlem Brundtland) report *Our Common Future*: 'Sustainable development is development that meets the needs of the present without compromising the ability of future generations to meet their own needs' (World Commission on Environment and Development, 1987). Here the future of humankind is put in the forefront, instead of nature, which means that culture is given a paramount role. This definition was regarded as controversial when it was first introduced due to its lack of focus on environmental matters, and it was never universally accepted (Manns, 2010). In 2012, the definition was expanded at the United Nations Conference on Sustainable Development held in Rio de Janeiro, Brazil (Rio+20):

> Sustainable development meets the needs of the present without compromising the ability of future generations to meet their own needs. Seen as the guiding principle for long-term global development, sustainable development consists of three pillars: economic development, social development and environmental protection.
> (United Nations Division for Sustainable Development, 2012)

According to the definition from *Our Common Future* in 1987, sustainable development implements ethical norms of welfare, distribution and democracy, while recognising nature's limited ability to absorb human-made encroachments and pollution. In the expanded definition from the Rio+20 Conference in 2012, the interrelation of environmental, social and economic goals are identified as separate, but parallel important factors, although these pillars were identified already in 2002.

The COST (European Cooperation in Science and Technology) Action IS1007 Investigating Cultural Sustainability (COST European cooperation in science and technology, 2011–2015) represents yet another stage in the definition of cultural sustainability. Initially, one of its main goals was to establish culture as a fourth and main pillar. It has since problematized the significance of culture and has identified three important roles *culture* plays in sustainable development: *in, for* and *as* sustainable development. These roles imply, first, 'culture *in* sustainable development', expanding the conventional sustainable development discourse by adding *culture* as a self-standing fourth pillar alongside separate *ecological, social* and *economic* considerations and imperatives. Second, 'culture *for* sustainable development' moves culture into a framing, contextualising and mediating mode, one that can balance all three of the existing pillars and guide sustainable development between economic, social and ecological pressures and needs. Third, 'culture *as* sustainable development' means that there can be an even more fundamental role for culture, which sees it as the essential foundation and structure for achieving the aims of sustainable development. In these roles, culture integrates, coordinates and guides all aspects of sustainable action (Dessein, Soini, Fairclough & Horlings, 2015). These three aspects have been further developed such that culture *in* sustainability is identified as cultural capital, *for* is considered a way of life and *as* is viewed as semiosis (Soini & Dessein, 2016). The activity of design is strongly involved in all of these aspects.

In the Kyoto Design Declaration, the International Association of Universities and Colleges of Art, Design and Media (Cumulus) declared that the aim should be as follows:

> ... to contribute to sustainable social, environmental, cultural and economic development for current and future generations, the Cumulus members will commit themselves to accepting their part in the further education of our youth within a value system where each of us recognizes our global responsibility to build sustainable, human-centred, creative societies.
>
> (Cumulus, 2008)

The Kyoto Design Declaration thus defined the crucial role of design literacy, i.e. the awareness and competence of the layperson to create sustainable development. We apply the concept of design literacy as developed by the research team Design literacy at Oslo and Akershus University College of Applied Sciences. The concept is not new, as it has been used to describe competencies in graphic design (Heller & Pomeroy, 1997) and to promote the lifelong learning of design (Nielsen & Digranes, 2012). Design literacy has also appeared within the European Union (EU) system, e.g. in the report *Design for Growth and Prosperity*, where the European Design Leadership Board (EDLB) provided 21 recommendations for the future development of Europe to the EU Commission (European Design Leadership Board, 2012). Recommendation 20 is to 'Raise the level of design literacy for all the citizens of Europe by fostering a culture of "design learning for all" at every level of the education system' by focusing on general design education for all (European Design Leadership Board, 2012, p. 73). Recommendation 21 focuses on professional design education, where member states of the EU are encouraged to support the development of design competencies for the twenty-first century by embedding the strategic role of design across disciplines in higher education (European Design Leadership Board, 2012, p. 73). Nielsen and

Brænne (2013, p. 6) conclude as follows: 'It is, however, time to be future oriented on behalf of the balance between nature and culture. The design literacy concept must be further discussed.' The design literacy research team has been focused on a continuum of design education from kindergarten to PhD in the research journal *FORMakademisk* (2008), the DRS//Cumulus conference in 2013 (Reitan, 2013), a cooperation between the Design Research Society (DRS) and the International Association of Universities and Colleges of Art, Design and Media (Cumulus), and in the research network DesignDialog (n.d.). The aim is to change the culture by providing design education to professionals and the general public in order to develop a more sustainable and democratic society.

In this book, we see design as a crucial component of culture. It includes a wide perspective of artefacts and professions and we thus utilise a broad interpretation of design: 'everyone designs who devises courses of action aimed at changing existing situations into preferred ones' (Simon, 1969, p. 55). There is a move towards understanding design products and processes as composed of symbiotic hybrids between design products, media types, services, architecture, communicative spaces, networks and modes of creation, production and exchange (Knutsen & Morrison 2010). We agree with Ezio Manzini, who argues as follows:

> Describing design as a problem solver means considering its role in the first world (physical and biological), but when we consider it as a sense maker, we are collocating it in the second (that of meanings and the conversations that produce them).
>
> (Manzini, 2015, p. 35)

This book is intended to offer insights into the conditions for the creation of sustainable development through design. Professional design is a discipline with its own culture, values and modes of operation and is based on a humanistic ideology. However, its practitioners and stakeholders have their own agendas and objectives, and the present conditions for utilising design in sustainable development are thus limited. How to approach these contradictions in a constructive way that opens up for fruitful cooperation presents a major challenge that demands to be met with various official measurements and other actions and the development of useful design approaches. Several chapters discuss and present examples of such efforts.

Thematic and conceptual framework

The contemporary preoccupation with non-practical matters related to aesthetic and personal sensations has resulted in an 'economy of experience' (Lash & Lury, 2007). As a result, aestheticisation has acquired paramount significance in all human activities (Welsch, 1998) and even in nature (Böhme, 2001). In this way, design as an aestheticizing component has become a key factor in the creation of sustainability, but it can still be used for other purposes. Design has often been associated with and criticised for stimulating superficiality and affluence – and not without reason (Foster, 2002; Baudrillard, 1998). This book examines the significance of design literacy (Nielsen & Brænne, 2013) as a powerful competence, which can fulfil, create and manipulate human needs. However, this research also focuses on the lesser known dimension of design as an activity that can contribute to the improvement of human well-being and sustainable development.

Worldwide environmental problems are closely linked to an increasing amount of waste and pollution related to the production, transportation and consumption of artefacts. Designers, decision makers, investors and consumers hold different positions in the design process, but they all make choices that will influence our future environment. In order to solve some of the crucial global challenges, designers and laypeople must cooperate. For this purpose, awareness of design qualities from a sustainable perspective is necessary. We include such an awareness of quality, longevity and sustainability in the design process of artefacts and solutions. It requires a variety of concerns and practices, such as user participation in the design processes, developing and displaying ethical responsibility and understanding and supporting sustainable aspects of production and consumption.

The concept of design literacy is used to address the complex matter of objectives and content in design education at the primary, lower secondary, upper secondary and university levels. We draw on work in areas such as visual literacy (Stankiewicz, 2003), media literacy (Buckingham, 2003; Erstad, 2010) and ecological literacy (Orr, 1992; Stegall, 2006). It is connected to the creation and understanding of artefacts and images in a broad sense (Heller, 2004). Design literacy is a competence not only for the professional designer, but also for laypeople in their position as users, decision makers and consumers (Nielsen & Digranes, 2007; Dong, 2008). The growing consumption of 'things we do not need' is an increasing problem. Design education of non-designers (in their role as consumers and decision makers) is seen as a stepping-stone for a cultural strategy for change (Nielsen & Brænne, 2013).

Overall, this book discusses the theoretical, methodological, practical and pedagogical aspects of the role of design in the creation of sustainability. These writings address both theoretical concepts and practical applications and include empirical studies of various scales (from minor objects to ideas, services and urban planning) covering various geographical and cultural entities. The book provides a foundation for future research, practices and policies in the field of culture and sustainability, and design and education.

The designer's approach

In contrast to the academic disciplines, the professional activity of design is based on practice and has been characterised as a 'making discipline' (Dunin-Woyseth & Michl, 2001). However, design also includes theoretic and academic approaches and reaches into other disciplines, such as art, technology, the humanities and social sciences. Mostly performed in teamwork with partners from various scientific disciplines and businesses, design is a multi- and transdisciplinary activity (Skjerven, 2004). This multifaceted approach is reflected in most of the contributions in the book and it is contextualised in the more theory-oriented chapters in Part I.

The process of globalisation has changed our lifestyles in many ways. It has promoted a certain universality and sameness, but has also led to renewed appreciation of the local (Lash, 2010). One consequence of globalisation has been a growing worldwide interest in the Nordic Way, which countries and other entities throughout the world understand as a societal model promoting democracy, social welfare and the desire to attain harmony with nature (Kildal & Kuhnle, 2005). There also has been a significant Nordic contribution to eco-philosophy closely connected to critical realism (Bhaskar et al., 2012), starting with the works of the late Norwegian philosophers Arne Næss, Peter Wessel Zapffe and Sigmund Kvaløy Setereng, followed by the Swedish philosopher Torsten Hägerstrand and the Finnish philosopher Georg Henrik von Wright. The Norwegian philosopher Arne Johan Vetlesen elaborates this contribution in his book *The Denial of Nature*:

> The trick, as I presently see it, is to ensure that what we formulate philosophically about value in nature is expressive of experience *of* and *in* nature, all the while being acutely aware that such experience and particular context are themselves at risk.
>
> (Vetlesen, 2015, p. 20, emphasis in the original)

He stresses that encountering nature through outdoor activities gives a first-hand, perceptual experience of nature and a completely different basis for developing empathy and accountability for nature. Further, Vetlesen stresses the significant role of objects, thereby relating the theme to design:

> … it would be more appropriate to say that we are not materialistic enough, in the sense that we care too little, much too little, about the world of objects, many of which are artefacts of human making, surrounding us.
>
> (Vetlesen, 2015, p. 172)

He then mentions the example given by Jean Baudrillard in 1968 that furniture once outlived its users, but today, we replace our furniture numerous times within our own lives due to planned obsolescence and ever more rapidly changing fashion. This behaviour causes many sustainability-related problems, generating waste and the overspending of materials and energy. Vetlesen criticises the *anthropocentrism* of theorists, such as Descartes, Kant and particularly Habermas, and the exploitation of nature for consumption caused by this view. He states that these theorists 'have been partly blind to the consequences of exploitation, not only for the "subhuman", non-human species, but also those that people in the future will experience living on a plundered planet' (Foros, 2016, p. 16, authors' translation from Norwegian). Thus, anthropocentrism can be seen as a threat to sustainability. However, it is crucial to change the culture through education to build a society more concerned about 'the way in which it spoils what it refuses to recognize as its moral equal, be it animals, the land or the biosphere' (Vetlesen, 2015, p. 3).

Vetlesen's point that we are not materialistic enough corresponds with Chapman's view on designing *emotionally durable design* in order to explore 'the idea of creating a deeper, more sustainable bond between people and their material things' (Chapman, 2015, p. 21).

In the field of design, this Nordic Way of eco-philosophy is seen in the ideal of Scandinavian design characterised by the extensive use of natural materials (Skjerven, 2002). Through its emphasis on nature, Scandinavian design has a close relation with sustainability. This aspect is implicit in several chapters of this book.

Structure of the book

Although this book presents a collection of independently authored chapters, it centres on a closely integrated series of debates. The authors come from various scientific disciplines and represent research programmes and national and international networks. This book builds on results and experience from the research projects 'Product Design: Materiality, Processes and the Future Environment' and 'Design Literacy: Design Education from Primary to University Level'. The work of these projects led to the creation of the Strong Research Group within the Faculty of Technology, Art and Design at the Oslo and Akershus University College of Applied Sciences. The research groups are closely related to the Design Research Society; (Cumulus, the International Association of Universities and Colleges of Art, Design and Media); the International Design History Society; the International Development Research Society Conferences and COST Action IS1007 Investigating Cultural Sustainability.

Part I Contextual perspectives

This first section emphasises contextual, normative and theoretical contributions and constructs a perspectival framework for the following sections. The chapters in the first section focus on three major themes: research traditions in the field of design, the conditions for creating human well-being and the significance of the historical legacy of modernism for cultural sustainability.

First, Astrid Skjerven introduces the special traditions of design research in her chapter 'Design research: contents, characteristics and possible contributions for a sustainable society'. Skjerven describes how, in recent decades, the design profession has undergone tremendous development, shifting from shaping products to contributing to social development in various fields on a global scale. This transformation has put new demands on the research competence of design professionals. Skjerven discusses how research traditions in design have always been related to culture and sustainability, while their research methods have fulfilled academic standards. In recent decades, the focus of design has changed from practical experience and a discourse on artefacts to a combination of these with academic traditions. Skjerven concludes that design research could become a decisive factor in the development of sustainability seen from a human and cultural perspective.

Ezio Manzini and Mugendi K. M'Rithaa's chapter 'Distributed systems and cosmopolitan localism: an emerging design scenario for resilient societies' focuses on an aspect of contemporary living conditions which has increasing relevance: resilience, or the ability to adapt to and withstand difficult social situations. So far, the discussion on resilience has been conducted from technical, economic and functional perspectives. Manzini and M'Rithaa's argue that the cultural dimension of resilience must also be considered. The chapter introduces the notions of distributed systems and cosmopolitan localism and the potential of design tools to connect and reinforce these notions. The authors observe that both distributed systems and cosmopolitan localism can be observed in the growing global wave of social innovations. Building on these innovations, Manzini and M'Rithaa's describe an emerging design scenario, the SLOC Scenario, and the new cultural fabric needed to implement it.

Another important theme is the conditions for developing wellfunctioning, sustainable societies. Peter Jones' chapter 'Social ecologies of flourishing: designing conditions that sustain culture' contributes to the discourse on the nature and consequences of human flourishing, which has been presented in the literature as the desired outcome of environmental and social sustainability. Recently, significant attention has been focused on the concept of flourishing as a normative and idealised state resulting from sustainability practices, contesting the narratives of sustainable development and modernism. Jones develops an account of the systemic conditions that contribute to a flourishing society based on the individual, organisational and societal factors of human development. This account advances the argument that agreements supporting the values of a flourishing society will sustain and benefit the many cultural resources and practices under threat from the on-going social movements towards urbanisation, globalisation and environmental change.

In the chapter 'The idea of simplicity as a pathway to cultural sustainability', Jorge Andres Caro del Castillo investigates how some ideas of modernism could be reconsidered to create products supporting future sustainability. Castillo addresses the idea of cultural sustainability through an analysis of the modernist ideas proposed since the late nineteenth century, which have deeply influenced the doings and behaviour of design throughout the past century and into the present. He explains how these ideas can be regarded as environmental and sustainable if viewed through the lens of their characteristics of leanness, simplicity and abstraction, and therefore they can be considered as true examples of cultural sustainability. Castillo proposes that cultural sustainability could be a good means to incorporate ethics into design and, finally, analyses how the processes, production, distribution and methodologies which follow these ideas could lead to better environmental and social conditions.

Part II Environments

The main topics of the book are objects and products. However, objects form part of a larger environment (on a scale from minor to major), and the two have many interrelations. The two chapters in this section focus on two major aspects of the environment on a greater scale: first, housing, and second, the outer environment and sense of place.

Petter Næss' chapter 'Housing culture, residential preferences and sustainability' deals with the environmental and social challenges faced by the housing sector. In wealthy countries, such as the Scandinavian nations, the shift towards a higher share of apartment buildings in close proximity to job opportunities, services and public transport facilities would seem to be favourable from a sustainability perspective. In recent decades, housing preferences and housing culture in Norway have seen a rise in the popularity of dense urban living, which has the potential to promote sustainability. However, at the same time, social and cultural trends driving higher per-capita floor area, fashion-motivated renovations and multiple-dwelling households are increasing the environmental load and aggravating social inequalities in housing.

Arild Berg argues in his chapter 'Designing a sense of place' that in order to develop a sustainable culture, people must care about their environment and identify with their physical surroundings. In other words, they must have a sense of place. Berg identifies success criteria for how a sustainable culture can be developed when people are invited into the designing of the built environment. As examples, he explores the participatory processes in the creation of an English school, a Norwegian hospital and a Finnish park. This cross-case analysis combines existing theory and empirical data to demonstrate how participatory design can contribute to more sustainable building practices.

Part III Products and cultures

This section deals with the relation between culture and products, from indigenous and local cultures to global cultures. It explores how products are at once the outcomes of the cultures to which they belong, but can also be altered by active intervention and attitudes.

In the chapter 'The importance of culture in design for sustainable behaviour research', Johannes Ludvig Zachrisson Daae addresses the importance of the environmental impact caused by our behaviour and the way we interact with products and how this has received increasing acknowledgement and attention during the last two decades. This has resulted in the development of a research field commonly referred to as 'design for sustainable behaviour' (DfSB). The identification and structuring of behaviour-changing principles and investigation of the factors affecting behaviour are among the topics that have received substantial attention in the DfSB research. Even though much of this work is strongly affected by the culture of the target group, the importance and effect of this has received very little direct attention. The purpose of this chapter is to remedy this situation by investigating the relationship between culture and DfSB and identifying how DfSB researchers and practitioners may benefit from drawing upon results from culture research.

In the chapter 'The social construction of child consumers: transmedia toys in light of Slavoj Žižek's notions of pleasure and enjoyment', Tore Gulden reflects on how the global toy industry can lock children into unsustainable behaviour through the marketing strategy of *transmedia storytelling* (TS), in which children learn about a toy through multiple media platforms, such as cartoons and games. Play experiments performed in Gulden's study indicate that children adjust to the play theme offered by a TS toy, while theory on product attachment suggests that the absence of personalisation of play themes makes children less attached to toys. This point is central to the discussion of how the personalisation of play themes relates to the longevity of toys.

In the chapter 'Contemporary traditional Inuit clothing as sustainable fashion', Janne Beate Reitan presents and discusses the indigenous traditions of Inuit, or Eskimo, women. The Inuit women of North Alaska make a new *atigi* parka every year simply by changing the cover of the garment. With the help of *atigi* covers, they create new clothing and change their self-presentation, which is also the case for those who do not produce their own clothing but choose to wear the garments. The expensive lining, similar to the clothing used in polar expeditions, lasts for many seasons. This use of clothing is discussed in connection to contemporary Western styles of clothing and other design items and relevant theories.

Veronika Glitsch takes up the question of whether improved fitting of clothes might lead to less waste and greater sustainability. In the chapter 'Fit in ready-to-wear clothing: why people dispose garments before they are worn out', she presents surveys from different countries showing that one of the main reasons for the disposal of clothing is dissatisfaction with fit. Sizing systems usually are not based on anthropometric measurements, and the grading practices influence the fit of a garment and the ease with which measurements are added. Glitsch discusses how changes in tailoring practices could encourage more sustainable behaviour, as fitted clothes are perceived as more attractive.

Part IV Design education for citizenship

This section discusses the importance of lay and professional education for sustainability. The chapters in this section address all stages and dimensions of education, from early childhood to adult and professional education.

Ingvill Gjerdrum Maus deals with school education in her chapter 'Developing holistic understanding in design education for sustainability'. Maus discusses design education for sustainability in the light of the ideas on students' development of understanding, as presented in Wolfgang Klafki's theory of kategorialen Bildung. The background for the study involves global political initiatives for the development of sustainable societies through education. The stepping stones for this discussion are students' perspectives on environmental concerns in product design as an educational topic in their creative and practical work. The data has been collected through group interviews with 15–16-year-old students attending Arts and Crafts classes in a Norwegian lower secondary school. The study indicates that in the design process for sustainability, students can perceive and alter the influence between products and environments. This makes the students understand design for sustainability as relevant for their present situation of creative and practical school work, as well as for their future. By informing the operationalisation of design education for sustainability among teenagers, this study contributes to empowering the youth for participation in the development of sustainable cultures.

Eva Lutnæs considers the importance of the layperson's critical literacy for sustainability in the chapter 'Rethinking consumption culture: educating the reflective citizen'. Lutnæs shows how education can build the capacity of younger generations to rethink consumption culture and transform deep-rooted social structures to develop ways of living within the support capacity of our eco-systems. She reviews three texts on reflective inquiry and asks how each might promote the education of aware, critical and empowered consumers. She identifies four common phases of reflective inquiry as a distinctive operation of thought. To trigger the exploration of new modes of production, trade and consumption, Lutnæs combines these phases of reflective inquiry with methods from systems-oriented design and proposes a model that fosters awareness of social inequities and the exploitation of nature and builds skills to rethink and transform unsustainable patterns of consumption.

Ragnhild Tronstad explores how the designed object can influence the user's behaviour. In the chapter 'Persuasion and play: crafting a sustainable culture', she argues that designing for a sustainable future not only arises from craftsmanship which produces sustainable products and solutions, but also has a rhetorical dimension, as the consumer must be persuaded to choose the sustainable option. In this chapter, theories and examples of persuasiveness and rhetoric in design are related to notions of cultural sustainability. Tronstad critically reviews recent debates on how play and game design can be employed as rhetorical tools and presents new perspectives on how the playful and the persuasive can be combined to form a particular kind of cultural sustainability.

Sabrina Brenner considers professional education in her chapter 'Teaching cultural sensitivity at architecture schools for more sustainable buildings:

lessons from reconstruction'. Brenner argues that students in today's architecture schools are typically trained in designing buildings only for their own context and the culture, climate and conditions to which they are accustomed. Consequently, most students and many architects have not reflected scientifically on architecture and the people for whom they build. The focus in architectural education has been on designing beautiful buildings according to aesthetic traditions within the architectural community. This way of designing utterly neglects the context and the people for which buildings are designed. In contrast, Brenner argues that *sustainability* is a synonym for *beauty* and that, consequently, only architecture that is the best suited for its environment can be considered to be sustainable.

References

Baudrillard, J. (1998). *The consumer society: Myths and structures.* London: Sage.
Bhamra, T., Lofthouse, V. & Cooper, P. R. (2016). *Design for sustainability: A practical approach.* Abingdon: Taylor and Francis.
Bhaskar, R., Høyer, K. G. & Næss, P. (2012). *Ecophilosophy in a world of crisis: Critical realism and the Nordic contributions.* London: Routledge.
Böhme, G. (2001). *Aisthetik: Vorlesungen über ästhetik als allgemeine wahrnehmungslehre* [Aesthetics: Lectures on aesthetics as a general perception of perception]. München: Fink, 2001.
Buckingham, D. (2003). *Media education: Literacy, learning and contemporary culture.* Cambridge: Polity Press.
Chapman, J. (2015). *Emotionally durable design: Objects, experiences and empathy* (2nd edn). London: Routledge.
Chick, A. & Micklethwaite, P. (2011). *Design for sustainable change: How design and designers can drive the sustainability agenda.* Lausanne: Ava Pub Sa.
COST European cooperation in science and technology (2011–2015). *ISCH cost action IS1007 – Investigating cultural sustainability.* Retrieved from www.cost.eu/extension/pdfExport/pdfexport.php?%5b10587%5d/%5b/COST_Actions/isch/IS1007%5d/%5bIS1007%5d/%5b%5d
Cumulus (2008). *The Kyoto declaration. Cumulus: International Association of Universities and Colleges of Art, Design and Media.* Retrieved from www.cumulusassociation.org/kyoto-design-declaration-signed-on-march-28-2008/
DesignDialog. (n.d.). Retrieved from www.designdialog.no/
Dessein, J., Soini, K., Fairclough, G. & Horlings, L. (eds). (2015). *Culture in, for and as sustainable development. Conclusions from the COST Action IS1007 investigating cultural sustainability.* Jyväskylä: University of Jyväskylä. Retrieved from www.cultural sustainability.eu/conclusions.pdf
Dong, A. (2008). The policy of design: A capabilities approach. *Design Issues, 24*(4), 76–87.
Dunin-Woyseth, H. & Michl, J. (2001). *Towards a disciplinary identity of the making professions: The Oslo millennium reader* (Vol. 4, 2001). Oslo: Oslo School of Architecture.
Erstad, O. (2010). Educating the digital generation. *Nordic Journal of Digital Literacy, 5*(1), 56–71.

European Design Leadership Board (2012). *Design for growth & prosperity. Report and recommendations of the European Design Leadership Board.* Retrieved from http://europeandesigninnovation.eu/wp-content/uploads/2012/09/Design_for_Growth_and_Prosperity_.pdf

FORMakademisk (2008). *Focus and scope.* Retrieved from https://journals.hioa.no/index.php/formakademisk/about/editorialPolicies#focusAndScope

Foros, Per Bjørn. (2016, 17 September). Arne Johan Vetlesen i samtale med Per Bjørn Foros. Det store altet [Arne Johan Vetlesen in conversation with Per Bjorn Foros. The large allness]. *Klassekampen,* pp. 16–19.

Foster, H. (2002). *Design as crime and other diatribes.* London: Verso.

Fry, T. (2009). *Design futuring: Sustainability, ethics and new practice.* Oxford: Berg.

Heller, S. (2004). *Design literacy – understanding graphic design* (2nd edn). New York: Allworth.

Heller, S. & Pomeroy, K. (1997). *Design literacy – understanding graphic design.* New York: Allworth Press.

Heskett, J. (2002). *Toothpicks and logos: Design of everyday life.* Oxford: Oxford University Press.

Julier, G. (1993). *Encyclopaedia of 20th century design and designers.* London: Thames and Hudson.

Kagan, S. (2013). *Art and sustainability: Connecting patterns for a culture of complexity.* Bielefeld: Transcript Verlag.

Kildal, N. & Kuhnle, S. (eds). (2005). *Normative foundations of the welfare state: The Nordic experience.* London: Routledge.

Knutsen, J. & Morrison, A. (2010). Have you heard this? Designing mobile social software. *FORMakademisk 3*(1). Retrieved from http://dx.doi.org/10.7577/formakademisk.188

Lash, S. (2010). *Intensive culture: Social theory, religion and contemporary capitalism.* London: Sage.

Lash, S. & Lury, C. (2007). *Global culture industry: The mediation of things.* London: Polity.

Manns, J. (2010). Beyond Brundtland's compromise. *Town & Country Planning,* (July/August), 337–346.

Manzini, E. (2015). *Design, when everybody designs: An introduction to design for social innovation.* Cambridge: MIT Press.

Nielsen, L. M. & Brænne, K. (2013). Design literacy for longer lasting products. *Studies in Material Thinking, 9*(art.1), 1–9.

Nielsen, L. M. & Digranes, I. (2007). User participation: Real influence or hostage taking. In E. Bohemia, K. Hilton, C. McMahon & A. Clarke (eds), *Shaping the future? The 9th International Conference on Engineering and Product Design Education* (pp. 305–310). Newcastle upon Tyne: The School of Design at Northumbria University.

Nielsen, L. M. & Digranes, I. (2012). Design literacy – from primary education to university level. In P. Israsena, J. Tangsantikul & D. Durling (eds), *Conference proceedings: Design Research Society 2012: Bangkok. Research: Uncertainty contradiction value* (Vol. IV, pp. 1348–1356). Bangkok: Chulalongkorn University & DRS.

Orr, D. W. (1992). *Ecological literacy: Education and the transition to a postmodern world.* Albany: State University of New York Press.

Papanek, V. (1971). *Design for the real world.* New York: Pantheon Books.

Reitan, J. B. (2013). DRS//CUMULUS conference. Retrieved from www.hioa.no/eng/About-HiOA/Faculty-of-Technology-Art-and-Design/DRS-CUMULUS-Oslo-2013

Saito, Y. (2007). *Everyday aesthetics.* Oxford, New York: Oxford University Press.

Simon, H. A. (1969). *The sciences of the artificial.* Cambridge: MIT.

Skjerven, A. (2002). *Goodwill for Scandinavian design: Lunningprisen 1951–70.* PhD dissertation. Oslo: University of Oslo.

Skjerven, A. (ed.). (2004). *Designkompetanse: utvikling, forskning og undervisning* [Design expertise: Development, research and education]. Oslo: KHIO.

Soini, K. & Dessein, J. (2016). Culture–sustainability relation: Towards a conceptual framework. *Sustainability Science, 6*(167).

Stankiewicz, M. A. (2003). Between technology and literacy. *International Journal of Art & Design Education, 22*(3), 316–325.

Stegall, N. (2006). Designing for sustainability: A philosophy for ecologically intentional design. *Design Issues, 22*(2), 56–63.

United Nations Division for Sustainable Development (2012). *What is sustainable development?* Retrieved from https://sustainabledevelopment.un.org/rio20/about

Vetlesen, A. J. (2015). *The denial of nature: Environmental philosophy in the era of global capitalism.* London: Routledge.

Vezzoli, C., & Manzini, E. (2008). *Design for environmental sustainability.* London: Springer.

Walker, S., & Giard, J. (2013). *The handbook of design for sustainability.* London: Bloomsbury.

Welsch, W. (1998). *Undoing aesthetics.* London: Sage.

Woodham, J. M. (2004). *A dictionary of modern design.* Oxford: Oxford University Press.

World Commission on Environment and Development (1987). Towards sustainable development. In *Our common future: Report of the World Commission on Environment and Development. UN documents: Gathering a body of global agreements.* Retrieved from www.un-documents.net/ocf-02.htm

Part I

Contextual perspectives

2 Design research

Contents, characteristics and possible contributions for a sustainable society

Astrid Skjerven

Introduction

The work of promoting a sustainable development that explicitly concerns not only physical but also cultural matters is a relatively new occupation. Thus, there are many blank spots related to this endeavour on the map of knowledge and understanding. This can only be improved through better cooperation between various professional fields. Such cooperation requires information from a variety of subject areas – from the natural sciences to cultural, philosophical and practical fields – to be put together to create a broader picture of the problem and thus generate fruitful solutions. There is a need for methodologies that exceed the traditional paradigm of academic research, and this has paved the way for incisive contributions from the creative and artistic fields with holistic views and complex paradigms of knowledge production (De Beukelar & Duxbury, 2014). These considerations make knowledge in the field of design, which aims to create environments for a better quality of life, of particular relevance. The birth of the design profession has its origin in the Industrial Revolution, the development that initiated our era's problems of sustainability in all their dimensions. Thus, the profession has always engaged with questions related to sustainability in the human environment and living conditions.

Although it is essentially a practical profession with the goal of creating concrete objects and environments, with practically-oriented research and development methods in accordance with this goal, the profession has also had a theoretical and academic foundation, along with a professional discourse. Thus, it fulfils the official international definition of research (*Frascati manual*, 2015). However, because of its practical and sometimes utopian approach, it exceeds the methods of traditional academic research. In this way, it makes a valuable contribution in the matter of research for a sustainable development.

Historical origin

The design profession's concern with issues of sustainability is perceived to have originated in the 1970s (Keitsch, 2012). In fact, it has a much longer history. The birth of the profession was a consequence of the need to solve problems of this kind, and it originated as a response to the Industrial Revolution in the nineteenth century, which was the starting point for today's environmental problems. The industrialisation of the production methods and the resulting urbanisation made it possible to produce goods in large quantities and at lower cost, thereby making products available for a larger part of the population. However, it also caused low aesthetic standards in the goods produced. They were regarded as unskilful imitations of handcrafted products, made without cooperation with the potential users (Pevsner, 1936). It also led to exploitation of natural resources, overcrowded and highly polluted cities with poor living conditions for the lower classes and the exploitation of natural resources. There was a need for a new profession that could improve the standard of the products and contribute to a better life in harmonious surroundings that would be fit for the emerging modern era. To find solutions to these problems, the new profession had to be research based and make use of both academic and practical methods.

The pioneers of the new profession were artists who had been trained and were working in the field of fine arts. Today, artists are regarded as belonging to a profession that is extremely different from that of designers, and they are viewed as lacking competence in scientific research. In the early 1800s, art – deriving from the Latin word *ars* – simply meant skill, and there was little or no division between the professions of art and design (Burton, 1999). Consequently, it was not regarded as inappropriate or amateurish to work in all art fields simultaneously.

Most of the first generation of designers were idealists, and many were 'utopianists'. From 1890, modernist artists and designers were increasingly committed to a holistic vision of art and society, and they supported the need for beauty and morality to be fundamentally conjoined (Greenhalgh, 2005). They wanted to create living areas shaped like idyllic villages or garden cities outside the big industrialised municipalities. These were often built on historic sources, some of which were medieval. The homes needed to be spacious and decorated with beautiful objects to enable a harmonious life to take place (e.g. Morris, 1890). Aesthetics was not regarded as an aim but rather as a means to create a meaningful life. The craftsman William Morris' escape from the polluted city of London to a nearby village and his erecting of a home and workshop built on medieval ideals is a good example of this.

The philosopher John Ruskin focussed on another aspect of human conditions in the new era, namely the amount of distance in the new industrial worker's individual relationship to the production process. The work methods were efficient, but they were mechanical and repetitive. In stonemasons' work on cathedrals in medieval times, each person's physical and individual encounters with the material were put forward as an ideal (Ruskin, 1849). Ruskin described a seemingly outdated work method and pointed to qualities associated with it that could easily be forgotten and had to be upheld for the sake of a meaningful life. He was thereby displaying the necessity of what we would call *cultural sustainability* today.

The aim of contributing to a better human life by designing practical, meaningful, beautiful artefacts available at an affordable price (Pevsner, 1936) was to become an ideology that would represent a leading star for the profession as it developed through the centuries. During the nineteenth century and the first half of the twentieth century, it was believed that people would prefer to buy products designed to meet these standards. It was also perceived that such objects had optimal and everlasting qualities. This would lead to limitation of consumption, thereby supporting sustainability. This ideology had a flourishing period during Functionalism; it was particularly evident in the Nordic countries, when the leader of the Swedish Design Society, a major figure in the profession, created the slogan 'More beautiful objects for everyday use' (Paulsson, 1919).

During the post-war period, when industrialisation accelerated and consumer behaviour followed other paths, this ideology was challenged. As a profession working in cooperation with commercial enterprises with different aims and views, compromises often had to be made, and their ideas and ideologies were sometimes overruled. Their work and the basis for product development was therefore also driven by economic interests that supported unnecessary consumption. This matter was identified as a problem at an early stage, mainly by the spokesmen of the Arts and Crafts movement (Crane, 2000). In our time, this dilemma has become a major issue, and there have been many severe criticisms of design professions (Baudrillard, 1998; Foster, 2000). In spite of this, the ideological aim of contributing to quality of life and sustainability has survived and continued to have followers. During our era, it has merged with the idea of sustainability and the related discourse.

The problem of working for commercial enterprises with the aim of profit has been part of the discourse since the Industrial Revolution, which brought about machine production. The critical view mainly came from the Arts and Crafts movement, which supported craft methods due to the independence of such enterprises. Among the main contributors to this movement were William Morris and Walter Crane (Frank, 2000).

Nature has always been a basic ideal for the design profession in terms of its forms and organic lifecycle. This is evident in the many theoretical works of the first generation of designers in the late nineteenth century. These works constituted the theoretical basis for innovation, and some were based on systematic research. The clearest example of this is Owen Jones' seminal book *The Grammar of Ornament*, published in 1856 (Jones, 1986). Through investigations of plant forms, he presented a set of 'laws' for ornamental decoration. As a standard work in most design education for several generations, the text's message has had a profound and lasting impact. In the 1980s, along with Postmodernism's interest in classical forms and ornaments, the book had a revival, and it was republished in 1986.

With its focus on aesthetics and research methods exceeding academic standards, design is strongly related to the field of art. The first professional designers were mostly artists who became engaged in the field. The main difference is that the intention of a practical function always forms part of a design process (Heskett, 2002; Pevsner, 1936). Fine art has traditionally been regarded as an activity that takes place with a critical distance from society and that is beyond or 'above' social and practical needs; thus, it also refuses the use of academic standards (Adorno, 1970; Heidegger, 1935). From the Romantic period on, artists have refused to follow academic standards in their research, and they have developed traditions based on experimentation with aesthetic means. Thus, there has always been a tension between the two professions of design and art, despite their many similarities.

In the twentieth century, the era of Modernism was dominated by the idea that a better life should be created through the integration of scientific methods taken from the technical sciences into the world of art and creativity. This constituted a basic notion in the idiom of functionalism. One of the many examples is the work of the architect Grete Schütte-Lyhotzky. To create an optimally functional kitchen with minimal space, she measured housewives' steps and other movements using American scientific methods (Noever, 1992). The unification of technology and art was a basic requirement for innovation during Walter Gropius' reign of the Bauhaus during its early years (Wolford, 1984). A Nordic example is Aino and Alvar Aalto's development of a method for making birch plywood that enabled them to produce their famous chairs (Schildt, 1984). This was a development of the design community's original ideology, which set the standards for modernist aesthetics and production methods.

The idea of harmony with nature was also represented, mainly by the French architect Le Corbusier's view of the significance of 'sun, light and air' in modern homes. This was particularly evident in the model house at the World Exhibition of 1925 and his Villa Savoie in Poissy (1929).

From eco-design to design for cultural sustainability

The post-war era, with its accelerating industrialisation and consumption, caused a new wave of concern about environmental problems. Some members of the design community realised that, in many cases, the profession contributed to this by designing objects that stimulated increased and affluent consumption. One of the leading figures in this movement was the Austrian-American designer Victor Papanek. He argued that designers should react against the role of being part of this development. Instead, they should act as facilitators for the creation of survival kits and products for basic needs. In his view, these products should be created locally out of reused materials, mainly in and for the so-called Third World. At the same time, they should represent an ideal for a change of attitude and production in the Western world (Papanek, 1971). Papanek won many supporters, particularly in the Nordic countries, which he visited frequently during the 1970s. Another example is the investigation of how more sustainable consumer patterns can be achieved (van Nes & Cramer, 2006; Zachrisson and Boks 2010).

The general concern about ecological questions from the 1960s on, which inspired increasing academic research on the topic, created a corresponding debate in the design community. Several designers started to develop methodologies that aimed to meet the challenge, and buzzwords like 'eco-design' and 'green design' started to flourish. A more lasting and better supported approach was that of 'cradle to cradle', which was based on principles found in nature's organic lifecycle (McDonough & Braungart, 2002). Today, the main trend is 'bio-mimicry', which attempts to incorporate nature and the way in which it recycles in the field of design (Monkogong, 2015).

During this era, emphasis was placed on physical environmental matters. The next stage of the discourse on sustainable development was a growing recognition of the significance of cultural matters and the importance of developing corresponding methodologies. This means that the designer ought to make use of methodological tools that could solve these types of problems. Despite the design profession's tradition of focussing on human well-being, this was realised relatively slowly, both inside and outside the design community. One of the pioneers and leading theoreticians of a holistic approach was the Italian designer Ezio Manzini, who introduced the question of the designer's role in the creation of social sustainability (Michel, 2007), and later that of human resilience in a troubled world characterised by cultural conflicts and increasing migration (Manzani, 2014). At present, there is growing comprehension of the importance of ontological and aesthetic traditions as a main ingredient in everyday life and a precondition for well-being. An important contributor to this movement has been the Japanese-American designer and philosopher Yuriko Saito. Her ideal is the Japanese notion of an organic lifecycle that comprises both nature and human beings – that is, culture. She puts forward the use of aesthetic traditions in contemporary design objects and their use in everyday life as basic requirements for human well-being (Saito, 2007). Phenomenological approaches based on the philosophers Martin Heidegger and Edmund Husserl are also being developed (Wendt, 2015). All of these approaches suggest that a sustainable development is dependent on both cultural and physical matters (Dessein et al., 2015).

At present, there is growing concern related to solving the often acute social and environmental problems that have arisen in urban areas all over the world. Therefore, governmental authorities and international organisations have initiated large-scale urban development projects. These are normally implemented by city planners and scientific experts, but in some cases, artists have been engaged in separate sub-projects where they affect and stimulate the citizens to generate solutions based on their own cultural traditions and ways of life, as well as through artistic experimentation (Duxbury, 2015; Kagan, 2013). Designers have engaged in similar projects, many of them related to the creation of sustainability and resilience in the Third World and areas that have been subject to environmental crises. One example of these is the Norwegian organisation Design without Borders (Ramberg & Verdu-Isachsen, 2012). In contrast to the artistic stance, the design profession does not claim to stand beyond society. Instead, they welcome cooperation with commercial enterprises. In this way, they are able to attain full inclusion in these projects and cooperate directly with the stakeholders.

The matter of gender

Female designers' significant role in design innovation has gradually been revealed by female design historians since around 1980. The contributions of the Bauhaus women – Eileen Gray, Ray Eames and others – have finally become recognised (Kirkham, 1998; Müller, 2009). There has been less focus on their influence on sustainability. The philosophy of ecofeminism proclaims that there are particular, significant connections between women and nature; these are illustrated by 'feminine' values, such as reciprocity, nurturing and cooperation, which are present both among women and in nature (Gaard & Gruen, 1993). The modern environmental movement began with a book by a woman (Meadows et al., 1972). Moreover, the first international definition of sustainability came from a commission led by a woman, the former Norwegian Prime Minister Gro Harlem Brundtland (United Nations, 1987).

Women's traditional role as housewives who decorate the home to provide a meaningful life, transfer cultural traditions to the next generation and frequently contribute to their husbands' work, thereby adding value, supports this argument. This has been the role of many designers' wives. They have also contributed with research- and experience-based innovative ideas.

Some women have had a more intellectual and freestanding role. An example of this is the Swedish philosopher and writer Ellen Key. From the 1890s, she was an active promotor of social reforms. She combined social engagement, care for children, focus on home decoration, modernity and appreciation of vernacular traditions in her views on design and decorating. This was most clearly expressed in her essay 'Skönhet för alla' ('Beauty for everyone'; Key, 1899). In this way, she promoted cultural sustainability long before the term was coined. In the design community, her theories paved the way for Swedish Functionalism and its famous slogan 'More beautiful things for everyday use' (Paulsson, 1919). With her many contacts among the élite of the Western world, like the American architect Frank Lloyd Wright, Key also had international influence.

The matter of gender also relates to homosexuality and trans-sexuality, as well as values representing non-Western traditions. One of the few researchers who have investigated the significance of gay male design for the environment is the British design historian Guy Julier (2011). Research in the field of gender and sustainable development is still scarce, and the topic needs to be further investigated.

A research paradigm in transition

In our era, new knowledge and understanding in the field of design has been considered to be mainly practice based, and research has been performed accordingly. In contrast to the academic disciplines, where the discourse is based on the written language, it has been carried out through an approach that may be characterised as a discourse of objects (Skjerven, 2005). Here, the innovation and alteration of products has been viewed as a kind of response or reaction to other products. These areas of design have therefore been called 'the making disciplines' (Dunin-Woyseth & Michl, 2001). Accordingly, design has often been seen as 'tacit knowledge', meaning a competence that is impossible to fully express through oral or written language (Polanyi, 1966). Considering the many verbal discussions and written technical documentation that form part of the design process, this is a viewpoint that focusses on a significant characteristic of the activity but fails to express the complexity of the activity and its discourse. In recent years, this view has been considered infrequently in the discourse.

In 1960–1980, there was a strong focus on methodology, and most studies were practice based. Moreover, many shifts occurred during this relatively short period (Cross, 1984; Reitan, 2007). At this time, there was an almost frenetic search for methods that corresponded with the 'core' of design and at the same time challenged its borders, sometimes even crossing them. These activities stimulated research as such and paved the way for the integration of practical and academic research.

In the last four decades, a certain rapprochement between the professional regimes of academic and practice-based research has taken place. This has mainly been due to three factors. First, the many amalgamations of institutions of higher education that have taken place since the late 1980s have led to an academisation of design education and research. Second, the academic world has become less reluctant to accept alternative practice-based approaches and has recognised their value. Third, and most importantly, the societal need to solve problems in a troubled world of increasing pollution, migration and cultural conflicts has made the necessity of coming up with concrete results a matter of urgency, regardless of the research field that is employed.

In addition to the basic differences in aims and methods, the barrier between academic research and design is built on the former's traditional requirement of a critical distance between the researcher and the research object, that is, the conflict between objectivity and subjectivity. As for research within the field of design, three different approaches have been identified, as follows: 'research on' (e.g. design history) and 'research in' (trying out new materials etc.), which may both fulfil the requirements of objectivity, as well as the controversial 'design through'. The latter means that the designer makes use of his or her professional creativity while simultaneously investigating a research question (Dixon, 2002). One of the first figures to confront and define these stances and to argue for a reconciliation between subjectivity and objectivity was Christopher Frayling (1993–1994). In our era of late Postmodernism, the belief in objectivity no longer exists, and this has been replaced by the argument for the use of intersubjectivity (Dixon, 2002). This has also led to a certain reconciliation between the two reigns of objectivity and subjectivity.

Conclusion

Since its birth in the mid-nineteenth century, the design profession has been research based. It has also been dominated by a holistic view that combines human culture and the natural environment. From the start, it has focussed on human culture and sustainability, both as a cultural and a physical matter. Moreover, it has comprised both theoretical and practical methods, and has undergone several stages, with shifting emphasis on theory and practice. Our era's perception that the profession has mainly been based on experience and a discourse through artefacts, with little use of written language, is a myth that has created unnecessary barriers to traditional academic research. Today's increasing demand for multidisciplinary and transdisciplinary approaches to attain cultural sustainability has resulted in a greater recognition of design research. If its potentialities are to be fully realised, a better understanding of this issue needs to be established. Research within design in a multidisciplinary setting may become a decisive factor in the development of the sustainability of both culture and the human environment.

From the perspective of the positive results of enterprises where design research and development have both been included, the future looks bright. The growing recognition of the advantages of cooperation between the various leading types of research should add to this. However, there still are some challenges that have to be met. In a situation of economic downturn and decreasing sales, competition is fierce and business enterprises are focussed on making rapid profits without considering future consequences. To some degree, this is countered by political authorities' increasing awareness of the global environmental situation and their related measurements in jurisdiction and international agreements. Another important factor is the growing consciousness of the significance of planning a sustainable physical and mental environment to secure a meaningful life is also an important factor.

References

Adorno, T. (1970). *Ästhetische Theorie*. Frankfurt: Suhrkampf.

Asplund, G., Galm, W., Markelius, S., Sundahl, E., Åhrén, U. & Paulsson, G. (1980). *Acceptera*. Arlöv: Berlings. (Original work published 1931.)

Atmanagara, J. (2015). Culture matters: Planning processes and approaches towards urban resilience in European cities and urban regions: Two examples from Brussels and Ljubljana. In J. Dessein, E. Battaglini & L. Horlings (eds), *Cultural sustainability and regional development* (pp. 176–188). London: Routledge.

Baudrillard, J. (1998). *The consumer society.* London: Sage.

De Beukelar, C. & Duxbury, N. (2014, December 30). Real sustainable development requires change through culture. *The Conversation.*

Burton, A. (1999). *Vision and accident: The story of the Victoria and Albert Museum.* London: Victoria and Albert Museum.

Crane, W. (2000). The importance of the applied arts, and their relevance to common life. In I. Frank (ed.), *The theory of decorative art* (pp. 178–183). New Haven, CT: Yale University Press. (Original work published 1892.)

Cross, N. (1984). *Developments in design methodology.* Chichester: Wiley.

Dessein, J., Soini, K., Fairclough, G. & Horlings, L. (eds). (2015). *Culture in, for and as sustainable development: Conclusions from the COST action IS1007 investigating cultural sustainability.* Brussels: COST.

Dixon, T. (2002). *Designforskning: En international Oversigt.* Copenhagen: CID.

Dunin-Woyseth, H. & Michl, J., (2001). Toward a disciplinary identity of the making disciplines: An introduction. *Oslo Millennium Reader, 4,* 1–20.

Duxbury, N. (2015). European cities as cultural projects: Where is culture in urban sustainability policy? In M. Hristova, D. Cesik & N. Duxbury (eds), *Culture and sustainability in European cities.* London: Routledge.

Foster, H. (2000). *Design and crime (and other diatribes).* London: Verso.

Frank, I. (2000). *The theory of decorative art: An anthology of European and American Writings 1750–1940.* New York: Bard.

Frascati manual. (2015). Paris: Organisation for Economic Co-operation and Development.

Frayling, C. (1993–1994). Research in art and design. *Royal College of Art Research Papers, 1*(1), 1–5.

Gaard, G. & Gruen, L. (1993). Ecofeminism: Toward global justice and planetary health. *Society and Nature, 2,* 1–35.

Greenhalgh, P. (2005). *The modern ideal: The rise and collapse of idealism in the visual arts from the Enlightenment to Postmodernism.* London: Victoria and Albert Museum.

Harvard, Å., Hjelm, S. I., Johansson, U. & Holm, E. S. (eds). (2007). *Under ytan: An antologi om designforskning.* Stockholm: Raster.

Heidegger, M. (1935). *Der Ursprung des Kunstwerkes.* Frankfurt: Klostermann.

Heskett, J. (2002). *Toothpicks and logos.* Oxford: Oxford University Press.

Jones, O. (1986). *The grammar of ornament.* London: The Studio Library of Decorative Art. (Original work published 1856.)

Julier, G. (2011). Design activism meets place-branding. In E. Pike (ed.), *Brand and branding geographies.* London: Elgar.

Kagan, S. (2013). *Art and sustainability: Connecting patterns for a culture of complexibility.* Bielefeld: Transcript.

Key, E. (1899). *Skönhet för Alla.* Stockholm: Verdandi.

Key, E. (2010). *Skönhet för alla* (Rev. edn). Stockholm: Alvastra.

Keitsch, M. (2012). Sustainable design: A brief appraisal of its main concepts. *Sustainable Development, 20,* 180–188.

Kirkham, P. (1998). *Charles and Ray Eames: Designers of the twentieth century.* Boston, MA: Massachusetts Institute of Technology.

Manzani, E. (2007). Design research for sustainable social innovation. In R. Michael (ed.), *Design research now* (pp. 233–245). Basel: Birkhäuser.

Manzani, E. (18–20 June 2014). *The cultures of resilience*. Keynote paper presented at the 20th Annual International Development Research Conference, Trondheim, Norway.

McDonough, W. & Braungart, M. (2001). *Cradle to cradle: Remaking the way we make things*. London: Vintage.

Meadows, D. H., Meadows, D. L., Randers, J. & Behrens, W. W. (1972). *The limits to growth: A report for the Club of Rome's project on the predicament of mankind*. New York: Universe Books.

Michel, R. (ed.). (2007). *Design research now*. Basel: Birkhäuser.

Monkogong, T. (2015). *Applying bio-mimicry to design a sustainable chain model*. London: Lambert.

Morris, W. (1890). *News from nowhere: Or an epoch of rest*. London: Kelmscott Press.

Müller, U. (2009). *Bauhaus women: Art, handicraft, design*. Paris: Flammarion.

Noever, P. (1992). *Die Frankfurter Küche: von Grete Schütte-Lihotzky*. Berlin: Ernst & Sohn.

Papanek, V. (1971). *Design for the real world: Human ecology and social change*. New York, Pantheon Books.

Paulsson, G. (1919). *Vackrare Vardagsvara*. Göteborg: Svenska Slöjdföreningen.

Pevsner, N. (1936). *Pioneers of modern design: From William Morris to Walter Gropius*. London: Faber.

Polanyi, M. (1966). *The tacit dimension*. London: Doubleday.

Ramberg, T. & Verdu-Isachsen, L. S. (eds). (2012). *Design without borders: Creating change*. Oslo: Norsk Form.

Reitan, J. B. (2007). *Improvisation in tradition: A study of contemporary vernacular clothing design practiced by Inuplaq women of Katkovik, North Alaska*.

Ruskin, J. (1849). *The seven lamps of architecture*. London: Dent.

Saito, Y. (2007). *Everyday aesthetics*. Oxford: Oxford University Press.

Schildt, G. (1984). *The white table*. New York: Rizzoli.

Skjerven, A. (2005). Gardinopphengningens talte Dager: Muligheter og Betingelser for Design i det nye FoU-bildet. In A. Skjerven (ed.), *Designkompetanse: Utvikling, Forskning og Undervisning* (pp. 47–51). Oslo: Akademisk Publisering.

United Nations (1987). *Report of the World Commission on Environment and Development: Our common future*. New York: United Nations.

van Nes, N. & Cramer, J. (2006). Product life time optimization: A challenging strategy towards more sustainable consumption patterns. *Journal of Cleaner Production, 14*, 1307–1318.

Wendt, T. (2015). *Design für Dasein: Understanding the design of experience*. Publisher: Author.

Wolford, F. (1984). *Bauhaus*. London: Thames and Hudson.

Zachrisson, J. & Boks, C. (2010, October). *When to apply different design for sustainable behaviour strategies*. Paper presented at the Knowledge Collaboration and Learning for Sustainable Innovation ERSCP–EMSU Conference, Delft, Netherlands.

3 Distributed systems and cosmopolitan localism

An emerging design scenario for resilient societies

Ezio Manzini and Mugendi K. M'Rithaa

What is "development" in a world where it is becoming increasingly clearer that, in the dominant models, economic growth brings environmental problems, growing social inequalities and physical and cultural desertification? In this chapter we will not dare to proffer a general answer to this question. We will only propose a tentative hypothesis: what if, on the long run, the fundamental goal, the one in relation to which we should evaluate if and how we are progressing, would be our ecosystem richness, that is its capability to resist to stresses and to learn from the unforeseeable events that, in any case, will happen? In other words, what if we consider the increase in our (global and local) ecosystems resilience as a meaningful indicator of human progress? Therefore, what if we assume "development" as the increase of the physical and cultural diversity, the redundancy and, most importantly, the capability to learn about the systems in which we live and which we contribute to building?

In our presentation, which is based on a reflection on our different experiences, we will introduce and examine these questions, discussing their implications for what design and design research are concerned. Within this perspective, the proposal for design researchers is not to re-invent the wheel, but to find in the reality of both the existing traditions and emerging technical and social innovation the raw materials with which new resilient and learning systems can be built.

Resilient systems in a risky society

For a long time we have known that whatever our future society will be, it will be a "risk society" (Beck, 1992) – a society likely to be affected by different kinds of traumatic events (from natural catastrophes, to war and terrorism, to financial and economic crises). So, we have known for a long time that the precondition for every possible sustainable society is its resilience – its capability of overcoming the risks it will be exposed to and the stresses and breakdowns that will inevitably take place (Walker & Salt, 2006). Today, the implications of this risk society are no longer only to be projected into the future. They are becoming evident worldwide in our daily life experiences and the fragility of our socio-technical system. Driven by that, the notion of *resilience* (intended as the system's capacity to cope with stress and local failures without collapsing) has become part of the vocabulary of more and more people and organizations and must rapidly come onto policy makers' agendas and be included among the aims and practical actions of the design community.

Consequently, for me, two observations must be done. First, the expression "resilient society" is not a synonym for sustainable society, if in the latter term we include – as in our opinion we should – its cultural dimension and the quality of life, in the profound fullness of its meaning. Resilience is rather a technical precondition, on the basis of which many different resilient societies may exist, endowed with different social and cultural characteristics.

On the other hand, and this is the second main observation on the current use of this term, since the current sociotechnical system is very fragile, transforming it in a resilient system would mean achieving a radical change of model (a prospect that is therefore the opposite of "resilience" in the sense of making the currently dominant model a little more adaptable). This observation clearly indicates a kind of paradox: to make our societies more resilient we must change them by moving away from the dominant ways of thinking and doing. In other words, against a background of mainstream fragile models, resilience is quite a disruptive concept – one that calls for radical transformations.

Proactive vs. defensive resilience

Until now, the notion of resilience in all its interpretations, including the most radical ones, has been used in the framework of a defensive discourse. Confronted by crises and catastrophic events, and because the likelihood of them occurring will increase in the future, the common reaction is one of survival: we have to re-organize our society and make it more resilient on current terms. Even though the manner of interrogating the notion of resilience has, of course, very strong motivations, it is intrinsically a limited approach: it implies what should not happen, not where, instead, we would like to go. But we can look at it also in a different, more positive and interesting way. If, technically, resilience means diversity, redundancy and continuous experimentation, it also means that the corresponding society must be a diversified, creative one. In other words, taking seriously the meaning of resilience, this compelling and deeply human image of society becomes much more than just a wish. It indicates the direction in which, very practically, we need to advance if our society is to have any hope of lasting. In short, in a resilient society, cultural diversity and creativity must flourish. Indeed, cultural diversity and creativity must be an integral part of any scenario of resilient societies.

Subsequently, we can also observe that, until now, the discussion on resilience has mainly adopted technical, economic and functional points of view, and the main questions have been: how can problems be solved in a resilient way? How can these solutions be made more viable? What could their economic model(s) be? It is important and necessary to raise these questions, and to search for their answers, but it is not enough. If resilience must be a characterizing feature of every potential future society, its cultural dimension, with its implications in terms of diversity and creativity, must be considered too. Therefore, new questions arise: what, in a resilient society, do we mean by development? How does the idea of democracy evolve? What is the relationship between the local and the global? And, more in depth: what about work, skill and creativity? What about trust? What about the very general ideas of time and space? A cultural approach to these questions would not attempt to solve 'problems' per se, but open up new possibilities in order to feed and support a social conversation about them. And this is exactly what design can do. Or more precisely, what design can contribute to in the framework of larger co-design processes.

How to design a resilient socio-technical system

How do we design a resilient socio-technical system? Let's look at natural systems. We can recognize that their tolerance of breakdown and their adaptation capacity (that is, their ability to withstand the test of time) may point to a way forward (Fiksel, 2003). As a matter of fact, it is easy to observe that lasting natural systems result from a multiplicity of largely independent systems and are based on a variety of living strategies. In short, they are diverse and complex. These diversities and complexities are the basis of their resilience – their adaptability to changes within their contexts. With this in mind, it should be feasible to devise something similar for man-made systems (that is, for the socio-technical systems that, when integrated with the natural ones, constitute our living environment). Assuming this wise approach, these systems should be made of a variety of interconnected elements capable of adapting and lasting through time (because even if one or more of their components break, given their number, and diversity, the whole system should not collapse (Johansson, Kish & Mirata, 2005).

How far are we (i.e., how far is our present society and the socio-technical systems on which it is based) from this complex, resilient, man-made environment? In our view, this question has no single, simple answer: contemporary society demonstrates a contradictory dynamism that forces us, on this point as on many others, to describe what is happening as a double trend: a mainstream one, enduring from the last century, and a new, emerging one. The two trends coexist and compete and in this competition we can see, on one hand, the big dinosaurs of the twentieth century, promoting large plants, hierarchical system architectures, process simplification and standardization (the result of which is to reduce bio and socio-technical diversity and consequently increase the overall fragility of the system). On the other hand, we can see the small and connected creatures of the new emerging world moving in the opposite direction, toward light, flexible, context-related distributed systems.

Resilient distributed systems

Over recent decades, a new generation of *distributed systems* (i.e., networks of various interconnected elements) have emerged, and in some cases spread, driven by the power of technological networks and by the enthusiasm of a growing number of people who tend to adopt such systems wherever possible (Biggs, Ryan & Wiseman, 2010). This trend has emerged and spread in three distinct waves of innovation.

The first of these occurred when the architecture of information systems shifted from the old hierarchical system to new, networked ones (*distributed intelligence*), with the radical changes in socio-technical organizations that this development made viable. The result has been that, as new distributed forms of knowledge and decision-making have become more common, the rigid, vertical models that were dominant in industrialized society have started to melt into fluid, horizontal ones (von Hippel, 2004; Bauwens, 2007). The success of this innovation has been such that today networked architecture is considered an obvious "quasi-natural" state (but of course this is not the case: before laptops and the Internet, concurrent with the mainstream model at the time, information systems were based on large mainframe computers and their consequently hierarchical – and therefore fragile – architecture).

The second wave of innovation has affected energy systems. In this case, a cluster of converging innovations has appeared, that put the energy sector in a new perspective: small, highly efficient power plants, renewable energy systems and the "smart" grids that connect them have made it possible to move toward distributed solutions (*distributed power generation*). These solutions are challenging the as yet mainstream systems, with their large power plants and hierarchical (untenable and fragile) grids. They are now a major field of investment and competition in the strong, ongoing "green technology" trend. It is therefore reasonable to conjecture that these technologies will strongly impact on the whole system and that, at the end of the day, the whole energy system will evolve following a trajectory similar to that of information systems, moving from a hierarchical architecture toward a decidedly distributed one (Pehnt et al., 2006).

The third wave of innovation toward distributed systems challenges mainstream globalized production and consumption systems. The signals of this trend include a variety of initiatives, ranging from the rediscovery of traditional craftsmanship and local farming to the search for small-scale, high-tech, fabrication systems capable of supporting new forms of networked microfactories (such as the ones proposed by *Fab Labs* and by the *makers movement*[1]).

Although this trend is still in its initial phase, we can foresee that, following a new principle of localization, it will grow stronger and that the whole production system will move in this direction, to design fabrication processes so that their products can be made as near as possible to where they will be used.

In the spirit of distributed production, this principle can be implemented by mixing different logics of design and fabrication that range from those of traditional industry, creating networks of small-medium enterprises, to supporting a craftsmanship revival and the application of high-tech, miniaturized production systems.

Similarly, the motivations behind these solutions may differ widely. One of these could be seen as an almost linear evolution of the lean production approach (a manufacturing model that has dominated industrial sector innovation for the last 30 years). In fact, distributed systems can be seen as the lightest and most flexible of fabrication systems, able to create products for specific clients not only when they need them (*customized* and *just-in-time production*), but also where they need them (or, at least, as near as possible to the place where they need them): "*point of use production.*"

The second strong motivation is the desire to optimize the use of local, renewable resources. Given that these are, by definition, highly context-specific, it follows that their best use is also, by definition, very context-specific. In other words, renewable resources "naturally" call for local uses. What is new today is that local production plants can be intelligently connected creating what we call distributed systems.

A third motivation is a growing interest in "the quality of proximity and self-sufficiency." That is, the value that a growing number of people recognize in local products: the search for "zero miles" food and the success of local microbreweries are well-known examples of this attitude (Petrini, 2007, 2010). However, the same attitude is expanding to other crafts and small-scale industrial activities, driven by both the recognition of local qualities and the political choice to support local economies and/or local self-sufficiency (in food, energy, water, and products), in order to promote community resilience to external threats and problems (Thackara, 2005; Hopkins, 2009).

Social innovation and cosmopolitan localization

Distributed systems are the result of complex, innovative processes in which technological components cannot be separated from social ones. While centralized systems can be developed without considering the social fabric in which they will be implemented, this is impossible when the technological solution in question is a distributed one. In fact, the more a system is scattered and networked, the larger and more connected is its interface with society and the more the social side of innovation has to be considered. In other words, with regards to our discussion here, we can say that no distributed systems can be implemented (and therefore, no resilient systems can be realized) without social innovation.

All this considered, the good news is that *social innovations* are spreading worldwide (Mulgan, 2006; Murray, Caulier-Grice & Mulgan, 2010) and that the emerging ways of living and producing they generate are largely conver-gent with the trend toward resilient distributed systems.

In fact, in its complexity and with all its contradictions, contemporary society is developing a growing number of interesting cases in which people have invented new and more sustainable ways of living (Meroni, 2007; Jeogu & Manzini, 2008; Manzini, 2015). For example we are increasingly seeing groups of families sharing services to reduce economic and environ-mental costs, while also improving their neighborhoods; new forms of social interchange and mutual help, such as time banks; systems of mobility that present alternatives to individual ownership and use of cars, such as car sharing, carpooling, and the rediscovery of bicycles; and the development of productive activities based on local resources and skills that are linked to wider global networks (e.g., certain products typical of a specific place, or the fair and direct trade networks between producers and consumers estab-lished around the globe). Further examples touch on every area of daily life and are emerging all over the world. (To read more about these examples, see DESIS, 2015).

Being localized, small, connected and open (to others' ideas, culture and physical presence), these promising social innovations actively contribute to the realization of resilient, distributed socio-technical systems. And, symmet-rically, distributed socio-technical systems may become the enabling infra-structure of a society where these kinds of social innovations can flourish and spread (Manzini, 2011).

Behind each of these projects (and behind the social innovations they refer to and promote) there are groups of creative and entrepreneurial people who have invented, enhanced and managed them. We can call them *creative com-munities*: people who invent and enhance solutions to everyday life problems by recombining an reconfiguring factors that already exist, giving them new functions and meaning and achieving results without waiting for wider changes in the system (in the economy, in institutions, in large infrastructures) (Meroni, 2007).

In challenging traditional ways of doing things, these creative communities introduce behaviors that often demonstrate unprecedented capacities for bringing individual interests into line with social and environmental ones. In so doing, these communities generate not only solutions to their everyday life problems, but also new ideas on society, production and well-being. They can therefore be seen as promising cultural experiments in line with the dis-tributed systems ethos we introduced in the previous paragraphs: initiatives that, in linking the technical opportunities of distributed systems with the wider socio-cultural trends associated with local-global interactions, become practical examples of a new kind of globalization: the *cosmopolitan localism* indicated years ago by Wolfgang Sachs (Sachs, 1992).

Observing contemporary society we can see that, contrary to previous per-ceptions, the joint phenomena of globalization and networking have given a new meaning to the local. The expression 'local' now refers to something very different from what was meant in the past – the valley, the agricultural village, the small provincial town, all isolated and relatively closed within their own culture and economy. Indeed, the term local now combines the specific features of places and their communities with new phenomena generated and supported worldwide by globalization and by cultural, socio-economic interconnectivity. Today, these phenomena are often characterized by extremely negative tendencies, that range from traditionalist stances that support local interests (including different forms of fundamentalism hidden behind the protecting veil of traditions and identity (Bauman, 1998; Beck, 2000) to turning what remains of traditions and landscapes into a show for tourist purposes (a "Disneyfication" of the local (Bryman, 2004)).

But luckily the overall scenario is better than that. The creative community driven social innovation we are referring to here, creates a variety of locality-oriented initiatives: from the rediscovery of neighborhoods and local food and crafts, to strategies to enhance the self-sufficiency of the local community. In other words, by inventing and enhancing new socio-cultural and economic activities, these creative communities are also generating a new *sense of place* and a new idea of *locality*.

Therefore, the emerging cosmopolitan localism can be seen as a creative balance between being rooted in a given place and community, and being open to global flows of ideas, information, people, things and money (Appadurai, 1990, 2001). A delicate balance that, of course, can be easily broken by slipping into a hermetic closure to the outside world or, vice-versa, into an openness to outside influence that destroys the locally specific features of the social fabric. Nevertheless, when this balance is successfully achieved, it creates a new idea of place that, in our view, is very contemporary: a place that is no longer an isolated entity, but that becomes a node in a variety of networks (where short networks generate and regenerate the local social and economic fabric, whilst long ones connect that particular place, and its resident community, with the rest of the world).

In the perspective of cosmopolitan localism, *small-scale* is to be considered an important quality for two sets of reasons. On the one hand, it permits the participating actors to understand and manage complex social-technical systems (in an open and democratic way). On the other hand, it enables individuals to carry out their activities, to fulfil their needs and build their desirable futures from within organizations where human relationships remain lively and personal.

At the same time, cosmopolitan localism produces a new idea of well-being largely based on *relational goods* (Uhlaner, 1989; Cipolla, 2009; Becchetti, Pelloni & Rossetti, 2015) such as: a lively social fabric, a healthy environment, a beautiful landscape and, last but not least, the richness of diversity that the place can express. That is, a well-being in which a major role is played by the recognition of how much the socio-cultural and environmental contexts contribute to the quality of life for people, and to the resilience of the overall society.

Emerging scenario and cultures of resilience

Distributed systems and social innovation are two sides of an emerging scenario. We will call it the SLOC Scenario, where SLOC stands for *Small, Local, Open, Connected*. These four adjectives together outline the main characteristics of this scenario. Individually, each one of these adjectives and its implications are easily understood, but together they generate a new vision of how a sustainable, networked society could take shape. In our view, this SLOC Scenario could become a powerful social attractor, capable of triggering, catalyzing and orienting a variety of social actors, innovative processes and design activities (Manzini, 2010).

More precisely, on the basis of what we have introduced in the previous paragraphs, we can see that the SLOC Scenario is neither a dream nor a forecast of the future. It is a motivating vision of what the future could be if a large number of social actors operated to reinforce and synergize on-going trends. So, the SLOC Scenario is proposing a possible future, but one which requires many converging efforts to become real and a new culture to emerge:

> the interwoven narratives, ideas, meaningful products and performances that, together, create the cultural fabric of an emerging society: a resilient society capable to face and navigate the turbulence of our time, learning from our experiences as to how best to thrive.
>
> (UAL, 2015)

Note

1 *Fab Labs* are small-scale workshops offering personal digital fabrication (http://en.wikipedia.org/wiki/Fab_lab); the *makers movement* is a subculture representing a technology-based extension of DIY culture (http://en.wikipedia.org/wiki/Maker_subculture).

References

Appadurai, A. (1990). Disjuncture and difference in the global cultural economy. *Theory, Culture & Society*, 7(2), 295–310.

Appadurai, A. (ed.). (2001). *Globalization*. Durham: Duke University Press.

Bauman, Z. (1998). *The human consequences*. New York: Colombia University Press.

Bauwens, M. (2007). *Peer to peer and human evolution. Foundation for P2P alternatives*. Retrieved from http://wiki.p2pfoundation.net/P2P_and_Human_Evolution

Becchetti, L., Pelloni, A. & Rossetti, F. (2010). *Relational goods, sociability, and happiness*. CEIS–University of Tor Vergata working paper n. 255. Retrieved from www.economia.uniroma2.it

Beck, U. (1992). *Risk society*. Cambridge, UK: Polity Press.

Biggs, C., Ryan, C. & Wiseman, J. (2010). *Distributed systems: A design model for sustainable and resilient infrastructure*. VEIL Distributed Systems Briefing Paper N3, University of Melbourne.

Bryman, A. E. (2004). *The Disneyization of society*. Thousand Oaks, CA: Sage Publications.

Cipolla, C. (2009). Relational services: Service design fostering sustainability and new welfare models. *Proceedings of the Second International Symposium on Sustainable Design (II ISSD)*. São Paulo.

DESIS. (2015). Retrieved from www.desis-network.org

Fiksel, J. (2003). Designing resilient, sustainable systems. *Environmental Science and Technology*, *37*, 5330–5339.

Jégou, F. & Manzini, E. (2008). *Collaborative services, social innovation and design for sustainability*. Milan: Polidesign.

Johansson, A., Kish, P. & Mirata, M. (2005). Distributed economies: A new engine for innovation. *Journal of Cleaner Production*, *13*(10–11), 971–979.

Hopkins, R. (2009). *The transition handbook: From oil dependency to local resilience*. London: Green Books.

Manzini, E. (2010). Small, local, open and connected: Design research topics in the age of networks and sustainability. *Journal of Design Strategies*, *4*(1), 8–11.

Manzini, E. (2015). *Design when everybody designs: Introduction to design for social innovation*. Cambridge, MA: MIT Press.

Meroni, A. (2007). *Creative communities: People inventing sustainable ways of living*. Milan: Polidesign.

Mulgan, J. (2006). *Social innovation: What it is, why it matters, how it can be accelerated*. London: Basingstoke Press.

Murray, R., Caulier-Grice, J. & Mulgan, G. (2010). *The open book of social innovation*. London: NESTA Innovating Public Services.

Pehnt, M., Cames, M., Fischer, C., Praetorius, B., Schneider, L., Schumacher, K. & Voss, J.-P. (2006). *Micro cogeneration: Towards decentralized energy systems*. Berlin: Springer.

Petrini, C. (2007). *Slow food nation: Why our food should be good, clean and fair*. Milan: Rizzoli.

Petrini, C. (2010). *Terra madre: Forging a new network of sustainable food communities*. London: Chelsea Green.

Sachs, W. (ed.). (1992). *The development dictionary: A guide to knowledge as power*. London: Zed Books.

Thackara, J. (2007). *In the bubble: Designing in a complex world*. Cambridge, MA: MIT Press.

UAL. (2015). Cultures of resilience. Retrieved from www.culturesofresilience.org

Uhlaner, C. J. (1989). Relational goods and participation: Incorporating sociability into a theory of rational action. *Public Choice*, *62*(3): 253–285.

von Hippel, E. (2004). *The democratization of innovation*. Cambridge, MA: MIT Press.

Walker, B. & Salt, D. (2006). *Resilience thinking: Sustaining ecosystems and people in a changing world*. Washington, DC: Island Press.

4 Social ecologies of flourishing
Designing conditions that sustain culture

Peter Jones

Introduction

In Jane Jacobs' (2004) final work, she explicitly warns the next generation of urban designers and policy makers of the critical risk to social sustainability through globalized economic development that fails to consider the loss of cultural knowledge.

> When a culture is rich enough and inherently complex enough to afford redundancy of nurturers, but eliminates them as an extravagance or loses their cultural services thought heedlessness of what is lost, the consequence is self-inflicted cultural genocide.
>
> (p. 160)

Her observations have unfolded much as she anticipated, and by any reasonable account, Western cultures have unravelled far beyond her moderate exemplars from the early 2000s. Since then, Western cultures, Anglo-American and European, have struggled through a global (Western) financial crisis of their own making, twelve years of the "global war on terror," the rise of a new Cold War alongside an ambiguous war against "terrorism," the new media hegemony of five Internet giants, the devolution of journalism and broadcast media into a small number of politically homogeneous corporate media owners, and the ongoing Middle Eastern refugee crisis. These problem systems reflect the outcomes of policy choices of neoliberal governance and directly erode cultural viability or the possibility of societal flourishing among human cultures. The foreseeable side effects of and social breakdowns from these macro-level dislocations, including economic globalization (Saul, 2005) and austerity programs, have led to significant distress for both urban and traditional settlements, as well as their associated cultures. Jacobs chose the culture as the unit of observation precisely to make the case that human flourishing expresses itself at the level of the culture, not the society or settlement. I consider Jacobs's argument a plea to sustain cultural viability, which is also the central concern of this chapter.

Cultural sustainability will ensure the continuity of human cultures as self-organizing social structures; the future viability of human generations within groups associated by settlements, arts, religion, and cosmological beliefs; and the continuity of knowledge practices. If social researchers believe the cultures comprising civilization to be put at risk by modernization and globalism, then we have the normative, ontological, and empirical responsibility to confront the issues involved in this crisis and present alternative design proposals that may yield preferable outcomes to cultural collapse and the imminent destruction of human knowledge, practices, languages, and art forms associated with these cultures. Largely due to global capital inequities and the concomitant displacement of settlements and populations, human cultures have never been at more risk of a collapse that would break the continuity of intergenerational learning, which defines cultures in human societies worldwide.

Both *culture* and *sustainability* are contested terms across disciplines, to the point of rejection in some discourses. From a systemic design perspective, these definitional challenges are necessary and implicit in any problem framing. In the framework that follows, the object of sustainability is to achieve *flourishing*, a value pursued via individual and social processes within a societal ecology that policies and education can define and measure. We might say cultural flourishing is found when people representing a given culture – that is, a group of people bound by identity and the self-production of historical values and symbolic meanings – articulate their culture as viable into the foreseeable future and are not threatened by external forces.

Can we design societies for cultural flourishing?

A central sociological concern addresses the meaning and articulation of flourishing in relevant social contexts and globalized societies, as well as the cultures eroded by globalization. A foundation for understanding the social, individual, and societal factors involved in human flourishing will enable committed actors to contribute to the sustainment of cultures and the individuals claiming inclusion in those cultures. The following framework and proposal aims to enable sociopolitical actors – policy makers, planners and designers, decision makers, social scientists, and engaged citizens – to facilitate the design of research, policies, and services to sustain cultural flourishing.

Cultural sustainability was placed on the global agenda by the UN World Commission on Culture and Development (1995), which stated the position that cultural resources must be sustained for the long-term needs of future generations. Among these resources are farming and food preparation; health and caring knowledge; the full range of arts, music, and creative expressive practices; religious practices and customs; aboriginal and developed crafts and practices; unique forms of knowledge and ways of learning; languages, dialects, and communicative practices; regional political and business practices; and numerous other forms of knowledge.

The concept of flourishing entails "a good life" and the sustainment of human life and all other forms of life (Ehrenfeld, 2008). In this proposal, flourishing is extended to the sustainment of culture. Cultures in many settlements are threatened by national disruptions, resulting in distressed migration; the structural loss of traditional craft and trades due to global trade regimes; and the loss of traditions, languages, and cultural knowledge practices due to the fragmentation of modern living arrangements that isolate individuals from indigenous or originating contexts. Among the many risks of the Anthropocene, cultural erosion is perhaps not considered as serious as the erosion of coastal settlements due to sea level rise caused by climate and oceanic ecological changes. The perceived threat or loss of cultural coherence is experienced by both migrants and settled communities in the form of the current transnational migration, which largely results from the dislocation of populations in Middle Eastern counties. Climate-related migration will become a much more significant and permanent force for dislocation, and innumerable cultural forms and practices may face an existential risk over a long period of continuous movement and resettlement.

Design proposals have not resolved the dilemma of a global, modernist sustainable development agenda rooted within a neoliberal political economy on the one hand and multiple-aligned citizen environmental movements on the other. We have continuous incremental policy proposals (such as the Kyoto Accord), industrial sustainability agreements (private supply chain governance), and scientific proposals, all based largely on the framing of science as "matters of fact." The redefinition of sustainability as a concern with regard to flourishing shifts the responsibility for decision making from evidence-based policy to betterment and amelioration, which are not policy or activist goals. Latour (2008) raised the distinction of designing for "matters of concern" as opposed to matters of fact as a perspective for framing complex societal problems as personally and collectively relevant:

> If the whole fabric of our earthly existence has to be redesigned in excruciating detail; if for each detail the question of good and bad has to be raised; if every aspect has become a disputed matter of concern and can no longer be stabilized as an indisputable matter of fact; then we are obviously entering into a completely new political territory.
>
> (p. 11)

In considering flourishing, we are challenged to revaluate the meaning of culture to stakeholders across the cultures of concern. As Latour contends, we must now extend the question of design to politics. The senior issue, a complex design problem, is nothing less than whether historical geographically located cultures can be sustained in the face of human-made global challenges.

A theory of social action must be sufficiently responsive to the complex and unknowable relationships of community and collective behavior. An inadequate theory of change with respect to the desired societal outcomes may result in ineffective and inconsequential actions addressed to the wrong issues, for example, the attempts to show progress on climate change by reporting on effects measures rather than taking the political action necessary to ameliorate large-scale industrial causes.

Over the past decade, designers and design schools have responded to the perceived necessity for socially engaged design by developing practices for social innovation and designing services for "bottom of the pyramid" innovations. Converging forces from 2008 included the economic deflation caused by the collapse of global mal-investment and the resulting massive unemployment after the global financial crisis, followed by sovereign debt crises. Since then, widespread disenchantment with globalization, the dislocating effects of the European monetary union, and distressed migration within Europe have eroded the vitality of and support for traditional and emerging human cultures. During this period, design schools and leaders in the field recognized the necessity of advanced design practices that play facilitative roles in strategic communication, as well as the framing of proposals for transformative change in communities and organizations. The design community signified this recognition with the signing of the Kyoto Design Declaration in March of 2008 (Cumulus Association, 2008). Design has since entered previously under-represented sectors such as healthcare, government, and international development, and in some schools and regions, these social sectors are the fastest-growing area of design contribution.

A systemic perspective is necessary to revalue culture as a social category and a locus of action. We adopt social systems perspectives (Luhmann, 1997, Christakis & Bausch, 2006), with the politically informed consideration of reflexive modernization (Beck, Bonss & Lau, 2003) and critical realism (Mingers, 2002). These frames share a view that humanity faces common continuing planetary problems in the Anthropocene era (Crutzen, 2002) that may demand future solidarities among members of specific cultural identities. This cultural solidarity will enable critical sustainability behaviors, including survivability and nurturing knowledge, to form within human groups facing common existential crises.

Luhmann (1997) pronounced that solidarity had waned as a cultural value when the stratification of market economies assumed precedence prior to modernism. He declared the Enlightenment value of happiness was likewise relegated to the mythos of history. Mingers (2002) critiqued and supported Luhmann's essential view of societal self-organization as underpinning the reproduction of culture. Mingers leaves it an open question as to whether societies self-organize within an environment that consists of other societies. His analysis opens the door to the present inquiry, which proposes design outcomes or goals for the sake of harmonious cultural relationships within societies.

The function of solidarity, or belonging to a culture as a self-organizing societal system, provides a knowable starting point for the design of flourishing societies. Luhmann defined a society as "a social system that can change its form of primary internal differentiation" and as an autopoietic (self-organizing by self-reproducing) system of social systems. Relating this to cultural flourishing, we can show how flourishing emerges within the components of culture as a social system, from the individual psychic system to the relationships within a bioregional ecosystem. We might therefore constitute a functional purpose of flourishing regarding which science, culture, and politics could potentially agree. While solidarity cannot be expected at every level of a societal system, the recognition of solidarity appears necessary to define the identity of a member of a culture. However, at the level of society, we can propose that a cultural-commons model consistent with polycentric governance (Ostrom, 2009) be adopted as a means toward creating the conditions for flourishing.

Background

Perspectives on modernist sustainability

In the history of social science's development from the pre-modern era, classical sociology conventionally defined a "successful" society without respect to human stewardship of the environment (Durkheim, 1982). We now recognize that we cannot isolate the definition of a flourishing society from a specific, located human settlement, with its own history, population dynamics, economics, and position in a situated environmental ecosystem.

The perspective known as strong sustainability emerged from the disciplines of ecological economics and environmental management over the last decade. A continuum from weak to strong sustainability perspectives has been argued (Ayres, 2008; Daly, 1987, 2001; Neumayer, 2013; Victor, 2008). The strong sustainability perspective acknowledges the macroeconomy as a subsystem of the natural ecosystem (Neumayer, 2013) informed by natural science. Weak sustainability "can be interpreted as an extension to neoclassical economics" (Neumayer, 2013, p. 28). Proponent of strong sustainability have recently argued for the necessity for a concomitant "strong social sustainability" (Upward & Jones, 2015; Colantonio & Dixon, 2011; Colantonio, 2007). The convergence of a strong social and ecological sustainability is consistent with the Ehrenfeld proposal of "flourishing."

The idealized proposal of flourishing is further articulated as a reflexive project that is consistent with the institutional redesign sought by reflexive modernization (Beck, Bonss & Lau, 2003; Law & Urry, 2004). Weak sustainability (or *sustainable development* as normally defined) adheres to the modernist principles of technological mastery and control of social and natural circumstances. The first era of modernism sought to control nature and to manage capital flows in an industrialized economy. It assumed clear boundaries between nature and society. The second era of modernism, inherent in the reflexive position, rejoins human societies to the natural world and redefines humanity's plurality of roles within the realism of a bounded ecology. Here, reflexivity recognizes the multiplicity of boundaries, the multiple claims to knowledge, our real limits of action, the limits of resources and their management, and the limits of institutional systems and governance. Reflexive modernization offers a multi-perspectival view of the sustainability predicament, recognizing that desired future states such as flourishing will be negotiated within institutions that are themselves limited and in constant reformation. The meanings of flourishing and of the beneficent outcomes of social design are not shared as universal aims.

The predominant understanding in modern cultures has been that "society is separate from the environment." This is an industrial era view that is not aligned with the reality of natural science. However, claims to scientific validity are no longer authoritative in political arguments. Climate change, energy production, population health, and the functions of economies have become shared cultural constructs and thus subject to restructuring. With respect to a cultural agency, everything "designed" becomes socially negotiated across a multiplicity of boundaries, and those boundaries are themselves redrawn or questioned as claims to power.

The "second modernity" calls into question the assumed goals, goods, and continuation of modern progressive projects. Ascribed social structures, such as those modeled in Figure 4.1 (the developmental model of flourishing) are vulnerable to competing claims and are contingent on perceived value and received utility. While significant social change and policy shifts are inherent in modernism, reflexive modernism requires rethinking how social meaning is constructed. Social behavior is reflexively shaped by our collective, pluralized understandings of the world as experienced and learned.

Reflexive modernization emerges as a theoretical frame that supports the "current consensus in related [natural science] disciplines" (Barkow, 2006, p. 29), which is necessary for moving toward flourishing or strong sustainability. It also promotes critical social reflection on action across the boundaries of a social ecosystem, encouraging a position removed from self-interest. We gain more thoughtful outcomes from scientific knowledge by questioning the validity of objectivist reasoning, or "matters of fact," because we discover that actors become polarized when faced with definitive propositions. While reflexive modernization acknowledges all disciplinary views as valid within their own epistemologies, it asserts a social theory that human action must follow from subjective agreement on decisions based on a multiplicity of values. Coordinated action on shared problems does not follow from the promotion of scientific or objective facts but from "matters of concern" (Latour, 2008). The lack of agreement with respect to "matters of fact" in sustainability science reveals the crux of the problem identified by Latour: value conflicts between stakeholder commitments and mindsets.

Societal flourishing as sustainability

There is no single common definition of flourishing we can apply to the current model. Ehrenfeld (2008) describes flourishing as a context for strong sustainability, as "the possibility that human and other life can flourish on this planet forever." The outcome that "sustainability" must sustain is flourishing. The conditions for flourishing differ by discipline and unit of analysis, across literatures and contexts. Flourishing conditions are well-summarized by Fredrickson and Losada as "to live within an optimal range of human functioning, one that connotes goodness, generativity, growth, and resilience" (2005, p. 678).

The qualities that contribute to human flourishing have been identified as those most beneficial and socially desirable experiences assumed to be nearly universal across the forms of human settlement. However, each human sciences discipline defines the function of flourishing differently. For psychologists, flourishing measures the engagement and personal growth of the individual in society (Keyes, 2002). For health planners and sociologists, flourishing qualifies the well-being of members of a society (Marks & Thompson, 2006). The functions of flourishing associated with an organization are related more to the values identified as system inputs (ecosystem services and stocks) and outputs (social and economic value), as opposed to the values of health and well-being directly. The starting point for a comprehensive cultural definition of flourishing may be the integration of these definitions into a meaningful social system, because they involve systemic relationships between the individual human, the social units of relationships, the structures of communities, and the solidarities that define allegiance to culture.

Individual and social flourishing

Keyes (2002) defines flourishing as a composite of individual qualities that in aggregate, demonstrate a healthy sense of well-being. He distinguishes six dimensions of psychological well-being that are indicative of a positive dynamic, as opposed to "languishing," or the downward spiral of negative trends. These include the following:

- self-acceptance;
- positive relationships with others;
- personal growth;
- purpose in life;
- environmental mastery;
- autonomy.

These six criteria are supported by research in mental health and studies of well-being in workplace and school contexts. These criteria for individual well-being may be significantly co-determined by social reinforcement, and individual flourishing, irrespective of social determinants, is not reducible to isolated measures. Depending on cultural and social group affiliation and personal history and preferences, social determinants may be significant criteria for individual well-being. Keyes (1998, 2002) further evaluated the social dimensions of individual flourishing with respect to publicly accessible social criteria, including the following five functions:

- social coherence;
- social actualization;
- social integration;
- social acceptance;
- social contribution.

While these factors may represent an individual's social well-being as reflected by participation in their society and culture, the contribution to overall flourishing is defined as an internal, subjective response to stimuli and social activity. However, any measure of a flourishing society should account for society's support for the possibility of achieving coherence, actualization, integration, and other conditions.

With respect to the relationship between an individual and his or her community and society, we might introduce the provision of *care*, or the concern for the conservation of health and growth in a person or collective. We can define self-care as an extended attribute of individual flourishing and social care as caring for one's own social groups and communities.

When we consider flourishing at the aggregate, community level, the values associated with livable cities and communities are developed by Gilroy (2008) and Timmer and Seymoar (2005). While their research into the social flourishing associated with healthy aging cannot be reduced to a set of community principles, their core principles of liveability are pertinent, including equity, dignity, accessibility, conviviality, participation, and empowerment.

At the societal level, we can identify flourishing *communities* as the social composite of institutions and organizations that satisfy human needs and co-produce value. The community level consists of many factors that we can identify based on research and initial models. Several authors define the social sustainability of cities or communities as equitable, diverse, and conducive to the social integration of multiple cultures while improving quality of life (Sachs, 1999; Barron & Gauntlett, 2002). Stren and Polese (2000) proposed an early definition of social sustainability for a city:

> development and/or growth that is compatible with the harmonious evolution of civil society, fostering an environment conducive to the compatible cohabitation of culturally and socially diverse groups while at the same time encouraging social integration, with improvements in the quality of life for all segments of the population.
>
> (p. 229)

McKenzie defined social sustainability as a "life-enhancing condition within communities, and a process within communities that can achieve that condition"

(2004, p. 12) and suggested several proposals intended to achieve social sustainability in communities, such as the following:

- equity of access to key services (health, education, transport, housing, and recreation);
- inter-generational equity;
- cultural resilience, wherein "positive aspects of disparate cultures are valued and promoted";
- widespread political participation among citizens;
- mechanisms via which a community can collectively identify its strengths and needs.

McKenzie posits a cultural ability to transmit awareness of social sustainability from one generation to the next and a sense of community needed to maintain that transmission. These functions might be reconceived as cultural aspects of flourishing, consistent with Throsby's (2003) definition of cultural capital. Throsby defines intergenerational equity as a key source of cultural capital, the stock of cultural resources inherited from ancestral heritage, a significant value in indigenous cultures.

Six principles for managing cultural capital are defined, all of which are found in indigenous cultures:

1   material and non-material well-being;
2   inter-generational equity;
3   intra-generational equity;
4   maintenance of diversity;
5   precautionary principle;
6   maintenance of cultural systems and interdependence.

Across these definitions, there are several other factors we might consider and evaluate:

- community livability;
- organizational participation;
- worklife satisfaction;
- positive community role;
- shared respect for common law;
- respect for commons;
- community care.

These factors defining conditions for social and individual flourishing are not yet integrated or measured by regional statistical samples. Case studies across these research areas are not analyzed using common variables. Empirical evaluations have not been made for the selection and development of these factors. These factors are selected due to their support in the literature and presented as design proposals for flourishing cultures and societies.

Models and methods

Design and planning methodologies

Cultural sustainability or flourishing can be viewed as organizing collective actions to achieve flourishing within a culture, which can be framed in numerous terms of identity and belonging, from highly local arts cultures to historically-defined national and ethnic cultures. The boundaries of a culture defined for diverse urban and social planning purposes may be circumscribed by a bioregion (such as a watershed and incorporated settlements), municipality, a subculture/enclave within a larger urban settlement, or an organization/ institution with a persistent identity. A national culture might be too large as a social system boundary, unless the nation was a contained population with a strong historically distinct identity.

While cultures can be conceived of as social systems, we can argue that flourishing cultures require a *settlement* context, a geographical location that corresponds to cultural or heritage assets and values. A culture should be construed as a socioecological system (Trist & Murray, 1997), even when considering technological cultures, such as start-up communities or workplaces. Design actions will be proposed regarding commons projects, such as the resolution of shared ecosystem or cultural services (historically shared parklands, fishing stocks, and heritage assets, such as ancient churches and monuments). The culture at large would rarely be at issue – an emergent, often crisis-related, concern may initiate the opportunity for cultural design. The opportunity to frame an intervention as a designing situation provides the necessary point of engagement with the socioecological design approach.

Various engagement methods are appropriate for flourishing-design contexts. The Transition Town (Smith, 2011), and transition design movements (Irwin, 2015) have championed localized alternatives to neoliberal and capitalist structures and living arrangements, which is consistent with many of the criteria for flourishing. While transition movements have not demonstrated a cultural sustainability orientation, the restoration of local governance and community self-organizing are consistent with cultural flourishing.

The inherent complexity and non-representability of cultural contexts may require hybrid approaches. Several methodologies have been perfected for multi-stakeholder collaborative planning for larger-scale social systems that cross cultural and organizational boundaries. A range of participatory planning methods, from normative planning (Özbekhan, 1969) to Oasis (Wheatley & Frieze, 2011) to collaborative foresight (Weigand, Flanagan, Dye & Jones 2014) methodologies, are proposed as an integration of collective action and participatory design that is consistent with stakeholder design in a cultural context.

Collaborative planning for a flourishing society may be framed as a redirective design proposal (Fry, 2008), wherein a deliberate shift in practices and values enables community members to define mutually desired outcomes that may not be achievable via conventional planning.

Social flourishing in an ecosystem model

We represent the criteria and relationships needed for flourishing based on Bronfenbrenner's (1979) socioecological theory of human development. Figure 4.1 presents this structure of social systems, which entails the individual, from family, and community contexts, as well as the boundaries of a cultural system. These are arranged topologically from the microsystem to the macrosystem (in Bronfenbrenner's terms).

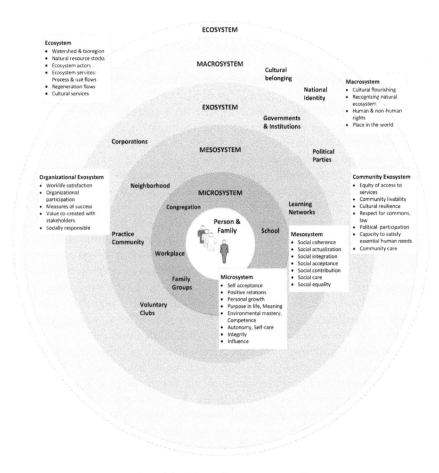

Figure 4.1 Socioecological model of flourishing system conditions.

Social ecology crosses multiple units of analysis and mediates between individual-, community- and culture-level relationships. A given settlement and its cultures entails a socioecological system, people, and resources, including people's assets, common resources, and relationships. This socioecological model represents four social contexts that are related in terms of proximity and temporality. The four contexts are arranged topologically from the microsystem to the macrosystem and contained within a natural ecosystem. The labels within each ring denote qualities of flourishing specified from sources at that unit of analysis and associated with each contained social system. The successive social systems are described in the figure in proximal relationship with one another:

Microsystem – The set of relations of a person to his or her immediate social context. For an adult citizen in a community, this entails his or her family and close relatives, individuals with whom he or she has close relationships, and immediate social groups. Consistent with Keyes's (2002) definition of individual flourishing, the microsystem criteria include individual well-being and social cohesion and inclusion. The values and measurable attributes consistent with individual flourishing are indicated in the diagram, ranging from self-acceptance to influence. These values are demonstrated by interactions between interpersonal relationships.

Mesosystem – The mesosystem includes individual microsystems and represents a stage in social development. The mesosystem involves social systems that reinforce engagement in society and cultures, yet it is not an aggregate of individuals. The meso level of the social ecosystem contains the workplace, schools (for younger people), and community or service organizations. In the diagram, flourishing criteria associated here include the Keyes (2002) criteria for personal social flourishing. These are consistent with behaviors in proximal communities, ranging from neighborhood to businesses and cultural organizations, where aspects such as social coherence and integration become observable in complex social relations.

Exosystem – The exosystem level includes processes that occur between the various settings within a culture and do not directly affect the individual but influence the social systems in which a person participates. These include the organizations and community institutions that all individuals within a social boundary would understand as part of society. Two exosystems are distinguished for definition purposes because they involve different values that may be associated with flourishing. The organizational exosystem entails the network of business relationships that affect a workplace and work life (which is, itself, located in the microsystem), and the community exosystem includes local institutions that are accessible within the experience of the individual. The McKenzie (2004) criteria for social flourishing (equity of access, intergenerational equity, cultural resilience, political participation, etc.) may be measured as outcomes of successful development at this level.

Macrosystem – A society and its cultures may be described as macrosystems in the societal flourishing model. The macrosystem defines the enduring archetypes and "blueprints" for societal functions that are repeatable across contexts. Bronfenbrenner defined the macrosystem as the experienced patterns in a society and its subcultures that influence belief systems, lifestyles, and the contexts of social interchange. The macrosystem includes institutional, infrastructure, media, and information structures that are expressed in relation to an individual within the levels contained by the macrosystem. Values and beliefs about one's culture and politics are formed via exposure to the larger macrosystem, and this macrosystem is the location at which emerging views of cultural and social flourishing, as relevant values, will be discovered and assessed. One's views of human rights, our "place in the world" as situated persons, and the rights of nature will be framed by the cultural frames expressed through the macrosystem.

Ecosystem – The final system ring necessarily includes the natural ecosystem, which was not defined as a boundary or social system by Bronfenbrenner but is required as a necessary spatial-ecosystem boundary and a system including the entire cultural-social system. While micro–macro systems can change in value and influence over time due to human interaction, the natural ecosystem changes both independently of social behavior and with direct and indirect human activities as a complex adaptive system (Levin, 1998). A regional bio-ecosystem is implicated in the life and development of all people within settlements because productive and agricultural activities are located within definable watersheds and are components in and effectors of resilient ecosystems. A regional ecosystem is highly interdependent due to the emergent effects of direct and indirect perturbation by organized commerce, extraction, agriculture, and settlements. The ecosystem level provides cultural services (landscapes, riparian areas, terrains, forests and woodlands, natural features) as sources for human cultural development. Regional and national values, identities, and spiritual beliefs are related to and drawn from the natural surroundings implicated in human histories.

Regardless of whether or not we, or humans in any societies, are cognizant of our role as reciprocal participants in an ecosystem, the local and regional ecosystems, by all scientific and moral rights, define the living boundaries for human development, flourishing, and culture. A comprehensive view of social flourishing will be incomplete without the explicit inclusion of natural resources and contributions to cultural development, health, lifestyle, food systems, and social identities.

Human cultures will be facing the struggle for sustainability within the very long ecological cycles of the Anthropocene era. This struggle implies the need for stewardship of regional ecosystems as living systems that ultimately determine all the human sources and systemic conditions of flourishing. Recent models of ecosystemic behavior (Heffernan et al., 2014) suggest that hierarchical-scaling ecosystems function as natural macrosystems that inclusively integrate all bio-ecosystems contained within their boundaries, from continental to regional to local watersheds.

Conclusion

The human need to form socially sustainable communities and societies, which will allow the possibility of flourishing, has never been more pressing. The globalization of all consumption trends, energy and food production, immigration in search of humane social conditions, placeless service provision, and the financialization of sovereign economies have exalted modernist values across almost all nations and contexts. However, the planetary limits on growth and continuous critical problems identified as existential threats in 1970, at the peak of modernism, have manifested as untenable in the era many geologists and social scientists have termed the Anthropocene.

In the near future, we might observe that the modern era ended after nearly destroying the differentiated human cultures that evolved from the medieval and Enlightenment periods. The commercial Internet has colonized the early cottage industries of Web 1.0. In many ways, corporations and resilient organizations can plan and protect themselves from the consequences of extreme climate dynamics, distressed migration, wage and job declines, and the many systemic effects of unethical political and societal governance. However, members of local communities, cities, and political settlements are embedded in the lived reality remain in precarious positions in the face of disruptive exogenous change.

While we tend to treat culture as the outcome and aggregate of innumerable individual choices, anthropological theories of culture reveal that culture manifests as collective practice by related individuals over long periods of time. With the continuous progression of modernism flattening the variations in cultures around the world, many traditional and regional cultures have become vulnerable to the loss of knowledge, skills, practices, and languages and ultimately the loss of meaning in human societies. Losses of culture result in the loss of the adaptable survivability that culture is theorized to represent. When human cultures and our systems of governance fail together, slowly, but in concert with the human erosion of capitalism, the family of human civilization is at risk.

The effects of the global problematique are most significantly experienced at home, among one's closest circles, as suggested by the microsystem of individual flourishing. However, actions in response to these conditions take the form of legitimated community and participatory governance. Community-centered and transformative design practices and participatory action research have become widely accepted and involved in all scales of citizen-led innovation and community building. Design leaders such as Thackara (2006, 2015) and Heller and Vienne (2003) have promoted engaged alternatives to professionalized design and methodological design practices to authentically participate in ecosystem restoration and cultural enhancement. Recently, comprehensive design approaches supported by research and new design education have been developed to address the inherent problem complexity and stakeholder conflicts consistent with diverse communities and policy change. The last decade has seen the evolution of redirective design (Fry, 2009), transition design (Irwin, Kossof & Tonkinwise, 2015), and systemic design (Jones, 2015; Jones, 2014) modes as proposals to advance design responses that will help create flourishing and socially-engaged education and socioecological sustainability.

The urgency for collective and policy action has led to numerous design-led proposals and methods, conferences, and now at least three decades of ecological design approaches. The relatively circumscribed methods of collective action in the context of cultural flourishing, while not developed with cases in this chapter due to its limited scope, can encourage flourishing in cultural settings that have the capacity to self-identify and self-organize as a social action movement.

We recognize that many societies with challenged cultures have limited abilities to support citizen engagement and thus develop practices and systems for flourishing. The framework for flourishing cultures is proposed to develop models from social science criteria to aid in formulating policy, facilitating civil society dialogues, co-designing community ecosystems, and organizing governance for inclusive participation in the creation of desirable social futures.

References

Ayres, R. U. (2008). Sustainability economics: Where do we stand? *Ecological Economics, 67*(2), 281–310.

Barkow, J. H. (2006). Introduction. In J. H. Barkow (ed.), *Missing the revolution: Darwinism for social scientists* (pp. 3–59). New York: Oxford University Press.

Barron, L. & Gauntlet, E. (2002). *Model of social sustainability (Stage 1 report).* Housing and Sustainable Communities Indicators Project, Western Australian Council of Social Service (WACOSS). Perth, Australia.

Beck, U., Bonss, W. & Lau, C. (2003). The theory of reflexive modernization. *Theory, Culture & Society, 20*(2), 1–33.

Bronfenbrenner, U. (1979). *The ecology of human development: Experiments by nature and design.* Cambridge, MA: Harvard University Press.

Christakis, A. N. & Bausch, K. C. (2006). *How people harness their collective wisdom and power to construct the future in co-laboratories of democracy.* Greenwich, CT: Information Age Publishing.

Colantonio, A. (2007). *Social sustainability: An exploratory analysis of its definition, assessment methods metrics and tools.* EIBURS Working Paper Series, 2007/01. Oxford Brooks University, Oxford Institute for Sustainable Development (OISD), International Land Markets Group, Oxford, UK.

Colantonio, A. & Dixon, T. (2011). *Urban regeneration and social sustainability: Best practice from European cities.* London: John Wiley & Sons.

Crutzen, P. J. (2002). The "Anthropocene." *Journal de Physique IV (Proceedings), 12*(10), 1–5.

Cumulus Association. (2008). *Kyoto design declaration.* Kyoto Design Conference, Japan.

Daly, H. E. (1987). The economic growth debate: What some economists have learned but many have not. *Journal of Environmental Economics and Management, 14*(4), 323–336.

Daly, H. E. (2006). Sustainable development-definitions, principles, policies. In M. Keiner (ed.), *The future of sustainability* (pp. 39–53). Dordrecht: Springer Netherlands.

Durkheim, E. (1982, translations of works written 1895–1917). In S. Lukes (ed.), *The rules of sociological method, and selected texts on sociology and its method*. London: Macmillan.

Ehrenfeld, J. R. (2008). *Sustainability by design: A subversive strategy for transforming our consumer culture*. New Haven, CT: Yale University Press.

Fredrickson, B. L. & Losada, M. F. (2005). Positive affect and the complex dynamics of human flourishing. *American Psychologist, 60*(7), 678–686.

Fry, T. (2009). *Design futuring*. New York: Berg Publishers.

Gilroy, R. (2008). Places that support human flourishing: Lessons from later life. *Planning Theory & Practice, 9*(2), 145–163.

Heffernan, J. B., Soranno, P. A., Angilletta Jr, M. J., Buckley, L. B., Gruner, D. S., Keitt, T. H. ... & Weathers, K. C. (2014). Macrosystems ecology: Understanding ecological patterns and processes at continental scales. *Frontiers in Ecology and the Environment, 12*(1), 5–14.

Heller, S. & Vienne, V. (2003). *Citizen designer: Perspectives on design responsibility*. New York: Skyhorse Publishing.

Irwin, T. (2015). Transition design: A proposal for a new area of design practice, study, and research. *Design and Culture, 7*(2), 229–246.

Irwin, T., Kossoff, G. & Tonkinwise, C. (2015). Transition design provocation. *Design Philosophy Papers, 13*(1), 3–11.

Jacobs, J. (2004). *Dark age ahead*. New York: Random House.

Jones, P. H. (2014). Systemic design principles for complex social systems. In *Social Systems and Design* (pp. 91–128). Japan: Springer.

Jones, P. (2015). Can we design for a flourishing society? A practice of cultural futures. In *Proceedings of Relating Systems Thinking and Design (RSD4) 2015 Symposium*. Banff, Canada, September 1–3, 2015.

Keyes, C. L. (1998). Social well-being. *Social Psychology Quarterly*, 121–140.

Keyes, C. L. (2002). The mental health continuum: From languishing to flourishing in life. *Journal of Health and Social Behavior*, 207–222.

Latour, B. (2008). A cautious Prometheus? A few steps toward a philosophy of design (with special attention to Peter Sloterdijk). In *Proceedings of the 2008 Annual International Conference of the Design History Society* (pp. 2–10).

Law, J. & Urry, J. (2004). Enacting the social. *Economy and Society, 33*(3), 390.

Levin, S. A. (1998). Ecosystems and the biosphere as complex adaptive systems. *Ecosystems, 1*, 431–436.

Luhmann, N. (1997). Globalization or world society? How to conceive of modern society. *International Review of Sociology, 7*(1), 67–79.

Marks, N. & Thompson, S. (2006). Towards a flourishing society: Economics, politics and well-being. *The Journal of the Royal Society for the Promotion of Health, 126*(6), 260–261.

McKenzie, S. (2004). Social sustainability: Towards some definition. *Hawke Research Institute Working Paper Series No 27*. Magill, South Australia: University of South Australia.

Mingers, J. (2002). Can social systems be autopoietic? Assessing Luhmann's social theory. *The Sociological Review, 50*(2), 278–299.

Neumayer, E. (2013). *Weak versus strong sustainability: Exploring the limits of two opposing paradigms* (4th edn). Cheltenham, UK: Edward Elgar.

Ostrom, E. (2009). A general framework for analyzing sustainability of social-ecological systems. *Science, 325*(5939), 419–422.

Özbekhan, H. (1969). *Toward a general theory of planning*. Management and Behavioral Science Center, University of Pennsylvania.

Sachs, I. (1999). Social sustainability and whole development: Exploring the dimensions of sustainable development. In B. Egon & J. Thomas (eds), *Sustainability and the social sciences: A cross-disciplinary approach to integrating environmental considerations into theoretical reorientation*. London: Zed Books.

Saul, J. R. (2005). *The collapse of globalism and the reinvention of the world*. Toronto: Viking Canada.

Smith, A. (2011). The transition town network: A review of current evolutions and renaissance. *Social Movement Studies, 10*(1), 99–105.

Stren, R. & Polese, M. (2000). Understanding the new sociocultural dynamics of cities comparative urban policy in a global context. In R. Stren & M. Polese (eds), *The social sustainability of cities: Diversity and the management of change*. Toronto: University of Toronto Press.

Thackara, J. (2006). Putting the future into perspective. *RSA Journal, 153*(5523), 36–41.

Thackara, J. (2015). *How to thrive in the next economy*. New York: Thames and Hudson.

Throsby, D. (2003). Cultural sustainability. In David Throsby & Ruth Towse (eds), *A handbook of cultural economics*. Northampton, MA: Edward Elgar Publishing.

Timmer, V. & Seymoar, N. (2005). *The livable city*. The World Urban Forum 2006: Vancouver Working Group Discussion Paper.

Trist, E. & Murray, H. (1997). *The social engagement of social science: A Tavistock anthology, volume 3: The socio-ecological perspective*. Philadelphia: University of Pennsylvania Press.

Upward, A. & Jones, P. (2015). An ontology for strongly sustainable business models: Defining an enterprise framework compatible with natural and social science. *Organization & Environment, 29*(1) 97–123.

Victor, P. A. (2008). *Managing without growth*. Cheltenham, UK Edward Elgar.

Weigand, K., Flanagan, T., Dye, K. & Jones, P. (2014). Collaborative foresight: Complementing long-horizon strategic planning. *Technological Forecasting and Social Change, 85*, 134–152.

Wheatley, M. J. & Frieze, D. (2011). *Walk out walk on: A learning journey into communities daring to live the future now*. Oakland, CA: Berrett-Koehler Publishers.

World Commission on Environment and Development (WCED). (1987). *Report of the world commission on environment and development: Our common future (the Brundtland Commission Report)*. New York: Oxford University Press.

5 The idea of simplicity as a pathway to cultural sustainability

Jorge Andres Caro del Castillo

Introduction

What is the role of culture in sustainability and why are cultural expressions and manifestations emphasised in sustainable development? Research on this topic demonstrates that culture, as an important motif and element of the human experience, cannot be discarded in the planning of futures or scenarios (Ramberg & Verdu-Isachsen, 2012). To analyse culture is to analyse the expression of humanity itself.

This chapter will analyse a specific cultural manifestation that had great influence on the work of designers and architects. Modernism, which is represented in the work of many individuals, such as Walter Gropius, Charles-Edouard Jeanneret and Henry van de Velde, as well as by organisations and movements such as the Bauhaus and the Werkbund, created the intellectual mould from which the minds of designers would emerge throughout the twentieth century. Because this influence was so important and powerful, it is certain that the simple, lean and minimalistic works of current designers are based on and inspired by these theories and influences (Walker, 2012). For these reasons, this chapter frames Modernism and its subsequent expressions as real and tangible cultural manifestations of the western world. If these movements are understood as manifestations of culture instead of mere theories or currents of thought, it will be possible to understand the mind-sets of the designers in our time.

Two examples of the work of two designers will be presented and explained. These examples will be useful in identifying the design styles and forms generated by Modernism and how these principles are manifest in contemporary development and environments, thus showing that they have not been replaced or forgotten but serve as a substantial basis for contemporary design.

The chapter then will focus on contributing new and useful knowledge to this field by proposing an alternative to production, manufacturing and distribution based on these previously mentioned manifestations. This alternative aims for leaner, simpler and truer processes of manufacturing, production and distribution based on the reconsideration of theories that were proposed before the Modern era in the work of individuals such as William Morris, Augustus Pugin and John Ruskin. Because these theories are closely related to artisanship and crafted means of production, they provide a useful framework for addressing ethical issues (Reid, 1986).

It is worthwhile for designers to analyse and comprehend what has been created and developed in history. With that knowledge, designers can create schemes and pathways that can be used to solve current problems and provide better environments for the people and spaces of our time.

Modernism as a manifestation of culture

This section will discuss Modernism and its heritage as an intrinsic manifestation of culture rather than a set of theories or propositions that were formulated in a given period. The justification for this approach is the major influence that this movement has generated in western civilisation throughout the past and present centuries. Certainly, the extensive cultural manifestation of Modernism is based on the influence of this movement on designers, architects and the public in a way that few movements have achieved. Paul Greenhalgh (1990) states, 'in terms of quality, the international style is the most successful "look" ever to have been invented' because it has influenced 'thousands of buildings and millions of objects'. Greenhalgh also renders a picture of the mind of the people in that time, stating,

> the millions of anonymous designers amongst us, the homeowners of Britain, painted their walls beige and boxed in their Victorian fixtures and fittings with hardboard. This was their oblique response to the modernist call for the rejection of historical style and enhancement of purity.
>
> (p. 4)

Similarly, Christopher Wilk states the following:

> Indeed, the build environment that we live in today was largely shaped by Modernism. The buildings we inhabit, the chairs we sit on, the graphic design that surrounds us have all been created by the aesthetics and the ideology of Modernist design. We live in an era that still identifies itself in terms of Modernism as post-modernist or even post-post-modernist. It simply is not possible to work in ignorance of the most powerful force in the creation of twentieth century visual culture.
>
> (2006, p. 12)

Wilk mentions that Modernism can, then, be conceived as a major twentieth century movement in art, architecture, design, literature and even culture. This statement is relevant because he refers to and identifies the Modernist approach as a true manifestation of culture that first flourished in some cities in Germany, as well as in the Netherlands, Paris, Moscow, Prague and New

York, and then spread to almost every country and society in the western world (Uphaus, 2008; Proctor, 2009).

Premises of Modernism as an influence

One of the most important premises on which Modernism rests is the concept of morality. The precursors of this movement understood that the way to address moral rightfulness in design and development was by exploding accepted conceptions of truth and demonstrating that the way to truth was through simplicity. Therefore, if a project were simple, it would be considered as morally correct. According to Greenhalgh (1990), 'truth meant the avoidance of contrivances which created an illusion of false impression'. These ideas were implemented and ameliorated by and through several members of the Modern Movement. However, it was usually necessary to demonstrate the way an object was made, which was an important characteristic. Therefore, its aesthetic value would be a result of the fabrication process.

The Modern Movement also proposed the systematic rejection of decoration and ornamentation because they could mask the structural and spatial 'trueness' of an object. These specific ideologies were in opposition to the ornamentation and decoration that was associated with the historicism that prevailed in the nineteenth century before the rise of the Modern Movement. The contemporary assumption was that if the human race was in the process of moving away from the past and the unsatisfactory conditions in which society was immersed, then the styles of the past should be seen as aesthetically and morally undesirable (Greenhalgh, 1990). An important concept of the Modern Movement was that purity was equal to truth. Subsequently, the Bauhaus Movement would reject ornamentation and decoration and embrace abstraction and a belief in the unity of all the arts (Wilk, 2006). It is worth mentioning that the concept of abstraction is defined as the process of removing or taking away the characteristics of a given concept in order to unveil a purer or more essential facet of it in order to reduce complexity, enhance efficiency and omit unwanted or unneeded attributes.

Some discrepancies

It is an undeniable truth that Modernism generated and incentivised positive changes, new theories and fresh knowledge. It is also true that these ideologies resulted in negative, undesirable and improvable conditions for some segments of the population, same as in the natural and the built environments. The posture of this work does not support the assumption that all the propositions Modern theories promote an adequate relationship between humans and the natural environments they inhabit. Therefore, some examples of this are presented.

The first example concerns the *homogenisation* and, in some cases, the alienation of design and cultural manifestations. In the proposition of an 'international style', efforts were made to standardise the conceptualisation and interpretation of aesthetic values. These efforts contributed to the devaluation of local manifestations of culture and individual interpretations of aesthetics. The minds of designers were also standardised according to strict parameters that required the forfeiture of personality for the sake of pursuing the simplicity of form (Greenhalgh, 1990). The second example refers to the importance Modernists placed on mass production and the industrialisation of manufacturing. Research shows that the minds of Modernists were oriented to bringing Modernism to the people through the means of mass production and prefabrication in an almost messianic way. They saw the machine and industrial technology as saviours and solvers of the problems they dealt with in that period. This sincere and passionate belief rather than being initiated or motivated by environmental causes, was a response to the economic, political and social circumstances in mainland Europe in that specific time. This concept is well explained by Paul Greenhalgh (1990):

> Their worship of the idea of mass production (in the absence of the political, economic, psychological and ecological reality of it) demonstrated the extent of the space between their quest and the material means with which they wished to accomplish it.
>
> (p. 16)

Lastly, it is relevant that these theories and works were an important influence on not only the mass consumption of goods but also fashion. The Werkbund viewed fashion as not a mere trend of changing clothes frequently. It represented a mind-set in which the new theories of capitalism, mass consumption and production were exemplified (Schwartz, 1996).

The idea of simplicity

In the past century, and surely in this current one, certain ways of thinking led to various methods of design, which were expressed as the famous 'less is more' by Mies van der Rhoe, 'doing more with less' by Buckminster Fuller and 'less, but better' by Dieter Rams. These similar ways of thinking led designers towards one simple goal: improve the way things are done by doing them in a simpler way. This principle, if understood literally, could generate useful insights. We are aware of examples such as Functionalism, Neoplasticism and the Bauhaus. These movements have been applied in many fields and areas in design, research and education (Wilk, 2006; Holt & Skov, 2008).

Perhaps Mies was not thinking of sustainable design when he decided to do things the way he did. Perhaps these ways of thinking were not intended to take care of the environment or to represent cultural manifestations. However, these ideas were transmitted through generations of designers, and they are a significant influence on the methods and procedures on contemporary design

(Greenhalgh, 1990). Today, sustainability is not an option or an added value; it is a must (Papanek, 1985; Fry, 2009).

The ideas of environmental preservation and social fairness might seem contemporary. However, research has demonstrated that the awareness of improving social conditions and generating positive changes in the ways mass manufacturing is performed have persisted for a long time. Indeed, they emerged more than a hundred years ago with the mechanisation of production and the distribution of labour. William Morris (1911) observed the following:

> Everything made by man's hands has a form, which must be either beautiful or ugly; beautiful if it is in accord with Nature, and helps her; ugly if it is discordant with Nature, and thwarts her.
>
> (p. 4)

This passage is relevant here because it raises the question of what could be more sustainable than placing nature as the main and most powerful inspiration, and focusing on maintaining and improving it (Dore, 1990). This example of the Arts and Crafts Movement, which was and is still a powerful cultural manifestation, is consistently related to current theories on sustainability, even if they were proposed and generated more than a hundred years ago. According to Peter Stansky (1985),

> Morris's views on the environment, on preserving what is of value in both the natural and 'built' worlds, on decentralising bloated government, are as significant now as they were in Morris's own time, or even more so. Earlier in the twentieth century, much of his thinking, particularly its political side, was dismissed as sheer romanticism. After the Second World War, it appeared that modernisation, centralisation, industrialism, rationalism – all the faceless movements of the time – were in control and would take care of the world. Today, when we have a keen sense of the shambles of their efforts, the suggestions that Morris made in his designs, his writings, his actions and his politics have new power and relevance.
>
> (p. 89)

This passage efficiently merges culture and sustainability. Stansky talks about cultural and natural preservation as well as human movements and institutions and how all these aspects interact and coexist. Consequently, the importance of this approach and pathway has not diminished through the years, and they are still relevant in a very strong and important way. Cultural sustainability refers to preserving not only cultural heritage, characteristics, aspects and methods but also the thoughts that lead to such preservation.

However, the idea of simplicity concerns more than form as the consequence of the aesthetic approach. It ought to include the actual construction of the project. Previously, the creators of the Arts and Crafts Movement worked to raise society's awareness of important considerations, some of

which can be summarised as follows: the necessity to make production processes and methods shorter, leaner, more local and closer to the people
(Morris, 1911; Naylor, 1971). Is not this also a principle of simplicity?

A contribution

Research has found that the idea of simplicity is rooted in the collective
thinking of contemporary design. Applied using several methods, simplicity is
common in many features of our daily lives, which of course refers to the
figure, form and aesthetic qualities and characteristics of designs and products.

The following example will show how a simple design can be considered
more sustainable than a complex one, which can be understood if the principles
of some already-mentioned styles are examined. The function is more
important than the form, and the function gives the product its beauty and
value (Wilk, 2006). The idea of the ultimate simplicity and abstraction of forms
is expressed in the use of fewer materials, simpler figures, simpler lines, fewer
combinations of materials, fewer colours, fewer textures, fewer processes, and
simpler and more efficient ways of production. The sense of simplicity and
abstraction that Modernism proposed can be used to develop fewer processes in
producing objects, therefore saving costs and reducing the amount of material,
energy, time and human resources. Simpler and less 'elaborate' forms and
figures require much less of all these aspects of producing an object.

Therefore, by pursuing the idea of abstraction, it might be possible to
include other novel characteristics, such as less distribution, fewer logistics,
less shipping, distribution, retail and supply (Kropotkin, 1906; Morris, 1911;
Papanek, 1985). It is important to mention this chapter does not propose that
the tendency of globalisation would be to cease supplying goods from one
side of the world to another. Instead, this work calls for a reduction or a systematic change in the way supply meets demand in the contemporary
context. Research has shown that these characteristics are sustainable, and
they are an ethical pathway for distributing products (Thorpe, 2007).

Two examples of the theory

In order to promote better understanding of the theory, two examples will be
analysed: the Bac armchair created by the British designer Jasper Morrison
(Cappellini, n.d.) and the Ekstrem chair created by Norwegian designer Terje
Ekstrøm (Varier, n.d.).

An aesthetic analysis of the first example reveals that its simplicity of form,
construction and materials correlates with the ideologies and later manifestations
of the Modern Movement (Boyer & Zanco, 1999). The truth and honesty of
the characteristics of the material used to fabricate this chair are visible. Morrison does not use any decoration or visual aid to enhance, alter or modify the
inherit characteristics of the wood (or polyurethane) in the product. Morrison
follows through in his design language a clear predisposition for clean and

simple figures, demonstrating that he has found substantial interest and inspiration in key representatives of the Modern Movement as stated by Buckminster Fuller and Le Corbusier (Morrison, 1990).

In terms of its aesthetics, this product is a positive representation of the idea of abstraction proposed by Modernists. Therefore, it is an example of the specific cultural manifestations that Modernism generated (Morrison, 2002).

When this first premise is displayed and the example is viewed as a representative of a given expression, then it is possible analyse it as an example of sustainability. The explanation is based on the physical and aesthetical attributes of the product. It is possible to say that this specific product incentivises the utilisation of few materials, few processes of manufacture, reduced time of production and a low degree of complexity of form. If these attributes are taken into consideration, it can be possible to imply that a 'simple' product involves fewer considerations and therefore fewer costs. Hence, the Bac chair can be seen as an example of a given cultural manifestation and a project that incentivises environmentalism. Hence, it is an example of cultural sustainability.

It is possible to think that many other products could better exemplify these theories (Uphaus, 2008). Moreover, some projects are more oriented to Modern movements than others are. Other projects are developed for environmentalism and cultural sustainability. Therefore, this product was chosen as an example first because it was developed by a very influential and well-known designer (Boyer & Zanco, 1999). Second, it is also important to explain the condition of a product that possesses 'sustainable characteristics without being planned for', which means that according to the previous research, it is recognised and understood that this product was generated because of the freedom of will and opportunity. It was not bound to any predisposition or influence of formal inspiration or ideology. These chairs exemplify that both manifestations coexist without being intentionally addressed.

Last, it is relevant to include and analysis of the ideology and attitude of Morrison towards design. Some consider Morrison as a "modernist scratching into post-modernism" (Fukasawa & Morrison, 2007). Morrison is critical of manufacturing, stating

> design, which used to be almost unknown as a profession, has become a major source of pollution, encouraged by glossy lifestyle magazines and marketing departments, it's become a competition to make things as noticeable as possible by means of colour, shape and surprise.

He also provides an interesting critique of functionalism, mentioning 'if a shape that follows function is too functional, its relationship to people may turn cold' (Fukasawa & Morrison, 2007).

However, as stated earlier in the text, the concepts of cultural sustainability and environmentalism can be expanded when this example is analysed. If the premise of abstraction and simplicity is extracted from the ideas of Modernism and is placed in a new context, it is elevated from the mere aesthetical qualities of a product and addressed it through the conception, manufacturing and distribution of the product. If this is achieved, the leanness and simplicity proposed by the Modern Movement proposed can flourish, providing a fertile ground for novel ways of conceiving design and interactions with goods.

The second example is the Ekstrem chair, which was designed in 1972 by the Norwegian designer Terje Ekstrøm. This project is considered here because it represents how postmodernism was initiated and addressed in a completely different setting for reasons that are different from previous ones. First, this project might seem humble in terms of the person who designed it and the manufacturer that fabricated it. Certainly, Ekstrøm is not as well known internationally as Morrison is, so this project is relevant. Even if not everyone in the world has heard of Ekstrøm, this particular project is well known and important in his country of origin, Norway. This chair is considered one of the first postmodern furniture products developed in the country; therefore, it has acquired iconic status.

The aesthetic attributes of this project also respond to the freedom of will because nothing similar was seen in the country before the conception of this chair (Høidal, 2001). This project was chosen because it is a different representation of the important concept of locality previously mentioned in this chapter. It is important to exemplify how postmodernism was generated and how it evolved in a local context as a personal and individual manifestation.

The alternative to craftsmanship

Some ideas that emerged as a response to the industrialisation and mechanisation of production generated by the Industrial Revolution can be used as a theoretical foundation to incorporate simplicity and abstraction into today's manufacturing of goods and products. Individuals such as William Morris and John Ruskin perceived the unfavourable conditions that the new means of manufacturing were causing in both society and the ecosystems of the late nineteenth and early twentieth centuries (Morris, 2009). They and other individuals perceived that industrialisation could and should help the worker by making his or her labour easier and faster (Kropotkin, 1900). However, instead, industrialisation transformed a skilled craftsman into a mechanised operative (Morris, 1911). Morris commented the following:

> Now as I am quite sure that no art, not even the feeblest, rudest or least intelligent, can come of such work, so also I am sure that such work makes the workman less than a man and degrades him grievously and unjustly, and that nothing can compensate him or us for such degradation: and I want you specially to note that this was instinctively felt in the very earliest days of what are called the industrial arts.
>
> (1911, p. 152)

John Ruskin also stated his position regarding the machine: 'life without industry is guilt, industry without art is brutality' (Ruskin, 1870). For these individuals, a production system that would narrow the gap between the manufacturer and the user was essential (Ruskin, 1981). This idea is relevant here because it exemplifies shortening the current production system. It is intended that a systematic and strong connection between the manufacturer and the public would lead to better mutual understanding and more efficient communication between these two entities.

A production system that would take into greater consideration the resources of craftsmanship would also benefit from the reduction of transportation, distribution, shipping, retail, and therefore all intermediaries (Reid, 1986). If all these activities were reduced, it would be possible to talk about a simple and lean way to address the design process by pursuing not only the abstraction of the form but also the abstraction of the conception and formulation of the project itself.

In addition, a reconsideration of the crafted means of production could contribute to a critical view of designers about their role in putting yet another product on the market (Fry, 2009). This might be relevant in a world where an increasing number of products are produced to be sold in in huge numbers on as many markets as possible (Papanek, 1985).

Finally, it seems natural and relevant that a systematic enhancing work crafted by hand can be an important source in addressing the ethical social circumstances of the design process. If a designer considers not only the individuals who will purchase and utilise the product but also the manufacturers of it, a true sense of ethical production would emerge.

The relation between the arts and crafts movement and modernism

Perhaps one of the very precursors of Modern Movement was Augustus Pugin. In 1835, he began generating propositions of the recognition of the identity and attributes of a given material and a construction process in which the joinery and solution of the structure were visible and revealed. He criticised the over-decoration of his time, in which the materials were hidden under a layer of other materials that served as 'imitators'. For example, plaster and papier-mâché were used to imitate stonework (Greenhalgh, 1990). Pugin was as a highly valuable source of inspiration for Morris and Ruskin. However, Pugin's work was also an important inspiration for other individuals who were not obviously influenced by his theories. Herman Muthesius, who was an extremely important inspiration for Walter Gropius, recognised Pugin's work in the areas of form imposition and craftsmanship. Subsequently, Le Corbusier acknowledged the work of Ruskin regarding the abstraction and truth of materials (Greenhalgh, 1990).

The work and propositions of Pugin and Ruskin took two distinctive pathways in the mind-set of the people who were inspired by their ideologies.

Individuals such as Muthesius and Gropius utilised Pugin's ideologies on the aesthetic and material level, whereas Morris applied this influence in manufacturing and labour-related contexts. We can thus infer that the Arts and Crafts Movement and the Modern Movement took two different directions. This fact separates them to the degree that they are completely different currents. This chapter recognises the deep differences between these two movements. Moreover, one of its main approaches is to show how they correlated and interacted based first on their origins and second on their development as separate ideologies.

The bond between Modernism and previous theories is exemplified by the connection between the Arts and Crafts Movement and the Bauhaus School. As stated in its programme of April 1919, the latter was inspired by Morris:

> Architects, painters, sculptors, we must all return to crafts! … A foundation in handicraft is essential for every artist … let us therefore create a new guild of craftsmen without the class distinctions that raise an arrogant barrier between craftsman and artist! Let us together desire, conceive and create the new building of the future, which will combine everything – architecture and sculpture and painting – in a single form which will one day rise towards the heavens from the hands of a million workers as the crystalline symbol of a new and coming faith.
>
> (Raizman, p. 181)

The Bauhaus praised the rejection of industrialisation and mechanisation, which seemed closely related to the First World War. The Bauhaus seem to have followed Morris's propositions, which called for a return to the handcrafted production and the manual skill that characterised the form (Stansky, 1985). Moreover, the school advocated work and manufacturing model that was closely related to the small-scale production that characterised the Middle Ages.

Morris was also an important influence on the development of the Deutscher Werkbund, particularly the ideas of not imitating hand-made goods in machine manufacturing and not promoting products as a mean to recreating the culture of the pre-capitalist era (Schwartz, 1996). Christopher Wilk (2006) commented the following:

> William Morris depicted an agrarian idyll in *News From Nowhere* (1890), reacting against the horrors of mechanised production and the problems of social dislocation associated with industrialisation in Britain during the nineteenth century. This vision fed the hopes and dreams of those associated with the Arts and Crafts movement both in Britain and elsewhere, inspiring the craftsmen and designers of the Wiener Werkstätte and the Deutscher Werkbund in the early years of the twentieth century.
>
> (p. 24)

Last, it seems relevant to mention some ideologies and norms that characterised the first stages of Modernism. The first phase comprised set of ideas of how the designed world could 'transform human consciousness and improve material conditions' (Greenhalgh, 1990). These sometimes were utopian ideas of a return to nature, in which a better world would be achieved not by improving the external accessories of life or implementing new technologies but by restoring the inner world of emotional and spiritual values.

In this period, the Modernists, similar to the Arts and Crafts movement, shared the notion that separating the practices of art and design and art from life was not optimal. Although the Modern Movement rejected the idea of implementing craftsmanship as a righteous means of production and replacing it by mass production, they integrated the concept of pristine form, enhancing of material qualities and rejection of the imitation proposed by architects and designers such as Pugin, Ruskin and Morris.

Conclusion

One of the aims of this work is to provide individuals related to design education or research with novel insights and discussions of the ways in which Modernism, post-Modernism and contemporary design can be perceived. This work aimed to provide relevant considerations for further research and the development of knowledge. Another aim of this work was to provide students and practitioners in design spheres with the knowledge and inspiration to perform their work. A wider understanding of history and theory will help to generate better and more conscious design.

Finally, this work was intended to reach every individual related to design and to state the imperative in addressing and generating appropriately sustainable and socially moral design. The utilisation of cultural sustainability as a means of incorporating ethics into the design process is a topic that should be studied intensively and then implemented efficiently in order to achieve the greater good. This chapter addresses the issue of cultural sustainability by examining previous theories and proposing the concept of incentivising the utilisation of crafted means of production. If the concept of cultural and environmental sustainability was considered in not only the aesthetical form of a given object but also the entire process of its design and production, better social and environmental conditions would result.

References

Boyer, C.-A. & Zanco, F. (1999). *Jasper Morrison*. Paris: Dis Voir.

Brower, C., Mallory, R. & Ohlman, Z. (2005). *Experimental eco design: Architecture, fashion, product*. Mies: RotoVision.

Cappellini. (n.d.). BAC chair. Retrieved from www.cappellini.it/en/products/chairs-and-armchairs/bac

Dore, H. (1990). *William Morris*. Secaucus, NJ: Chartwell Books.

Fry, T. (2009). *Design futuring: Sustainability, ethics and new practice*. Oxford: Berg.

Fukasawa, N. & Morrison, J. (2007). *Super normal: Sensations of the ordinary*. Baden: Lars Müller Publishers.

Greenhalgh, P. (1990). *Modernism in design*. London: Reaktion Books.

Høidal, E. (2001). Møbelmuseet. Retrieved from http://mobelfagligsenter.no/publikasjonar-og-artiklar/om-stolen-ekstrem/

Holt, S. & Skov, M. H. (2008). *Manufractured: The conspicuous transformation of everyday objects*. San Francisco: Chronicle Books.

Kropotkin, P. A. K. (1900). *Fields, factories and workshops, or industry combined with agriculture and brain work with manual work*. London: Thomas Nelson.

Kropotkin, P. A. K. (1906). *The conquest of bread*. London: Chapman and Hall.

Morris, W. (1911). *Hopes and fears for art: Five lectures*. London: Longmans, Green and Co.

Morris, W. (2009). *Signs of change*. [Waiheke Island]: Floating Press.

Morrison, J. (1990). *Jasper Morrison: Designs, projects and drawings 1981–1989*. London: Architecture Design and Technology Press.

Morrison, J. (2002). *Jasper Morrison: Everything but the walls*. Baden: Müller.

Naylor, G. (1971). *The arts and crafts movement: A study of its sources, ideals and influence on design theory*. London: Studio Vista.

Papanek, V. (1985). *Design for the real world: Human ecology and social change*. London: Thames & Hudson.

Proctor, R. (2009). *1000 new eco designs and where to find them*. London: Laurence King Publishing

Raizman, D. (2003). *History of modern design: Graphics and products since the Industrial Revolution*. London: Laurence King Publishing.

Ramberg, T. & Verdu-Isachsen, L. S. (2012). *Design without borders: Creating change*. Oslo: Norsk Form.

Reid, H. (1986). *The furniture makers: A history of trade unionism in the furniture trade, 1865–1972*. Oxford: Malthouse Press.

Ruskin, J. (1981). *The stones of Venice*. London: Faber and Faber.

Ruskin, J. (1870). *Lectures on art*. New York: Allworth Press.

Schwartz, F. J. (1996). *The Werkbund: Design theory and mass culture before the First World War*. New Haven, CT: Yale University Press.

Stansky, P. (1983). *William Morris*. Oxford, UK: Oxford University Press.

Stansky, P. (1985). *Redesigning the world: William Morris, the 1880s, and the arts and crafts*. Princeton, NJ: Princeton University Press.

Thorpe, A. (2007). *The designer's atlas of sustainability*. Washington, DC: Island Press.

Uphaus, N. (2008). *Ecological design*. Kempen: teNeues.

Varier. (n.d.). Ekstrem chair. Retrieved from www.varierfurniture.com/en_no/Movement-Chairs/Ekstrem/Variations-Ekstrem/Ekstrem_Black_KNI009

Walker, S. (2012). The object of nightingales: Design values for a meaningful material culture. *Design and Culture, 4*(2), 149–170. doi: 10.2752/175470812x13281948975459.

Wilk, C. (2006). *Modernism: Designing a new world: 1914–1939*. London: V&A Publications.

Part II
Environments

6 Housing culture, residential preferences and sustainability

Petter Næss

Introduction

The purpose of this chapter is to discuss the prevailing Norwegian[1] housing development and housing culture from a sustainability perspective and assess to what extent current trends toward more acceptance of dense forms of living are sufficient to bring us closer to sustainability goals. In Norway, political focus on sustainable urban development and sustainable housing was already strong in the late 1980s, boosted by the fact that the UN Commission that put the very concept of sustainable development on the international political agenda (World Commission on Environment and Development, 1987) was headed by Gro Harlem Brundtland, who was Norwegian Prime Minister from 1986 to 1989 and from 1990 to 1996. This paper takes as its point of departure the fact that the single-family house has for a long time been the most common form of housing in Norway and also a widely preferred dwelling type. This housing type is associated with high land consumption and energy use and is in its suburban form highly problematic judged against sustainability criteria (see the section *Housing and sustainability* in this chapter). Housing cultures are, however, not static, and they can be influenced by the kind of housing types actually being built. During the latest decades, housing development as well as housing preferences changed toward higher popularity of denser forms of living (see the section *Norwegian housing culture and residential preferences* in this chapter). The positive sustainability consequences of this are, however, counteracted by growth in floor area per capita, frequent fashion-motivated renovations and increasing second-home ownership (see the section *A consumerist housing culture* in this chapter). Sustainable development within the housing sector would require housing provision and housing cultures to be based on a radically different paradigm than the prevailing consumerist and growth-oriented conditions (see the section *Concluding remarks* in this chapter).

Often, the typical Norwegian housing culture has been associated with the single-family house. Around 60 percent of the Norwegian population lives in this housing type (Statistics Norway, 2013a), although its share has decreased somewhat during the most recent decades, especially in the largest urban regions. Judged from the overall high share of single-family house residents, the characterization of the detached single-family house as the typical Norwegian way of living seems to have some merits. The picture is still more nuanced. For one thing, there are obvious differences between urban and rural contexts. Moreover, in the cities, suburban life in a single-family house was, before World War II, an option for a much smaller part of the population than after the strong suburban development in the 1950s, 1960s and 1970s. The conceptualizing of the Norwegian housing culture as one closely tied to the single-family house therefore needs to be differentiated in terms of spatial as well temporal contexts. And regarding the latter, it is not given that the single-family dwelling will – or should – retain its dominating position in the future. As will be shown in the next section, this kind of dwelling performs poorly against most sustainability criteria in an urban context. Given that an increasing part of the future Norwegian population is expected to be living in urban areas, prevalence of the single-family house as a dominant housing ideal and aspiration for the residential career of households raises several problems, seen from a sustainability viewpoint.

Before discussing the sustainability merits of different housing types, a clarification of my interpretation of the terms of sustainable development and urban sustainability is necessary.

Housing and sustainability

Sustainable development and criteria of urban sustainability

As the saying goes, a pet child gets many names. Concerning the use of the concept of sustainable development, one might perhaps as well say, 'a pet name gets many children.' Today, a manifold range of strategies and projects is promoted with the claim that they are derived from the very concept of sustainable development. It has become politically impossible not to be a supporter of sustainable development, so there is a clear danger that the concept will be watered down. For example, sustainability is sometimes presented as being a matter of sustaining the growth potential of a particular city or urban region in competition with other geographical areas (e.g., Municipality of Aalborg, 2003). Such an understanding is very different from the way in which the concept of sustainable development was presented in the document that put the concept on the international political agenda, namely the report 'Our Common Future' launched by the Brundtland Commission in 1987. My discussion below is based on the Brundtland Commission's definition of sustainable development as

> development that meets the needs of the present without compromising the ability of future generations to meet their own needs. It contains within it two key concepts: the concept of 'needs,' in particular the essential needs of the world's poor, to which overriding priority should

be given, and the idea of limitations imposed by the state of technology and social organization on the environment's ability to meet present and future needs.

(World Commission on Environment and Development, 1987, p. 43)

Sustainable development, as understood in this definition, combines ethical norms of welfare, distribution and democracy while recognizing that nature's ability to absorb human-made encroachments and pollution is limited. What would such a development imply for housing development in a wealthy country like Norway? Based on the conception of sustainable development in the Brundtland Commission's report, the 1992 conference on Environment and Development in Rio de Janeiro, and the subsequent work of the UN committee on Environment and Development and the United Nations Human Settlements Program, the following environmental, social and economic goals of sustainable urban development emerge as important:

- Environmental goals: Reducing energy use and emissions, minimizing encroachments on ecosystems and arable land, minimizing the use of environmentally harmful construction materials, replacement of open-ended flows of substances with closed loops, and a sound environment for the city's inhabitant.
- Social goals: Promote accessibility, affordability, democracy, fair distribution and social cohesion – locally and in a global context.
- Economic goals: Resource efficiency, meeting vital needs among the population.

Housing and environmental sustainability

Housing development is closely related to the overall development of cities. Among the four largest cities in Norway,[2] accounting for nearly one third of the total Norwegian population, residential areas accounted for on average 37 percent of the total urban area and 52 percent of the built-up parts[3] of the urban area. The extent to which urban development entails conversion of previously undeveloped land into urban areas is closely related to the kind of housing development taking place. Different kinds of housing put different demands on land for construction. Whereas housing development based on apartment buildings often requires only 50 to 100 square meters of land per dwelling, the construction of single-family house areas typically consumes around 1000 square meters of land per dwelling. Single-family houses thus add up to low-density, land-consuming neighborhoods and cities, whereas apartment buildings are compatible with compact, dense urban development. Needless to say, this translates into different extents of pressure against undeveloped land resulting from different kinds of residential development (single-family houses, row houses, apartment buildings). The less land-consuming types of housing are thus friendlier to the protection of farmland, forests, biotopes and areas for outdoor recreation activities like hiking, skiing, bathing and picking of berries or mushrooms.

Densification, rather than urban sprawl, seems more favorable for the protection of natural landscapes, arable land and biodiversity (Beatley, 2000; Pinho et al., 2011). This is particularly the case if densification can incorporate 'brownfield' sites, obsolete harbor areas and parking areas incompatible with a goal of reducing car traffic in the urban center. Since land values usually vary with the distance from the city center (Alonso, 1964) and cultural conceptions of appropriate densities differ between inner-city and suburban contexts (e.g., Fishman, 1996), there is usually a clear center-periphery gradient in the density of population as well as jobs, with higher densities in the inner than in the outer parts of cities. If residential development primarily takes place as the construction of single-family houses, new dwellings are likely to be built mostly as suburban extension of the built-up areas on undeveloped land. Conversely, housing development in the form of apartment buildings or other more concentrated housing types is much more compatible with in-fill and transformation of vacant or poorly utilized areas within the existing urban fabric. A program for housing development in a city where apartment buildings make up the bulk of construction therefore creates much stronger incentives for re-use of such urban areas, which might remain derelict or under-utilized if housing production is geared mainly toward the provision of more single-family houses.

Moreover, multifamily houses require less energy for space heating and cooling per square meter than detached single-family houses (Høyer & Holden, 2001; Brown & Wolfe, 2007). Besides, the floor area of a single family house is usually larger than in apartments and terraced dwellings. This implies a further increase in the differential in space heating requirement between concentrated and area-demanding housing types.

There is overwhelming evidence that low-density cities and residential locations in outer suburbs or exurbs contribute to longer average traveling distances, higher proportions of car usage and higher energy use for transport, compared to denser cities and more central residential neighborhoods (Newman & Kenworthy, 1999; Ewing & Cervero, 2010; Næss, 2012). The densities and locations typical for single-family houses are thus much less favorable in terms of transport energy use and greenhouse gas emissions than the settings associated with apartment buildings and other concentrated types of housing. Since distances between various facilities such as dwellings, jobs, shops, restaurants, etc. will be longer in a low-density than in a dense city, low-density housing contributes to a larger need for transportation. This also affects the modes of travel, since it is economically unfeasible to provide a dense network of public transport lines with frequent departures in urban districts with a sparse population living along the lines. Walking distances from the dwelling to public transport stops as well as waiting times for departures are therefore typically longer in single-family house areas than in higher-density housing districts. Needless to say, this makes public transit less attractive, compared to the private car.

Low-density urban development also discourages an extensive use of non-motorized modes of travel, since most trip destinations in a low-density city will typically be located beyond what the inhabitants consider as acceptable walking or biking distances.

Car driving is also facilitated in single-family house areas because this kind of housing normally provides parking space on each individual site in a garage or in the driveway. Although some apartment buildings also offer parking space in private basement garages, it is much more common that residents in apartment buildings (and also terraced houses) have to walk to a common parking area some distance away from the entrance of the individual dwelling, or simply have to park along curb of the street.

Housing and social sustainability

As can be seen above, the widespread association of suburbia with single-family houses in popular literature (e.g., 'Crossing California,' 'Virgin Suicides' and 'The Ice Storm') and movies (e.g., 'Burbs,' 'Neighbors' and 'Revolutionary Road') is for a reason, as is urban planners' frequent association of single-family houses with car-dependent urban sprawl. And as indicated by the above-mentioned literature and films, suburban single-family house districts are also associated with several social problems. One of them is social segregation. Especially in the USA, suburban development has been tied to social segregation. Through market-based sorting mechanisms, poor people in general, and particularly those belonging to ethnic minorities, are prevented from settling in affluent, white suburbs. The rapid suburbanization that took place in American cities in the decades subsequent to World War II entailed an exodus of high- and middle-income people from the core cities to suburban municipalities, leaving behind central municipalities with a poor tax base for maintenance and improvement of their technical and social infrastructure. The result was the emergence of so-called donut cities, with a ring of affluent suburbia surrounding a 'hole' of poor inner districts. This spatial separation was strongly correlated with cleavages in income levels, color and immigrant status. In a European context, suburban development has to a greater extent than in the USA also included denser types of housing development, such as the construction of apartment buildings along the newly established metro lines in Eastern Oslo in the 1960s and 1970s. In such cases, the socio-spatial segregation occurs to a greater extent within the suburban area itself, with predominantly white and affluent single-family house areas contrasted by denser working-class suburban districts populated by high proportions of immigrants of non-western origin.

According to Power (2001), social integration is dependent on high density, mix of uses and affordability. Single-family house suburbs very often represent the opposite. The suburbs are also being criticized for reducing the opportunities for social contacts, in particular with people from other social groups than one's own (Putnam 2000). Single-family house areas are usually socially more homogeneous than dense inner-city districts. Residents of single-family house areas are therefore usually not 'disturbed' in their local environment by social groups perceived as alien or different. This 'undisturbedness' may at the same time give rise to ignorance and prejudice against people with a different social and cultural background.

Because we cannot live as 'undisturbed' in dense urban environments as in rural and low-density suburban areas, high-density living forces us to train our ability to show consideration and tolerance. Arguably, this is an important and valuable quality of urban social life. Learning to show consideration and to tolerate different fellow human beings is an important part of the process of becoming socialized into civilized humans.

Furthermore, suburbia has been accused of contributing to the maintenance of oppressive patterns of gender roles (Friedan, 1963). Studies in several cities have shown that the jobs of female and male workforce participants living in inner-city districts are located approximately equally far away from home, whereas the jobs of female suburbanites tend to be located within a shorter radius from the dwelling than those of their male counterparts. Among suburbanites, there is thus a tendency for women to find it necessary to choose among a narrower range of job opportunities (and also leisure facilities) than their male counterparts, whereas women's accessibility to facilities is more equal to that of men if they live in the inner districts (Hjorthol 2000; Næss 2008).

Regarding traffic accidents (Røe & Jones, 1997), noise (Kolbenstvedt & Hjorthol, 1987), as well as local pollution, the location of developmental areas has its impacts on the distribution of burdens and benefits between the city's own inhabitants. Metaphorically, as illustrated by Krier (1996), suburban single-family houses are 'bombarding' the inner city with cars and their associated environmental problems. If the construction of new residences takes place in the outer parts of the urban area, those who move into the new suburban single-family houses will benefit from a local neighborhood less polluted and less exposed to traffic accidents than the urban average, while themselves contributing to an increased overall amount of transport burdening residents living closer to the city center with more through traffic, noise, air pollution and a higher risk of accidents. Conversely, those who move into new dwellings made available through inner-city densification typically generate only a small amount of traffic and pollution but will be exposed to the negative impacts of car traffic originating mostly in the suburbs (Røe & Jones, 1997).

Suburban single-family house development thus leads to increased polarization by aggravating the local environmental problems facing those inhabitants who are at the outset exposed to the least satisfactory local traffic situations, while providing a sheltered situation for those who move into the new suburban residences. On the other hand, densification in terms of building more apartments in the inner districts contributes to a less unequal distribution of traffic-related environmental nuisances, since the suburbs will then 'bombard' the city center with fewer cars.

Economic aspects

Multifamily houses require less material for the construction of the buildings. Construction costs per square meter of floor area are still most often higher for apartment buildings than for single-family houses, since the 'wet rooms' of the dwelling (bathroom, toilet and kitchen) are more expensive to build than the remaining rooms and normally make up a larger share of the total floor space in apartments than in the usually more spacious single-family houses. Due to this difference in average floor area size, the building costs per dwelling still vary little across building types, at least in a Norwegian context (Kvinge, Langset & Nørve, 2012).

If we change the view from the individual dwelling to the level of the city, apartments and other dense forms of housing stand out as considerably less costly for society than single-family houses. Multifamily houses require less material for infrastructure construction (roads, sewers, cables, etc.) at city level as well as at neighborhood level and thus reduce the costs of these elements in urban development (Burchell et al., 1998). Operational and maintenance costs for infrastructure show the same pattern. Considering the costs for the construction of residential buildings and infrastructure together, multifamily housing is considerably less expensive for society than single-family dwellings (Mønnesland, 1991). Housing costs are still often higher in the inner city than in the suburbs – in particular when measured per square meter of floor area. This reflects higher demand than supply of centrally located dwellings in many cities, allowing developers to sell at high prices. There is also often a hidden subsidizing of suburban building sites, since road taxes and fees for water, electricity and sewer use are usually 'flat,' independent of location.

Summary so far

Summarizing from the above, the key elements of sustainable housing development in urban areas would be:

- The re-use of urban land instead of greenfield development, with densification channeled to areas already technically affected
- Building resource-efficient housing types. No more construction of detached single-family houses in the major urban regions – those already existing are more than sufficient
- Locating most new residential development to inner-city districts and close to other major public transport nodes.

How well do such principles fit with the current housing culture and residential preferences in Norway?

Norwegian housing culture and residential preferences

The concept of housing culture is rather elusive, and it is hard to make any distinct definition. Some authors, such as Rapoport (2000), hold that it is impossible to relate culture to housing (or any built environment), because these concepts are too broad, general and abstract. Housing cultures do, however, manifest themselves through more concrete attitudes or practices. According to Støa and Aune (2012), housing cultures can be viewed as a coproduction of built environment, social organization, local practices and everyday life, constructed through processes of shaping and reshaping built environment and local practices (domestication). They change from decade to decade and vary between as well as within societies.

Housing ideals are one kind of such attitudes. Like housing cultures, such ideals are also changing (Guttu, 2003), and they vary geographically and between social groups. In Norway, a suburban residential ideal is claimed still to hold a strong position (Aamo and Aspen, 2002). It is often stated that the Norwegian housing culture is particularly focused on single-family houses (Støa and Narvestad, 2005). The very concept of home has been widely understood as a retreat for resting and regaining strength to go back out into the world. Drawing on the architectural theorist Joseph Rykwert, Støa and Aune (2012) find the term 'home' to be linguistically rooted in the fireplace and the gathering around it. The material representation of this conception is most commonly the detached, suburban house. Some authors hold that housing tends to become 'suburban' as soon as a certain affluence level has been reached (e.g., Rapoport, 1998). Haveraaen (1993) claimed that the investment in a single family house was considered a demonstration that a couple really intended to go for a long-lasting relationship – if you did not move to a single-family house, this would be interpreted as an indication of ambivalence about the relationship.

As evident from above, it is often stated that Norwegians have a particular predilection for detached single-family houses. However, single-family houses are hardly more dominating as a preferred dwelling type in Norway than in other Nordic countries, let alone compared to North America and Australia. Moreover, a considerable change in residential preferences among Norwegians has occurred over the last 25 years.

Housing cultures could be considered as a particular kind of discourses within a society, and as such being part of the wider concept of social structures (Bhaskar, 1993; Archer, 2000). Such structures influence the actions, conceptions and well-being of human agents, but they are also subject to influence and change caused by human agency, possibly via changes in other structures in society such as legislation, economic conditions or the built environment. The predominant housing cultures exert an important influence on the residential preferences of individuals. But these preferences may also be influenced by other sources, such as movies, music videos, impressions from tourist trips to cities in foreign countries, etc. They can also be influenced by what is actually being constructed. For example, the more new apartments are built, the more normal and acceptable will this type of housing probably be regarded.

Residential development in Norway, particularly in the recent decade, has indeed contributed to making apartments a more common type of dwelling. At least this is true for the four largest cities, where apartments accounted for 68 percent of new dwelling constructed in the period 2000–2013, whereas single-family houses only accounted for 21 percent. (It should be noted that the cities as defined here also include the suburban municipalities.) As can be seen in Figure 6.1, the proportion of apartments has particularly been high since 2004. As a consequence of the high share of apartments and the low share of single-family houses among newly constructed residences, the share of the total dwelling stock of the four largest Norwegian urban regions accounted for by single-family houses decreased from 36.4 percent to 35.6 percent over the seven-year period 2006–2013, whereas the share of apartments rose from 37.3 to 38.4 percent. The shift toward denser form of housing development has been an important contributor to the density increase taking place in most of the larger Norwegian cities since the turn of the millennium. Since 2000, population densities within the urbanized land have increased in eight of the ten largest Norwegian cities. This tendency has been particularly pronounced in Oslo (see below).

In the 1970s and 1980s, the smaller Norwegian towns and urban settlements (say, below 10,000 inhabitants) had very few apartment buildings. Living in an apartment in a small urban settlement in these days was in many ways stigmatizing, since benefit claimers and other low-status groups made up a relatively large proportion of the apartment dwellers. After more than two

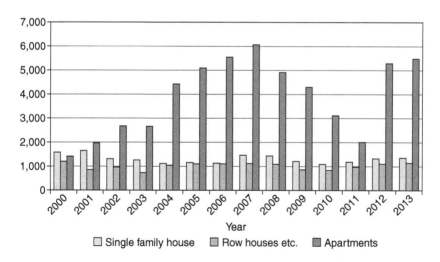

Figure 6.1 Proportions of new dwellings constructed in the four largest Norwegian urban regions 2000–2013 accounted for by different housing types.

Source: Statistics Norway (2014).

decades of densification, the number of apartments has increased considerably, also in the small towns and urban settlements, and living in an apartment has become much more normalized and maybe even fashionable. In the bigger cities, a large number of apartments already existed when the densification trend started three decades ago, but the massive construction of new apartments since then has made this housing type increasingly common among the middle class and high-income groups. New kinds of urban housing cultures have emerged and are apparently still proliferating.

Changing housing preferences have to do with shrinking household sizes as well as cultural trends. The average number of residents per dwelling has declined sharply over the past half century. Nationally, the number has dropped from 3.3 persons in 1960 to 2.2 persons in 2011, with even lower figures in the biggest cities (yet with a slight increase again during the most recent years in Oslo due to strong population growth not compensated by a sufficient pace or new housing development). In the municipality of Oslo, more than one half of all households in 2011 consisted of only one person, and for Norway as a whole the share was 40 percent, with 45 percent on average for the four largest cities (up from 43 percent in 2001) (Statistics Norway, 2011a).

It is reasonable to assume that households consisting of one single person or only two persons will be less likely to prefer a single-family house than persons belonging to a large household. The changes that have taken place in the household composition could therefore be expected in themselves to contribute to a change in residential preferences. But there also seems to be a more general trend toward a higher acceptance of dense living. This can be seen by comparing changes in residential preferences among different household categories.

Among couples aged 35–54 without any children living at home in the Norwegian cities of Oslo, Bergen and Trondheim, the proportion who preferred to live in an apartment building increased from 22 percent in 1988 to 39 percent in 1995. A similar, but even stronger tendency was found among single people between 25 and 34 years. In this group, the proportion favoring apartment buildings increased from 17 percent to 42 percent in the same period. However, among young couples with children, the single-family house held a strong and stable position as the most popular type of residence, favored by about 90 percent both in 1988 and 1995 (Hansen, 1997). No comparable later surveys of residential preferences appear to have been conducted in Norway. However, a survey by Elnan (2011) indicates that there is, at a national scale, an under-supply of 237,000 apartments and over-supply of 208,000 single-family houses, compared to the residential preferences among the population. This is despite a reduction already having taken place in the proportion of single-family houses from 58.1 percent of the Norwegian stock of inhabited dwellings in 1990 to 52.9 percent in 2011 (Statistics Norway, 2011b).[4] The under-supply of apartments compared to the existing residential situation is evident among all age groups above 40 years and particularly high among those more than 55 years old. Given the fact that nearly two thirds of the forecasted population growth in Norway over the next two decades is expected to be due to an increase in the number of elderly people, there is reason to expect a continuing trend toward higher preferences for apartments and a correspondingly lower demand for single-family houses.

The above-mentioned changes in attitudes and preferences may be partially caused by the fact that a decreasing proportion of urban residents are newcomers from rural areas or have their roots in rural traditions through parents or grandparents living in the countryside. According to a Finnish study, urban residents without any family ties to the countryside consider the single-family house as the goal of their residential career to a lesser extent than first- or second-generation urbanites. Moreover, one could also speculate that the increasingly multicultural population of Norwegian cities, especially Oslo, may have contributed to increase the share of the population who prefer other types of housing than the detached single-family house. Apart from demographic changes, the spreading of more urban lifestyles and housing preferences is probably also boosted by our increasing exposure to international impulses, notably through international media channels.

It has been argued (e.g., Krizek, 2003; Van Wee 2013) that a change in housing supply toward higher shares of apartment construction as densification within existing urban area demarcations may prove to yield less positive (from a sustainability perspective) results than expected, because such a policy may suppress market demand for suburban neighborhoods within the cities and hence force people with preferences for single-family houses to move to exurban areas. However, this argument disregards the fact pointed to above that residential preferences are not static. There is a two-way influence between housing cultures and residential development. Housing culture influences what is built, but what is built also influences housing culture. Demands and preferences can be influenced by what is being supplied. If no new single-family areas are built, the demand for new dwellings will be directed toward other residential environments. There is considerable wisdom in the Aesop fable about the fox and the grapes: you may no longer feel a need for something that is anyway out of reach. (The fable's analogy with urban residential development is, however, not very accurate, since there would even in the absence of any further construction of single-family houses be a large number of existing single-family houses available on the market.)

The spatial urban development in Greater Oslo may serve as an illustration. The core municipality (Oslo) and its neighboring municipalities have pursued a pronounced densification policy since the mid-1980s (Næss, Næss & Strand, 2011). As a result, the population density within the continuous urban area (Greater Oslo, comprising 980,000 inhabitants in 2016) increased by as much as 37 percent over the period 1985-2016. The population density increase has been especially high in the central parts of the core municipality. Within the so-called Inner Zone, the number of inhabitants grew from

132,700 in 1989 to 220,000 in 2016, with no increase in the urbanized land, representing a population density increase of as much as 66 percent.[5]

One might perhaps think that this would cause widespread dissatisfaction among parts of the population who had in the beginning of the period a preference for single-family houses. According to theories of residential self-selection, a considerable exodus of people with a predilection for single-family houses to exurban areas might perhaps be expected. However, nothing like this has happened. The population of Greater Oslo has grown by 215,000 over the last two decades (three quarters of which in the core municipality) and is forecasted to increase by another 300,000 over the next 20 years (Statistics Norway, 2013b). Population densities have also increased in the settlements in the part of the metropolitan area outside Greater Oslo. The acceptance, and even popularity, of denser forms of living among Oslo residents is also indicated by a study by Sjaastad, Hansen and Medby (2007), who identified preferred residential neighborhood types (except single-family house areas, which were not included among the investigated neighborhoods) in Oslo as indicated by sales prices per square meter. According to this study, the following characteristics of the neighborhood were positively assessed: location in the inner city; traditional blocks; small, well-maintained green areas within dense neighborhoods; clearly indicated differentiation between public, semiprivate and private outdoor areas; and multifunctional interplay between private facades and public street space. On the other hand, large, non-maintained lawns and green areas in the suburbs were negatively assessed.

A consumerist housing culture

Housing preferences and housing culture have developed toward the higher popularity of dense urban living, which has been favorable from a sustainability perspective. But trends contributing to more floor area per capita, fashion-motivated renovation and multiple-dwelling households are all increasing the environmental load.

Despite lower shares of single-family houses, the total environmental load of the Norwegian housing stocks keeps on increasing, in absolute terms as well as per capita, since floor area per capita is still increasing. Residential floor area per inhabitant nearly doubled from $30\,m^2$ in 1970 to $58\,m^2$ in 2009, with an increase of 7 percent over the period 2001–2009 (Bartlett, 1993; Statistics Norway, 2010). Shrinking household size and part-time childcare responsibilities push toward more floor area per capita, as well as does a wish for more spaciousness. The 'renovation mania,' where dwellings are renovated more and more often to conform with shifting interior design fashions, is also putting considerable loads on the environment. Cultural trends associated with 'urbanity' and 'creative class' have promoted shifts toward more resource-efficient dwelling types, but TV programs like 'Extreme makeover' and 'lifestyle' magazines and newspaper sections pull in the opposite direction of sustainability.

This strong and continuing growth in housing standards has been facilitated by the general economic growth. According to the Ministry of Finance (2013), the purchasing power per inhabitant in Norway will be nearly doubled over the period 2012–2060. It seems unlikely that such growth will not also imply an increase in housing consumption per capita, if for nothing else at least due to a need for more space to accommodate all the new items bought or for frequent renovations to keep up with changing architectural and interior fashions. In Norway, the item "residences, lighting, and space heating" accounted for 31 percent of household expenditures in 2012 (Holmøy & Lillegård, 2012). Suppressing consumption within the residential sector would have strong repercussions on the total economic development and would likely be considered a threat against the growth-dependent economy as such.

An emerging multi-home society

Families increasingly have more than one dwelling they have a feeling of as a 'home.' Between 2001 and 2014, the number of cabins, summer houses etc. in Norway increased by nearly 20 percent up to a total of 450,000. More than one out of five Norwegian households now own a vacation home, and in addition a nearly equally high proportion have regular access to a vacation home not owned by themselves. The latter group includes relatives (children, grandchildren, siblings, nephews etc.) of the owners as well as those who rent a vacation home on time-share basis. Altogether, 40 percent of Norwegian households have a vacation home at their disposal (Forskning.no, 2009).

The standard and size of vacation homes has increased considerably in the recent decades in Norway as well as in other wealthy countries. In international research vacation homes are often called second homes, which highlights the fact that some people have two homes (some might have more) and in that sense a form of double settlement. This has been made possible by an affluent society proving substantial freedom within the family and work structure. The use pattern for Norwegian vacation homes has changed from consisting of few but long stays toward more frequent short stays. Improved transport infrastructure, a high rate of car ownership and flexible working hours have made it possible to work at your second home, travel long distances extending the weekend-recreational zone and regularly travel to the second home. Such multiple-dwelling-home lifestyles include not only traditional cabins and apartments in mountain villages, but also urban second homes and second homes abroad (e.g., along the Spanish sun coast).

Local services are usually situated at longer distances from the vacation home compared to primary dwellings located in urban areas. This may become increasingly important in terms of travel-related environmental impacts if current trends among some middle-class professionals with geographically flexible jobs of living for considerable parts of the year in vacation homes where they can combine recreational activities with internet- and

82   *P. Næss*

computer-based work become more common (Arnesen & Skjeggedal, 2003; Arnesen & Overvåg, 2006; Arnesen, Overvåg, Skjeggedal & Ericsson, 2011). In addition, owning a vacation home could also request the ownership of a car, which for some people living in urban areas might otherwise not have been necessary.

According to Aall, Klepp, Engeset, Skuland and Støa (2011), the energy consumption during stays in Norwegian vacation homes has increased by almost 100 percent from 1973–2005. Along national highway stretches leading to important vacation home areas, cars bound for or returning from vacation homes account for a considerable part of the total traffic at weekends (Ericsson, Skjeggedal, Arnesen & Overvåg, 2011). But increasingly Norwegians also own (or rent on a long-term contract) vacation homes in other countries, notably in southern Europe. Air travel to and from vacation homes in foreign countries has increased considerably in recent years (Aall, Klepp, Engeset, Skuland & Støa, 2011).

Rebound effects of living densely?

In a growth-oriented economy, the lower flows of energy and other resources made possible by higher efficiency tend to rebound to higher levels because of the quest of the economy for higher flows. The above-mentioned more frequent use of vacation homes both within Norway and abroad might be partially a 'rebound effect' of living in 'climate-friendly' permanent dwelling types and locations (Holden & Norland, 2005, Næss, 2006; Nørgaard, 2008; Skjeggedal et al., 2009). Current notions of a climate-friendly urban form suggest, as mentioned above, that high-density rather than sprawling cities are better at mitigating climate-related emissions. However, Norwegians tend to have a strong desire to 'connect' with nature, which is a factor that might result in urban dwellers compensating the lack of nearby nature in urban residential settings with ownership and more frequent use of vacation homes. Different spatial contexts might therefore result in different preferences toward owning and using vacation homes in Norway and abroad. On the other hand, owning a vacation home might tie up both time and economic resources to a degree that reduces vacation home owners' ability to spend time and money on other kinds of vacations such as long distance international flights or cruise ship trips in the Mexican Gulf. This could be considered as a positive rebound effect of vacation home ownership in relation to climate impacts.

Investigations conducted by the author of this chapter in the metropolitan areas of Oslo, Stavanger and Copenhagen (Næss, 2016) do show certain individual-scale rebound mechanisms, counteracting to some extent and among some residents the effects of resource-saving principles in urban planning and housing development. However, these mechanisms are not very strong, and countervailing mechanisms also exist. At an aggregate metropolitan scale, any rebound effects are not strong enough to change the environmentally favorable effects of inner-city living for weekend travel, where the effect of a central residential location in terms of reducing car travel is nearly as strong as on weekdays. Neither does our material show any effects of residential location on the frequency of private long-distance trips. Rebound effects of inner-city living on secondary home access also seem to be moderate, and for usage of secondary homes no such effect is found at an aggregate level. Neither is there any support in our material from the urban regions of Oslo and Stavanger of the hypothesis of an environmentally favorable rebound effect in terms of a reduced number of flights among persons who visit secondary homes frequently. We do find, however, a tendency of more frequent private flights among inner-city residents of Oslo, Stavanger as well as Copenhagen, corresponding with similar results reported by Holden and Norland (2005). However, it is difficult to find causal explanations explaining this correlation. An 'urban' and cosmopolitan lifestyle contributing both to an increased propensity for flights and a preference for inner-city living seems a more plausible explanation, together with the opportunity to spend money saved through low daily-life travel costs on other types of consumption (Næss, 2006, 2016).

Indirect rebound effects due to money saved are probably hard to avoid. As long as the purchasing power remains the same or increases, resource efficiency improvement resulting in money-saving is like squeezing the balloon (and in a growing economy, the balloon is on top of that steadily pumped up with more gas). This points to some serious challenges for policies aiming at sustainable housing and more environmentally friendly housing cultures within a society generally oriented toward growth. The relationship between economic growth and sustainable housing is indeed an uneasy one (Xue, 2012). I will not here go more deeply into these issues, which I have dealt with in other publications (Næss & Høyer, 2009; Næss, 2011).

Concluding remarks

In wealthy countries like Norway, a shift toward a higher share of apartment buildings in proximity of job opportunities, service and public transport facilities is favorable, seen from a sustainability perspective. During the latest decades, housing preferences and housing culture in Norway have developed in this direction. However, at the same time, social and cultural trends contributing to more floor area per capita, fashion-motivated renovation and multiple-dwelling households are increasing the environmental load and aggravating social inequalities in housing.

The Norwegian level of housing consumption (nearly 60 square meters of floor area per inhabitant) is among the world's highest and is in Europe only surpassed by Luxemburg (Dol & Haffner, 2010). In a world of finite natural resources, a further increase in the average size and standard of Norwegian dwellings is highly problematic from a perspective of globally just distribution of resource use and environmental footprints.

However, even in Norway and other wealthy North European countries, some population groups live in substandard dwellings. If satisfaction of these needs is to be combined with a requirement for the nation as a whole to keep its consumption level within an 'ecological scope,' it will be necessary to practice a principle of *selective standard improvement* (Næss, 2001). Instead of producing dwellings to meet demands rooted in a wish to use the dwelling as a symbol for social status and success[6] (a competition pushing consumption along a continual upward spiral), housing policies should be directed toward meeting needs based on socially agreed-on norms, within boundaries set by environmental sustainability and global responsibility. This is, of course, something that would sound utterly strange within the prevailing neoliberal policy discourse. But so, probably, does the very concept of sustainable development, understood as meeting needs, especially the basic needs of the world's poor, without undermining the environment's possibility to meet the needs of future generations.

Notes

1 The focus on Norway reflects my own national background and accordingly better knowledge about urban development, housing policies and housing culture in Norway than in other countries. I do think, however, that the sustainability challenges pertaining to the Norwegian housing culture are largely relevant to the situations in other affluent European countries as well as in North America and Australia.

2 Oslo, Bergen, Stavanger and Trondheim. 'Cities' are here defined as continuous urban areas regardless of municipal borders, i.e., in accordance with the definition of urban settlements stated by Statistics Norway.

3 Excluding parks, sports fields, farmland, forests, water bodies etc. within the urban area demarcations.

4 Some of this reduction may be due to single-family homes in remote areas being abandoned or converted into second homes.

5 Together with Norway, Sweden stands out as a country where urban densification during recent decades has been particularly noticeable. For example, whereas the population density within the continuous urban areas of Oslo increased by 7 percent over the period 2006–2011, the corresponding figure for Stockholm over the years 2005–2010 was 8 percent (Statistics Norway, 2015; Statistics Sweden, 2013). In Copenhagen and other Danish cities, densification was for several years less pronounced, but during the last decade, there has been a strong trend of urban densification especially in the municipality of Copenhagen (Statistics Denmark, 2015). In contrast especially to Norway and Sweden, Helsinki and other Finnish cities are still developing in a more sprawling way (Ristimäki & Söderström, 2015).

6 'We want our homes to impress others.' Norwegian National Broadcasting (NRK) website news, February 9, 2015, retrieved from www.nrk.no/norge/kjoper-_wow-faktor_-av-interiorarkitekter-1.12186906

References

Aall, C., Klepp, I. G., Engeset, A. B., Skuland, S. E. & Støa, E. (2011). Leisure and sustainable development in Norway: Part of the solution and the problem. *Leisure Studies, 30*(4), pp. 453–476.

Aamo, A. S. & Aspen, J. (2002). *Høyhus i Oslo. Delutredning III. Bolighøyhusets kvaliteter*. Oslo: The Municipality of Oslo, the Planning and Building Agency.

Alonso, W. (1964). *Location and land use*. Cambridge, MA: Harvard University Press.

Archer, M. S. (2000). *Being human. the problem of agency*. Cambridge: Cambridge University Press.

Arnesen, T. & Overvåg, K. (2006). Mellom fritidsbolig og bolig. Om eiendomsregistrering og bruksendring. *Utmark* 1/2006. Retrieved from www.utmark.org

Arnesen, T. & Skjeggedal, T. (2003). Spekulasjoner om å bo, utmark og urbanitet. *Plan* 2/2003, pp. 10–14.

Arnesen, T., Overvåg, K., Skjeggedal, T. & Ericsson, B. (2011). Transcending orthodoxy: Multi-house home. Leisure and the transformation of core–periphery relations. In Danson, M. & de Souza, P. (eds), *Peripherality, marginality and border issues in Northern Europe*. London: Routledge.

Bartlett, S. (1993). *The evolution of Norwegian energy use from 1950 to 1991*. SSB Reports 93/21. Oslo: Statistics Norway.

Beatley, T. (2000). Preserving biodiversity: Challenges for planners. *Journal of the American Planning Association*, 66(1), pp. 5–20.

Bhaskar, R. (1993). *Dialectic – the pulse of freedom*. London: Routledge.

Brown, M. & Wolfe, M. (2007). *Energy efficiency in multi-family housing: A profile and analysis*. Washington, DC: Energy Program Consortium.

Burchell, R., Shad, N. A., Listokin, D., Phillips, H., Downs, A., Seskin, S., Davis, J. S., Moore, T., Helton, D. & Gall, M. (1998). *The costs of sprawl – revisited*. Washington: National Academy Press.

Dol, K. & Haffner, M. (2010). *Housing statistics in the European Union 2010*. The Hague: Ministry of the Interior and Kingdom Relations. Retrieved from www.hofinet.org/documents/doc.aspx?id=661

Elnan, K. (2011). *Scenarieanalyse 2010–2020: Boligbehovet i Norge*. Oslo: Prognosesenteret. Retrieved from http://boligprodusentene.no/rapporter/scenarioanalyse-boligbehov-i-norge-article119-176.html

Ericsson, B., Skjeggedal, T., Arnesen, T. & Overvåg, K. (2011). *Second Homes i Norge. Bidrag til en nordisk utredning*. ØF-rapport nr. 1/2011. Lillehammer: Østlandsforskning.

Ewing, R. & Cervero, R. (2010). Travel and the built environment. *Journal of the American Planning Association*, 76: 1–30.

Fishman, R. (1996). Bourgeois utopias: Visions of suburbia. In Fainstein, S. S. & Campbell, S. (eds) *Readings in urban theory* (pp. 21–31). Cambridge, MA: Blackwell.

Forskning.no (2009). *Bolig: I hus og hytte*. Oslo: Research Council Norway. Retrieved from www.forskning.no/artikler/2008/juni/184543

Friedan, B. (1963). *The feminine mystique*. New York: W.W. Norton and Company Inc.

Guttu, J. (2003). *Den gode boligen: Fagfolks oppfatning av boligkvalitet gjennom 50 år*. Dr. Art thesis 11. Oslo: Oslo School of Architecture.

Hansen, T. (1997). Unpublicized results from Boforholdsundersøkelsen 1995. Oslo: Norges byggforskningsinstitutt.

Haveraaen, M. (1993). *By, bosted, lokalsamfunn, bolig. Fire stedsrettete arbeider hvor planlegging møter sosiologi*. Dr. Scient. Thesis. Ås: Norwegian Agricultural University.

Hjorthol, R. J. (2000). Same city – different options. An analysis of the work trips of married couples in the metropolitan area of Oslo. *Journal of Transport Geography*, 8, pp. 213–220.

Holden, E. & Norland, I. T. (2005). Three challenges for the compact city as a sustainable urban form: Household consumption of energy and transport in eight residential areas in the greater Oslo region. *Urban Studies*, 42(12), pp. 2145–2166.

Holmøy, A. & Lillegård, M. (2012). Forbruksundersøkelsen 2012. Dokumentasjon-srapport. Oslo: Statistics Norway.

Høyer, K. G. & Holden, E. (2001). Housing as basis for sustainable consumption. *International Journal of Sustainable Development, 4*(1), pp. 48–58.

Kolbenstvedt, M. & Hjorthol, R. (1987). *Bytrafikk, bomiljø og helse. Resultater fra NTNF-programmet Trafikk og miljø's førundersøkelser på Vålerenga/Gamlebyen i Oslo 1987.* TØI-rapport 0073/1990.

Krier, L. (1996). *Architecture choix ou fatalité.* Paris: Norma.

Krizek, K. J. (2003). Residential relocation and changes in urban travel: Does neighborhood-scale urban form matter? *Journal of American Planning Association, 69,* pp. 265–281.

Kvinge, T., Langset, B. & Nørve, S. (2012). Hva betyr kvalitetskrav for byggekost-nader og boligtilbud? NIBR Working Paper 2012:112. Oslo: Norwegian Institute for Urban and Regional Research.

Ministry of Finance. (2013). *Meld. St. 12 (2012–2013) Perspektivmeldingen 2013.* Oslo: Ministry of Finance. Retrieved from www.regjeringen.no/nb/dokumenter/meld-st-12-20122013/id714050/

Municipality of Aalborg. (2003). *Plan- og Bæredygtighedsstrategi.* Aalborg: Aalborg Kommune.

Mønnesland, J. (1991). Natur- og miljøvennlig tettstedsutvikling – en vurdering av økonomiske hindringer. [Environmentally sound urban development – an assess-ment of economic obstacles.] NIBR-notat 1991:114. Oslo: Norwegian institute for urban and regional research.

Newman, P. W. G. & Kenworthy, J. R. (1999). *Sustainability and cities: Overcoming automobile dependence.* Washington DC and Covelo, California: Island Press.

Næss, P. (2001). Urban planning and sustainable development. *European Planning Studies, 9*(4), pp. 503–524.

Næss, P. (2006). Are short daily trips compensated by higher leisure mobility? *Environment & Planning B, 33,* pp. 197–220.

Næss, P. (2008). Gender differences in the influences of urban structure on daily-life travel. In Priya, T. & Cresswell, T. (eds) *Gendered mobilities* (pp. 173–192). Aldershot: Ashgate.

Næss, P. (2011). Economic growth, urban development and environmental sustain-ability/Crescita economica, sviluppo urbano e sostenibilità ambientale. In Moccia, F. D (ed.), *Abitare la Città Ecologica/Housing ecocity* (pp. 48–77). Naples: CLEAN.

Næss, P. (2012). Urban form and travel behavior: Experience from a Nordic context. *Journal of Transport and Land Use, 5*(2), pp. 21–45.

Næss, P. (2016). Urban Planning: Residential Location and Compensatory Behaviour in Three Scandinavian. In Santorius, T., Walnum, H. J. & Aall, C. (eds), *How to improve energy- and climate-policies? Understanding the role of rebound effects.* pp. 181–207, Berlin: Springer.

Næss, P. & Høyer, K. G. (2009). The emperor's green clothes: Growth, decoupling and capitalism. *Capitalism, Nature, Socialism, 20*(3), pp. 74–95.

Næss, P., Næss, T. & Strand, A. (2011). Oslo's farewell to urban sprawl. *European Planning Studies, 19*(1), pp. 113–139.

Nørgaard, J. S. (2008). Avoiding rebound through a steady-state economy. In Horace Herring, H. & Sorrell, S. (eds) *Energy efficiency and sustainable consumption: dealing with the rebound effect* (pp. 204–223). Basingstoke: Palgrave Macmillan.

Pinho, P., Santos, S., Oliveira, V., Barbosa, M., Silva, M., Galera Lindblom, P., Weber, R., Reardon, M. & Schmitt, P. (2011, November 27). *Report On approaches and strategies for a metabolically sustainable city*. SUME Working-Paper 3.3, Oporto. Retrieved from www.sume.at/project_downloads

Power, A. (2001). Social exclusion and urban sprawl: Is the rescue of cities possible? *Regional Studies, 35*(8). pp. 731–742.

Putnam, R. D. (2000). *Bowling alone. The collapse and revival of American community*. New York: Simon & Schuster.

Rapoport, A. (1998). Using 'culture' in housing design. *Housing and Society, 25*(1&2), pp. 1–20.

Rapoport, A. (2000). Theory, culture and housing. *Housing, Theory & Society, 17*(4), pp. 145–165.

Ristimäki, M. & Söderström, P. (2015). Development of the urban form in Helsinki and Stockholm metropolitan regions. Paper presented at The 7th Nordic Planning Research Symposium, Stockholm, August 20–22, 2015.

Røe, P. G. & Jones, K. (1997). *Bystruktur og trafikkulykker. Hvilke byplanforhold har betydning for ulykkessituasjonen i norske byer?* Prosjektrapport 1997:12. Oslo: Norwegian institute for urban and regional research.

Sjaastad, M., Hansen, T. & Medby, P. (2007). *Bokvalitet i by og etterspurte bebyggelsestyper*. Oslo: SINTEF Byggforsk.

Skjeggedal, T., Overvåg, K., Arnesen, T. & Ericsson, B. (2009). Hytteliv i endring. *Plan* 6/2009, pp. 42–49.

Statistics Denmark. (2015). *Folketal den 1. i kvartalet efter kommune, køn, alder, civilstand, herkomst, oprindelsesland og statsborgerskab*. Copenhagen: Statistics Denmark. Retrieved from www.statistikbanken.dk/statbank5a

Statistics Norway. (2010). *Boliger, etter bruksareal, tid og statistikkvariabel*. Oslo: Statistics Norway. Retrieved from www.ssb.no/statistikkbanken

Statistics Norway. (2011a). *Bebodde boliger og bosatte, etter region, tid og statistikkvariabel*. Oslo: Statistics Norway. Retrieved from www.ssb.no/statistikkbanken

Statistics Norway. (2011b). *Bebodde boliger og bosatte, etter bygningstype*. Oslo: Statistics Norway. Retrieved from www.ssb.no/statistikkbanken

Statistics Norway. (2013a). *Folke- og boligtellingen, boliger, 19. november 2011*. Oslo: Statistics Norway. Retrieved from www.ssb.no/befolkning/statistikker/fobbolig/hvert-10-aar/2013-02-26

Statistics Norway. (2013b). *Framskrevet folkemengde, etter region, tid og statistikkvariabel*. (Population forecast by region, time and statistical variable.) Oslo: Statistics Norway. Retrieved from www.ssb.no/statistikkbanken

Statistics Norway. (2014). *Boligbygg, etter region, bygningstype, tid og statistikkvariabel*. Oslo: Statistics Norway. Retrieved from www.ssb.no/befolkning/statistikker/fobbolig/hvert-10-aar/2013-02-26

Statistics Norway. (2015). *Tabell: 04859: Areal og befolkning i tettsteder (T)*. Oslo: Statistics Norway. Retrieved from www.ssb.no/statistikkbanken

Statistics Sweden. (2013). *Tätorternas landareal, folkmängd och invånare per km2 2005 och 2010*. Stockholm: Statistics Sweden. Retrieved from www.scb.se/sv_/Hitta-statistik/Statistik-efter-amne/Miljo/Markanvandning/Tatorter-arealer-befolkning/#c_li_335300

Støa, E. & Aune, M. (2012). Sustainable housing cultures. In Smith, S. J., Elsinga, M., O'Mahony, L. F., Eng, O. S., Wachter, S. & Eastaway, M. P. (eds), *International encyclopedia of housing and home*, Vol. 7 (pp. 111–116). Oxford: Elsevier.

Støa, E. & Narvestad, R. (eds) (2005). *Bokvalitet og bærekraft under endrede rammebetingelser.* Trondheim: NIBR, Byggforsk, SINTEF and NTNU.

Van Wee, B. (2013). Land use and transport. In Van Wee, B., Annema, J. A. & Banister, D. (eds), *The transport system and transport policy. An introduction* (pp. 78–100). Cheltenham, UK and Northampton, USA: Edward Elgar Publishing.

World Commission on Environment and Development (1987). *Our common future.* Oxford: Oxford University Press.

Xue, J. (2012). *Economic growth and sustainable housing: An uneasy relationship.* London/New York: Routledge.

7 Designing a sense of place

Arild Berg

Creating a sense of place for a sustainable environment

'Sense of place' has become a central concept in both geography (Massey, 1991) and sociology and the sociologist Baldwin describes it as 'a way to understand the wider world through localized human–environment relationships' (Baldwin, 2012, p. 208). From a design perspective this concept is relevant because not only can sense of place be studied and analysed, it can be created and designed to the needs and potentials in local communities. In most local communities there are change processes and there is a need to gain more knowledge about the relationship between sense of place and landscape perceptions, and on the relationship between sense of place and peoples' willingness to contribute to rural landscape management (Soini, Vaarala & Pouta, 2012, p. 124). Soini et al. found that although a strong sense of place is often assumed to lead to care of place, the willingness to contribute to the landscape did not differ significantly between four different local communities. Instead they found that inhabitants tended to see the landscape in two main categories; landscape as scenery or landscape as a dwelling place. Therefore the relationship between sense of place and how people can be enabled to contribute to such landscape management should be further studied.

People's willingness – and ability – to engage in places, not only rural but also urban – can be connected to how their attachment can give place meaning. One example of this was shown in a study on sense of place at a shopping street in Kuala Lumpur in Malaysia (Shamsuddin & Ujang, 2008). They found that Rhwie's definition of 'sense of place' included 'the point where the physical element, activity and meaning are intertwined in the people experience of place' (Shamsuddin & Ujang, 2008, p. 399). They discovered that there was a strong attachment to the traditional streets. The streets were seen as essential in 'sustaining the economic activities and meaningful in accentuating cultural diversity and self and group identity'. Their research concluded that place attachment had a significant contribution to the concept 'sense of place' and therefore should be considered in the design of urban places especially when redevelopment was one of the options.

In such development of the environment unfortunately the pure technical materialization often seems to overrule the influence from people on site (Marres, 2012). Although sustainability is a new turning point in political frameworks such as Horizon 2020 where eco-friendly materials has been in focus (Pacheco-Torgal, 2014) and where sustainable innovation is a goal, too little attention has been given to the cultural aspect of sustainability, although the cultural perspective is of essential importance, claims Soini and Birkeland (2014). Their claim is in line with the view of the social anthropologist Barnett (1953) who stated that sustainable changes must be adapted in unique ways in different cultures, because various social systems have different values and practices. Barnett showed how innovation is related to social behaviour and social manners. To change social patterns and to get more people to do things in new ways is a part of innovation: there is often a need for a social implementation of a technical solution – the technical solution is not an innovation before it is implemented in use by people in a practice. According to definitions of the concept of sustainability, it is not only dependent on ecological and economic values, but also on social values (Soini & Birkeland, 2014). If a solution is not socially rooted, people are less likely to accept a new way of doing things, and this reduces the implementation of the solution and it may not become permanent. New ways of thinking can change behaviour, but it requires a different approach than simply delivering a technical aid or a new invention. It concerns how technical solutions become related to human use and adjusted accordingly. People's behaviour is linked to their traditions, their ways of seeing the world and eventually this concerns how people will behave in the encounter between technology and culture. Parts of the debate have therefore lately turned towards the concept of cultural sustainability and whether this is already sufficiently covered in the social part of sustainability, or whether there are reasons for the cultural aspect to be enhanced more (Skjerven, 2012; Soini & Birkeland, 2014).

A culturally sensitive perspective

Culture has therefore been launched as a new and possibly fourth pillar in discussions about sustainability (Soini & Birkeland, 2014), as equally important as social, economic and ecological values. Culture can be seen as an integral part of the social because both the social domain and the cultural domain are related to human behaviour, peoples' traditions and their cultural heritage. Therefore a new perspective might emerge by looking at the culture linked more closely to the other two pillars: ecology and economy. The reason why this is rewarding is that it is challenging to envisage both ecology and economy without understanding how they relate to different cultural understandings. The interwoven and reciprocal affiliation between culture and economics on the one hand and culture and ecology on the other hand can help to shed new light on the subject.

Culture and economy are linked through historical examples with various forms of the economy. Throughout history there have existed various types of economies that have been linked to different cultures (Giljum et al., 2008). In some cultures where people made their living by fishing and from resources in the sea, for example, pearl shells have been payment, and have served as valid currency over large areas. In other cultures, the ownership number of goats, cows or reindeers explains people's financial situation. A contemporary example is how credit cards have replaced coins and banknotes in many places. These examples show how economy and culture are inextricably linked, and that it is not so easy to point out exactly what is the value in different cultures. Therefore cultural awareness is very central to finance and economy.

Ecology is another established pillar of sustainability. Ecological qualities are often linked to what is materially recyclable, but it can also be seen in connection with intangible values and cultural variations. For example, the social anthropologist Taussig has shown how an indigenous view of nature is that spirits of the ancestors animate nature (Taussig, 2009). Some people handle phenomena in nature with great circumspection and see it as a sin to take everything from one place, and therefore always leave something for the animals and spirits. This in turn provides a greater opportunity for the spread of seeds. Such a sustainable ecology, based on cultural values, is in contrast to modern society's consumer culture. Views on ecology are therefore closely connected to cultural practice.

Although culture can be seen as intertwined with the three pillars of sustainability concept – the social, ecological and economic – the debate has concerned whether culture should be a fourth pillar in the sustainability concept. The lack of this concept might be a reflection of the view that this is unnecessary because culture is anyway implicit in the existing concepts. However, the criticism has been raised that, in discussions about sustainability, decision makers do not sufficiently treat culture from consciously and culturally sensitive perspectives (Soini & Birkeland, 2014). Through establishing culture as a fourth pillar in sustainability a more conscious approach to culture can emerge.

People's connectedness to their environment is described in material culture studies (Tilley, 2006) with knowledge about relationships between people, environment, artefacts and artworks. Tilley describes how material artefacts are closely associated with cultural rituals, values and activities. The design of these objects is therefore crucial and design is such an activity that can explain and deepen understanding of the values that are prevailing in a culture. There have been several studies of the design of objects and how this practice can relate to sustainable cultures (Keitsch, 2012b; Sanders & Stappers, 2008; Skjerven, 2012). A more system critical perspective of design practice has been proposed (Aagaard Nielsen, 2010). Some studies have stressed that recycling principles should be introduced already in the conceptual phase of a design process (Melles et al., 2011). Others have focused on system ideologies that influence practice in a determinable direction. A few have focused on participatory design that contributes to innovative products (Asaro, 2000; Bang, 2010; Berg et al., 2014; Buur & Larsen, 2010).

According to Soini and Birkeland there should be more studies on how the story lines of the cultural sustainability discourse should be explored in more detail to focus on communication with the associated stakeholders, interests and actors (Soini & Birkeland, 2014, p. 221). In spite of this, there has been little research on how participatory design can contribute to new products seen in a holistic social context, related to different cultures. Despite these earlier studies in this field there was a knowledge gap that justified the research question of how participatory design can contribute to sustainable cultures. This approach was chosen because participatory design can contribute to local engagement which is necessary to change a culture into sustainable communities.

Central concepts in designing a sense of place

As methodical perspective case study was a suitable response to the research question because it was possible to explore existing theory in other real life contexts than in the initial theories (Yin, 2009). Using case study methods Yin recommends establishing some theoretical propositions to enhance the validity of the study by bridging theory and empirical research through pattern matching in cross-case analysis. Some central propositions in cultural sustainability were therefore identified from the initial theories through concept mapping (Maxwell, 2005). As shown in the background introduction, these initial propositions were existing concepts that were relevant in a preliminary theoretical framework for designing a sense of place. These were:

1 People's willingness to management of environment (Soini et al., 2012).
2 People's attachment to traditional places (Shamsuddin & Ujang, 2008).
3 Accentuation of cultural diversity (Shamsuddin & Ujang, 2008).
4 Stimulation of self – and group identity (Shamsuddin & Ujang, 2008).
5 Sustainable changes must be adapted in unique ways in different cultures (Barnett, 1953).
6 Technical solutions should be adjusted to human use for cultural sustainability (Marres, 2012).
7 Cultural awareness of systems of economy (Barnett, 1953).
8 Avoiding over consumption (Melles et al., 2011).
9 A system critical approach based on local engagement (Aagaard Nielsen, 2010).
10 Inclusion of recycling principles (Melles et al., 2011).

Through a hermeneutic approach (Gadamer, 2004) the aim was to deepen the understanding of these initial concepts through Soini and Birkeland's proposal of exploring more story lines for the discourse in cultural sustainability (Soini & Birkeland, 2014, p. 221) and with a pragmatic approach aiming to identify success criteria for project management (Westerveld, 2003). The cases were chosen because they contributed to complementary perspectives as recommended in ethnographic approaches (Hammersley, 2007). In this case, these complementary perspectives were represented by a political and demo-cratic level, an institutional and professional level and a personal and leisure time level. The first context was about participation in the development of a school in the UK (Ghaziani, 2008). This was chosen because it shed light on political processes and democratic aims that were difficult to realize in prac-tical building processes. The second case showed participation in developing health promoting environments in a hospital in Norway (Ingeberg et al., 2012). This was chosen because it showed the roles of the patient and health professionals in relation to a creative process where stringent and formalized ethical guidelines were integrated in the process. In the hospital study, key people took part in establishing focus group interview participants, similar to how the group leader was essential in implementing social change in a neigh-bourhood area (Whyte, 1981). The third case was participation in a park in Finland (Isohanni et al., 2013) and this was chosen for a third complementary perspective that involved a whole urban area, involving the local community. The participants in the case studies were, in various degrees, involved in the conceptual and material phases of the design process but these aspects were emphasized in this study because Eriksen claims that in a participatory design process material and physical examples could stimulate new imaginative spaces (Eriksen, 2012).

Designing a sense of place in a school

The first story line exemplifying the cultural sustainability discourse was from a school in the United Kingdom where politicians reflected on the high ideological aims of pupil participation but where the strategy failed in practice because of a lack of realistic procedures (Ghaziani, 2008). The reason for focussing on pupil participation in the school environment was that the amount of time young people spend in school, from preschool to twelfth grade, was so significant that it is important to recognize that much of this time is devoted to 'living' as well as learning (Ghaziani, 2008, p. 225). With a series of project examples, Ghaziani showed various ways of including pupils in the development of the school environment. One example was when

> children worked as clients with a number of the UK's leading names in design and architecture. The main aim of this project was to identify what children and young people wanted to change in their schools and how their proposed design solutions could lead to useful improvements.
>
> (p. 228)

Ghaziani found that the pupils' voices for school environmental issues were divided to two main categories: (1) their 'needs' and (2) 'physical features' of their school environment.

The 'physical features' highlighted by children about the school environment were classified into six categories, which were:

1   Indoor spaces (interior) – the interior of school buildings and how
    they look.
2   Comfort and control – the comfort levels of pupils and teaching staff in
    school buildings and the extent to which these can be controlled.
3   Activity spaces – specific design features required for different activities.
4   Nature and outdoor – the extent to which pupils have contact with the
    natural world whether they can see and access nature both indoors and
    outdoors.
5   Facilities – those facilities that are important for pupils.
6   Exterior – the exterior of school buildings and their appearance.

Despite these findings, the study reflected a culture with little aim for
participation in the paper work but where there in general was room and
need for more real participation in practice. This was important, Ghaziani
claimed, because the environment can work as structural elements for
thoughts, behaviour and well-being. The atmosphere in a school should
therefore be inclusive and based on users' participation, because the school is
a place to live, and not only to learn:

> A school should be looked upon as not only a place to learn, but also a
> place for socialising, relaxation and fun. Pupils have special needs that
> require special spaces. Therefore, the whole experience of schooling is
> important.
>
> (Ghaziani, 2008, p. 234)

Ghaziani's study demonstrated the value of including pupils in school planning although there seemed to be a gap between what was written in the
political aims of participation, and what was done in reality.

Designing a sense of place in a hospital

The second story line exemplifying the cultural sustainability discourse was
from a hospital in Norway where health professionals co-created public art
(Ingeberg et al., 2012). This case was the final project in my doctoral study
about participation in public space (Berg, 2014), and in this study new knowledge could be enhanced through the 'sense of place' perspective. The methodological approach was participatory research. The staff and elderly patients
in a ward for mental health care were invited into a creative process of having
ideas, making the art objects and installing them in their hospital environment
for everyday use. The research project was a collaboration between the nurses
and me, an artist and doctoral student. We wanted to investigate in which
ways art could contribute to communication in a hospital. Through both

workshops with health workers and my individual experiments in an art studio, artworks were developed that were installed in the hospital in the mental health ward. Material based art experimentation was combined with participatory design processes.

From a conceptualization perspective, the context of a hospital was chosen by the artist, but a participatory aspect emerged as the specific ward was suggested by the nurse researcher. Her aim in positioning the art project in a geriatric ward was that these patients represented a group that was unrecognized in health research. Whereas heart disease gets much attention in health research, elderly people in mental health care get less. Her idea was, therefore, that art could contribute to their everyday situation, but also that the dissemination of the research results that included art works through communication could contribute to another type of attention to this group.

During the materialization of the project, the ideas of the nurses contributed significantly to the final expression, both in the execution of material specific qualities, and in the principal choice of motif that had to be both figurative and nonfigurative. The nurses contributed to the form development. One example was that the tactile line in the middle of a form should be enhanced, according to the nurses, to enable the patients to connect their thoughts to 'a border', to 'a break in a structure'. This was because a break in the thoughts to create communication was often needed in mental health care diagnostics in order to connect to patients who could possibly be depressed, isolated or suffering from paranoia. The size of one of the ceramic art objects (45×43×16 cm) enabled several people to touch it, to enhance communication. Further, they contributed to a process that engendered a series with a larger variety of forms than I intended from the beginning, both larger and smaller than my initial artistic idea. They said: 'There should be as much variation as possible, as people are all different.'

Changes in the interior of the ward had to follow central interior decoration guidelines. Although the department was temporarily located in an industrial area they had to follow the same guidelines as for the rest of the hospital. Another subject of discussion was why there was a door that looked like a prison door in a locked ward. According to the doctor the art pieces with blue and white colours would fit the door better. A discussion on why this 'prison door' not had been painted previously took place. The ward leader said that painting the door would require further permission from the manager and that the art project could possibly enable such permission. Further, when the corridor was discussed a psychiatric nurse suggested that lines maybe could be painted on the wall and on the floor, horizontally and vertically, to serve as a pedagogical structure.

As soon as the Regional Committee for Medical Research Ethics (REC) accepted the project, the project was intensified and creative proposals came from the health professionals. Their reflections were connected to, and emerged from, material samples in ceramics. Additional ceramic forms of communication were thus produced in consultation with health professionals and patients (Figure 7.1). However, these objects, with abstract and figurative patterns, were not to be put in the patient ward, as some of the employees were afraid that they could trigger violence in psychotic patients. The subject was much discussed, as they always had admission other objects on the wards,

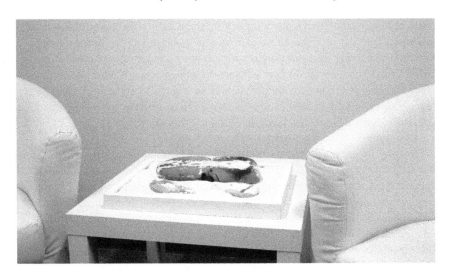

Figure 7.1 Ceramic forms developed by Arild Berg through participatory design for a more communicative environment in a psychiatric ward.

Source: photos Arild Berg.

such as coffee cups, which could also be used to harm others, but these were not seen as a danger. Instead we placed a basket of ceramic stone-like objects in the dining room for employees. The availability of the stones affected the staff. One of the nurses reported how a physiotherapist unexpectedly got the idea of taking the basket of stones into a physical training session with patients. She observed communication that was nonverbal, using touch. The patients' actions were evaluated and explained by the health professionals.

Having placed the stones in the lunch room the staff used to point at the dissimilar stones, lift and touch them, and discuss their likes and dislikes. The contact person said that as time passed by the stones gradually disappeared from the lunch room to reappear on the desktops of different staff members. After a while, the stones were moved to the light therapy room where we placed them in a box with marble sand. Some of the stone-like forms were placed in the light-therapy room for patients. The stones were placed in picture frames filled with sand (Figure 7.1). This was done to enhance the feeling of mental change and mental stimulus. The stones, partly sheltered by sand, could be seen as disappearing memories. By moving the stones and turning them around in the sand, new imageries and marks would appear; my intention was to create a similar situation as to how memories are lost. Placed in the light-therapy room they would be available to stimulate dialogues in therapy. The larger stone forms were placed by the staff in the public entrance corridor outside the locked ward. The purpose of the bigger stone forms had been to enable more people to touch them at the same time, to enhance a specific kind of communication.

The project created a change of communication at the ward where the environment, to a larger extent, became a part of the everyday dialogues and it also initiated more therapeutic dialogues with health professionals. A theoretical outcome was that the pedagogical structure developed in the implementation stage was published in a journal of psychosocial nursing (Ingeberg et al., 2012), and this was a sustainable aspect in addition to a change of practice.

Designing a sense of place in a public park

The third story line exemplifying the cultural sustainability discourse was from a community-based development of public art in an urban park in Finland: the Wirkkala Park in Arabianranta area (Isohanni et al., 2013). The intention of the art consultant Isohanni was that through the planning of the park there should be a dialogue between the people and the architecture in the environment. Through designing a sculptural landscape, and by including sculptural, interior-like objects in the park, the branding of the area changed. It changed from being an urban environment with little social activity to becoming a social meeting point and a landmark in the city.

In Isohanni's documentation of how the Arabianranta art contributed to public space it was shown that individual art projects offer points of contact, topics for discussion and a sense of community, as well as augmenting the collective memory of the specific living environment (Isohanni, 2008, p. 8). Similarly, through a participatory process perspective it shows how the process can be carried out to materialize art in public spaces. In this example, the initial study of the residential area of Arabianranta informed and inspired the art consultant Isohanni; 'after a while walking became a dialogue with the place – not unlike the discussion a painter has with her work when painting'. A feeling of merging outer landscape and inner life was experienced and described by Isohanni: 'I strived to remain open to thoughts and encounters within the place.... Art coordination is not only about generating results, but also becoming a part of the building process and local artistic activities' (Isohanni, 2008, p. 2).

How can participatory design contribute to cultural sustainability?

The different case studies show how various perspectives are characterized by a professional background constituted by fore-meanings and fore-understanding (Gadamer, 2004, p. 207). This, seen from the design perspective, can represent a worldview that is connected to research traditions in material cultures where there is no sharp distinction between humans and the environment and where the aim is to investigate both the banal and the extra-ordinary in peoples' relation to their environment (Tilley, 2006, p. 70). This approach to the environment can also be seen as an ecological and sustainable view of the world where self-realization is an aim in the sense that the self is widened by seeing ourselves in others and in our environment, leading to a deepened perception of reality and our own self – a deepened realism (Næss, 1986, p. 29). The environment should ideally create social meeting points. By the use of material objects it is possible to create physical structures that are inclusive, not only of people but also in relation to the materials in the environment. Materialized art and design can 'talk back' in a material language to the architecture. Thus it can be created in such a way that it responds both materially and conceptually to the people involved.

Studies on sustainable cultures have been developed through new methods in architecture, design and housing (Keitsch, 2012a). With perspectives from sociology, ecology and economy, the action researcher Aagaard Nilsen demonstrated the relationship between sociopedagogical approaches, action research and how to develop sustainable cultures on a systemic level (Aagaard Nielsen, 2010). This is highly relevant for participatory design. Another organizational perspective on how participation can contribute to sustainable cultures comes from Llamas-Sanchez' study of the innovation that can happen in local communities and which considers both the culture within the organization itself as well as external contexts such as institutional factors (Llamas-Sanchez et al., 2011). This study identified some relevant issues for sustainable design practices. These were empowerment, receptiveness to change, the climate of implementation, support for the implementation, culture organizational, institutional pressures, communication and coordination and participation of stakeholders. Therefore both institutional and organizational factors affect the innovation process in sustainable practices

'A central issue is that culture, in its many forms, has to be sustained. When the sustainability of development is in question, cultural aspects in addition to economic, social, and economic aspects need to be taken into account' (Soini & Birkeland, 2014, p. 220). Soini and Birkeland demonstrate how cultural sustainability can be presented through storylines and political contexts to strengthen sustainable environment. They express how the heritage and cultural vitality story lines can be seen most clearly as a fourth, cultural pillar of sustainability, equal to ecological, social, and economic sustainability.

These case studies have contributed to a deeper understanding of the obstacles and incentives in public environment processes, because in these studies participation actually did happen and the people actually had an influence on the result. Through cross-case analysis (Yin, 2009) and concept mapping (Maxwell, 2005) some issues for designing a sense of place were identified.

The issues emerging from the case studies modified the initial propositions. These were formulated to success criteria (Westerveld, 2003), for higher relevance to design in a cross-disciplinary practice.

Ten success criteria for designing a sense of place

Finally, as a conclusion to how participatory design can contribute to cultural sustainability, ten success criteria were identified. The concepts emerged from combining the initial theoretical propositions (Aagaard Nielsen, 2010; Barnett, 1953; Marres, 2012; Melles et al., 2011; Shamsuddin & Ujang, 2008; Soini et al., 2012) with the empirical documentation from the case studies. These are interconnected as shown by the lines in Figure 7.2.

Including engagement is the first success criterion for designing a sense of place, meaning that people should be included in the design process. When they participate they must also be willing to contribute to the management of the environment (Soini et al., 2012). This way they can contribute in transforming a place into social meeting points by actively creating ideas and contributions about indoor spaces. This requires a sensibility towards the environment and a meaningful awareness of the built environment. This might also lead to a built environment with a connectedness to nature (Ghaziani, 2008). Exploring attachment is the second success criterion for designing a sense of place, where the intention is to approve and search for peoples' attachment to traditional places (Shamsuddin & Ujang, 2008). This can be understood and respected through cultural and physical exploration (Ingeberg et al., 2012; Isohanni et al., 2013) such as awareness of the unique values of a place and by considering and taking advantage of site-specific professional practice and the specific architectural traits in the environment.

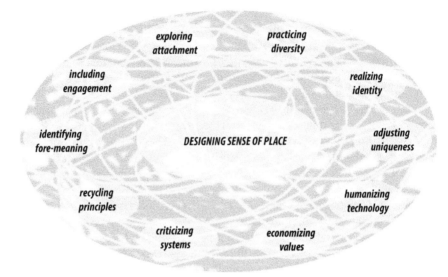

Figure 7.2 A visualization of ten success criteria for designing sense of place.
Source: by Arild Berg.

Practicing diversity is the third success criterion for designing a sense of place, meaning that cultural diversity should be accentuated (Shamsuddin & Ujang, 2008) so that a variety of people recognize the relevance and importance of the place. This can be achieved through using a variety of communication cultures, including design proposals and experiments (Ingeberg et al., 2012) that are connected to existing practices at the place. Realizing identity is the fourth success criterion for designing a sense of place, meaning that both self- and group identity should be stimulated (Shamsuddin & Ujang, 2008). This can be done through the design of the exteriors of buildings and the activity spaces that over time enable various kinds of self-realization through gaming and social meeting points as well as spaces for reflection (Ghaziani, 2008; Isohanni et al., 2013).

Adjusting uniqueness is the fifth success criterion for designing sense of places in the sense that sustainable changes should be adapted through designing in unique ways in different cultures (Barnett, 1953; Ghaziani, 2008; Ingeberg et al., 2012). Pupils at a school will have different needs to patients in a hospital, but even the geographical location, the existing local culture and traditions, as well as future political plans, should be considered to create a long-lasting design solution. Humanizing technology is the sixth success criterion for designing a sense of place, implying that technical solutions should be adjusted to human use (Marres, 2012) such as facilities for groups should be designed based on specific needs (Ghaziani, 2008; Ingeberg et al., 2012). The technical planning and realization should be based on peoples' practice and should strengthen and help human activity. Economizing values is the seventh success criterion for designing a sense of place where the intention is to have cultural awareness of systems of economy (Barnett, 1953). This could be achieved through the participants' identification of various value creations enabled by design (Ghaziani, 2008; Ingeberg et al., 2012). This means the ability to analyse activity in the place from various perspectives to identify economic, social and religious, health and aesthetic values.

Criticizing systems is the eighth success criterion for designing a sense of place, meaning to encourage and enable a system critical approach based on local engagement (Ingeberg et al., 2012; Aagaard Nielsen, 2010) by including participants in the local area in the design process and using visual and material examples to stimulate imaginative spaces of new, future practices. This often means that adjustments to the system are needed. Therefore participants should be not only users, but decision makers and various stakeholders should also all take part in the process in order to enable a sustainable solution. Recycling principles is the ninth success criterion for designing a sense of place, where the intention is to make sure that recycling principles are included and that over consumption is avoided (Melles et al., 2011). This means that an awareness of existing values should be an overall attitude: these are physical values such as materials and environmental resources but they are also mental values such as knowledge and competence. New values can be recycled from existing values. Over consumption is to be avoided, such as attitudes that claim that all that is old should be rejected and replaced by something new.

The last, tenth success criterion for designing a sense of place is to identify fore-meaning to make sure that all participants in the design collaboration are reflective about their agenda: how their values and fore-meanings are related to their professional and personal background (Gadamer, 2004). Interest in each other's background and agenda contribute to a shared understanding of a goal, where there might be a fusion of the horizons of understanding. In a cross-disciplinary collaboration, such common ground can strengthen a sustainable change in designing a sense of place.

Thus the ten success criteria identified for designing a sense of place that contribute to cultural sustainability are: including engagement, exploring attachment, practicing diversity, realizing identity, adjusting uniqueness, humanizing technology, economizing values, criticizing systems, recycling principles and identifying fore-meaning.

Finally, in conclusion, it has been shown that participatory approaches can contribute to communication and cooperation in the development of the physical environment to create a 'sense of place' and cultural sustainability. This was exemplified in the school where politicians, pupils, researchers, and teachers contributed to new spaces for schooling. It was shown in the hospital where nurses, co-researchers, patients and relatives developed a new use of the environment for dialogues. Finally it was shown in the park where the project contributed to augmenting the collective memory of the environment and where art consultants, architects, city planners, artists and local community members all contributed to an emerging place identity. Existing theory on 'sense of place' has thus, through the case study approach, been adjusted to a cross-disciplinary field of design collaboration that contributes to cultural sustainability.

References

Aagaard Nielsen, K. (2010). *A new agenda for sustainability*. Farnham: Ashgate.

Asaro, P. M. (2000). Transforming society by transforming technology: The science and politics of participatory design. *Accounting, Management and Information Technologies*, *10*(4), 33.

Baldwin, J. (2012). Putting Massey's relational sense of place to practice: Labour and the constitution of Jolly Beach, Antigua, West Indies. *Geografiska Annaler Series B-Human Geography*, *94B*(3), 207–221. doi: 10.1111/j.1468-0467.2012.00410.x.

Bang, A.-L. (2010). *Emotional value of applied textiles: Dialogue-oriented and participatory approaches to textile design*. Kolding: Kolding School of Design.

Barnett, H. G. (1953). *Innovation: The basis of cultural change*. New York: McGraw-Hill.

Berg, A. (2014). *Artistic research in public space: Participation in material-based art (Vol. 33/2014)*. Helsinki: Aalto University.

Berg, A., Stoltenberg, E. & Reitan, J. B. (2014). Sustainable design technology: A case study of a master student's lamp project. In *Design Education & Human Technology Relations. The 16th International Conference on Engineering & Product Design Education* (pp. 632–637). Bristol: The Design Society.

Buur, J., & Larsen, H. (2010). The quality of conversations in participatory innovation. *Codesign-International Journal of Cocreation in Design and the Arts*, *6*(3), 121–138. doi: 10.1080/15710882.2010.533185.

Eriksen, M. A. (2012). *Material matters in co-designing: Formatting and staging with participating materials in co-design projects, events and situations, (new media, public spheres, and forms of expression)*. Malmö: Malmö University.

Gadamer, H.-G. (2004). *Truth and method* (2nd, rev. edn, translation revised by Joel Weinsheimer and Donald G. Marshall, eds). London: Continuum.

Ghaziani, R. (2008). Children's voices: Raised issues for school design. *CoDesign: International Journal of Cocreation in Design and the Arts*, *4*(4), 225–236. doi: 10.1080/15710880802536403.

Giljum, S., Behrens, A., Hinterberger, F., Lutz, C. & Meyer, B. (2008). Modelling scenarios towards a sustainable use of natural resources in Europe. *Environmental Science & Policy*, *11*(3), 204–216. doi: 10.1016/j.envsci.2007.07.005.

Hammersley, M. (2007). *Ethnography: Principles in practice*. London: Routledge.

Ingeberg, M. H., Wikstrøm, B.-M. & Berg, A. (2012). The essential dialogue: A Norwegian study of art communication in mental health care. *Journal of Psychosocial Nursing and Mental Health Services*, *50*(8).

Isohanni, T., Wilson, R. & Wirkkala, T. (2013). *Wilson meets Wirkkala: The story of Tapio Wirkkala Park, designed by Robert Wilson*. Helsinki: Aalto University.

Keitsch, M. (2012a). Sustainable architecture, design and housing. *Sustainable Development*, *20*(3), 141–145. doi: 10.1002/sd.1530.

Keitsch, M. (2012b). Sustainable design: A brief appraisal of its main concepts. *Sustainable Development*, *20*(3), 180–188. doi: 10.1002/sd.1534.

Llamas-Sanchez, R., Munoz-Fernandez, A. & Maraver-Tarifa, G. (2011). The local agenda 21 in Andalusia, Spain: A model for sustainable innovation. *African Journal of Business Management, 5*(32), 12653–12663. doi: 10.5897/ajbm11.2381.

Marres, N. (2012). *Material participation: Technology, the environment and everyday publics.* Basingstoke: Palgrave Macmillan.

Massey, D. (1991). A global sense of place. *Marxism Today, 38*, 5.

Maxwell, J. A. (2005). *Qualitative research design: An interactive approach.* Thousand Oaks, CA: Sage Publications.

Melles, G., de Vere, I. & Misic, V. (2011). Socially responsible design: Thinking beyond the triple bottom line to socially responsive and sustainable product design. *Codesign-International Journal of Cocreation in Design and the Arts, 7*(3–4), 143–154. doi: 10.1080/15710882.2011.630473.

Næss, A. (1986). *Self-realization: An ecological approach to being in the world* (Vol. 4). Murdoch, WA: Murdoch University.

Pacheco-Torgal, F. (2014). Eco-efficient construction and building materials research under the EU Framework Programme Horizon 2020. *Construction and Building Materials, 51*, 151–162. doi: 10.1016/j.conbuildmat.2013.10.058.

Sanders, E. B.-N. & Stappers, P. J. (2008). Co-creation and the new landscapes of design. *Codesign: International Journal of Cocreation in Design and the Arts, 4*(1), 5–18.

Shamsuddin, S. & Ujang, N. (2008). Making places: The role of attachment in creating the sense of place for traditional streets in Malaysia. *Habitat International, 32*(3), 399–409. doi: 10.1016/j.habitatint.2008.01.004.

Skjerven, A. (2012). Cultural traditions for the sake of innovation: The concept of Scandinavian design as a potential tool in the development of a sustainable China. *Sustainable Development, 20*(3), 230–238. doi: 10.1002/sd.1539.

Soini, K. & Birkeland, I. (2014). Exploring the scientific discourse on cultural sustainability. *Geoforum, 51*, 213–223. doi: 10.1016/j.geoforum.2013.12.001.

Soini, K., Vaarala, H. & Pouta, E. (2012). Residents' sense of place and landscape perceptions at the rural-urban interface. *Landscape and Urban Planning, 104*(1), 124–134. doi: 10.1016/j.landurbplan.2011.10.002.

Taussig, M. (2009). *What color is the sacred?* Chicago, IL: University of Chicago Press.

Tilley, C. Y. (2006). *Handbook of material culture.* London: Sage.

Westerveld, E. (2003). The Project Excellence Model®: Linking success criteria and critical success factors. *International Journal of Project Management, 21*(6), 411–418. doi: http://dx.doi.org/10.1016/S0263-7863(02)00112-6.

Whyte, W. F. (1981). *Street corner society: The social structure of an Italian slum.* Chicago: University of Chicago Press.

Yin, R. K. (2009). *Case study research: Design and methods.* Thousand Oaks, CA: Sage.

Part III

Products and cultures

8 The importance of culture in design for sustainable behaviour research

Johannes Ludvig Zachrisson Daae

Introduction: design for sustainable behaviour

According to a report by the British Design Council (Design Council, 2002, p. 19), "80% of a product, service or system's environmental cost is determined at the design stage". Although one might argue that many of the decisions made at the design stage are beyond the control of the designer, there is no doubt that the designer has the opportunity to make a difference. Designers must be aware of their responsibility to contribute to reducing the negative environmental impact caused by their products (Manzini, 2009).

In recent years, increasing attention has been directed towards the environmental impact caused during the use phase of products (Dietz et al., 2009; Van Hemel & Brezet, 1997), and the significance of the way people behave and interact with products has been acknowledged (IPCC, 2007; House of Lords, 2011). Understanding "the ways in which end users interact with products" is one of the goals of design research (Kannengiesser & Gero, 2012, p. 50). It has long been acknowledged that the design of products and systems strongly affects the way people interact with them. Buckminster Fuller stated,

> I made up my mind ... that I would never try to reform man – that's much too difficult. What I would do was to try to modify the environment in such a way as to get man moving in preferred directions.
>
> (Tomkins, 1966, p. 17)

This consequence of design provides designers with opportunities to reduce environmental impact by designing products and systems that alter people's behaviour and make them interact with products in more sustainable ways.

This realization has resulted in the development of a research field often referred to as Design for Sustainable Behaviour (DfSB) (Pettersen & Boks, 2009). The field builds on the work of Jelsma, who in 1997 connected Akrich's (1992) concept of script to the task of reducing environmental impact through the way people interact with products (Jelsma, 1997). The idea behind scripts is to provide "a kind of user manual inscribed into an artefact", where the design of a product guides the way it is being used (Jelsma, 1997); which again is strongly related to Donald Norman's (1988) concept of affordances.

The field as we know it today began to be systematically explored about a decade ago (Bhamra, 2004; Rodriguez & Boks, 2005) and has since resulted in an active research community from which valuable research has emerged (e.g. Lilley, 2007; Lockton, 2013; Pettersen, 2013). User-centred design and interaction design have been found to be promising approaches to inform this development (Wever et al., 2008). In addition, DfSB research draws upon concepts and insight from behavioural psychology and sociology. Topics in focus have been the identification of principles for how products can be designed to affect behaviour (e.g. Lockton et al., 2010), investigations into questions of when the different principles are most likely to result in the intended behaviour (e.g. Daae, 2014) and case studies related to these questions (e.g. Tang & Bhamra, 2012).

Among the tools that have been developed specifically to support design practitioners, "Design with Intent" by Lockton et al. (2010) has probably been most widely used. The tool consists of a card deck with 101 design principles (or patterns) for how one might affect people's behaviour through design. On each card, there is a question about a particular behaviour change and a picture and explanation of an example of a design answering the question. There are several ways to utilize the card deck, but one of the most common uses is to generate new ideas during brainstorming.

Another of the tools developed to support design practitioners is "Dimensions of Behaviour Change" by Daae and Boks (2014). The aim of this tool is to help designers make informed design decisions that will lead to the desired behaviour change and will also be accepted by the target group. The tool draws heavily upon the behavioural factors identified by behavioural psychology and utilizes these to provide indications for the type of design solutions that are more likely to be successful. This tool also consists of a card deck, but this deck presents nine dimensions along which design principles can be adjusted: Control, Obtrusiveness, Direction, Empathy, Encouragement, Meaning, Importance, Timing and Exposure.

Although DfSB has been a dedicated research field for more than a decade and has resulted in conference tracks and special issues in journals, a number of aspects and directions still need to be investigated. One of these, which may turn out to have a significant impact on the further development of DfSB research and the practical application of its results, is the inclusion of cultural factors and the effect they may have on how design affects behaviour.

Culture and design

There are several indications in the literature that culture plays an important role in influencing behaviour (e.g. Fullerton et al., 1996; Shaw & Clarke, 1998).

Consumer concerns are likely to be influenced by different local and national peculiarities, with local culture affecting the meanings assigned to specific issues. These different interpretations in turn affect how these issues are prioritized by consumers, with variation in cultural influences potentially leading to different patterns of consumption behaviour.

(Shaw & Clarke, 1998, p. 166)

Whether culture affects behaviour directly or indirectly (through the various factors that determine behaviour) depends on how *culture* is defined. For instance, Linton defined culture as "the configuration of learned behaviours and results of behaviour whose component parts are shared and transmitted by the members of a particular society" (Linton, 1947, p. 21). This definition creates an inseparable link between culture and behaviour by presenting culture as behaviours itself and as a result of behaviours. In contrast, Spencer-Oatey defined culture as "A fuzzy set of attitudes, beliefs, behavioural norms, and basic assumptions and values that are shared by a group of people, and that influence each member's behaviour and his/her interpretation of the 'meaning' of other people's behaviour" (Spencer-Oatey, 2000, p. 4). From this perspective, culture affects behaviour indirectly through its various components. This perspective on culture has a long tradition in ethnographic circles and bears clear similarities to Taylor's classic definition: "Culture ... is that complex whole which includes knowledge, beliefs, arts, morals, law, customs, and any other capabilities and habits acquired by man as a member of society" (Taylor, 1871, p. 1).

The analysis in this chapter builds upon an understanding of culture similar to that of Taylor and Spencer-Oatey: Culture is considered to affect people's behaviour both directly and indirectly through its effect on other behavioural factors. Interestingly, there is a strong overlap of the components that Spencer-Oatey and Taylor identified as cultural components and the behavioural factors commonly identified in the behavioural psychology literature (e.g. Jackson, 2005; Klöckner & Blöbaum, 2010). This overlap heightens the potential importance of connecting the two research fields and creates an obvious approach for investigating the relationship between them.

The multitude of different types and levels of cultural influence makes it challenging to understand the influence of culture and to take cultural influence into consideration when designing products. "Culture is a complex concept, and its effect upon behaviour is, therefore, difficult to assess" (Shaw & Clarke, 1998) p. 165). This is an issue particularly when investigating the totality of the ways behaviour may be affected by culture. However, it is possible to identify particular aspects of culture and behaviour that have a more obvious connection. One such study, of particular relevance to DfSB, was published by Moray (2004). This was a meta-study in which Moray reviewed a number of studies investigating the effect of national culture on usability. By comparing how people with different nationalities understand various practical challenges, Moray found that the way we expect systems to work strongly depends on where we come from. For instance, he found that North Americans expect a light switch to turn the light on when pointing upwards, whereas Europeans when the light switch points downwards.

The expectation of how a system should react to a particular manipulation, or how a system is structured, is what Norman and Draper call the "conceptual model" (Norman & Draper, 1986). It is very difficult to interact successfully with a product if one has an incorrect conceptual model of how the product works and responds to different input. For the user to interact with the product as intended, it is crucial either to design products and systems with the same conceptual model as the target expects or to communicate the correct conceptual model in an intuitive manner. The user's culture both provides information and a lens through which to interpret information; "Culture allows people to fill in the blanks. The major point for discussions of culture's influence on behaviour is to reiterate the conclusion that culture presents detailed knowledge and this knowledge is taken for granted" (Brislin, 1993, p. 16).

Because the conceptual model of the user is affected by his or her cultural background, it is relevant for us to consider the culture of the target group when we want to affect user behaviour through design.

Discussion

To date, the majority of DfSB research has not actively taken cultural factors into consideration when investigating how behaviour could be affected by design. The only exception is the work of a few researchers who advocate investigation of foreign or older cultures as a source of inspiration to find more sustainable ways of living (Kuijer, 2014; Matsuhashi et al., 2009). The connections between culture and behaviour presented in the literature, as summarized previously in this chapter, indicate that DfSB research may benefit greatly from including cultural considerations. However, how this should be done, and what consequences this may have for DfSB research and the design of behaviour-changing products and systems, will probably require substantial investigation and experience from practical application to be answered. Nevertheless, a number of aspects may still be discussed.

First, whether it is consciously included or not, the influence of culture cannot be ignored. To ignore this influence is, in effect, the same as assuming a mono-culture (de Jong & Mazé, 2010). Not considering the behavioural implications of cultural variations may possibly be justifiable if the target group for the design is a well-defined and homogenous group, with no cultural variations, but it is questionable if this situation is ever encountered in reality. Regardless, when investigating fundamental principles or designing solutions for a global market, this approach has obvious shortcomings, and even if the cultural differences within the target group do not affect their behaviour or the way they react to behavioural interventions, this cannot be known unless it has been investigated.

One might argue that many of the behavioural factors DfSB researchers already consider are directly or indirectly affected by culture. For instance, people's norms and values, or the social norms of other relevant people, are among the factors often associated with culture. Thus, culture is already included in the current approaches, although it is not stated so explicitly. However, by explicitly considering the cultural influence, one might not only be pushed towards distinguishing between variations within the target group but might also gain a wider perspective.

Thus, it is necessary to consider cultural influence when investigating how design can influence behaviour. Doing so not only potentially reduces the risk of rebound effects and unexpected reactions to the design due to cultural aspects but may also provide additional elements to consider in the design. This may again lead to higher granularity in the understanding of the target group and better precision in the selection of behaviour-changing design principles, which may increase the likelihood of successfully affecting the target behaviour.

Acknowledging the need to consider the influence of culture leads to another central question: What is the most effective and precise way to introduce the influence of culture to DfSB? Should it be considered as an additional factor, to be dealt with on an equal basis with other behavioural factors, or should it be considered as a filter, to which the behaviour analysis or design recommendations should be adjusted accordingly? As culture has been found to affect behaviour both indirectly and directly, it is possible that both approaches may be beneficial. There may be aspects of culture that affect behaviour independently and thus should be considered as additional factors. However, as the influence of culture is strongly connected to the behavioural factors already considered by DfSB, and no obvious independent factor is available, it is likely that it would be most beneficial to consider the cultural influence as both a filter for adjusting the behavioural factors and as an additional perspective from which to approach and understand the behavioural factors.

It is, however, relevant to consider whether cultural research may contribute with even more than additional perspectives for investigation and as a filter through which to interpret behavioural factors. Does cultural research also provide other contributions which DfSB may draw upon? The literature related to cultural research is extensive and contains contributions from a variety of academic disciplines and thus may contribute with a multitude of valuable ideas, methods or approaches for categorizing and analysing behaviour. This may not only improve our ability to understand and interpret behaviour but may also enable better informed design of behavioural interventions and more precise adjustment to the target group.

Whether the influence of culture will become more or less important in the future is an open question. It will depend, among other things, on whether or not increased globalization results in increasing homogenization of global cultures. This is the topic of an academic debate often referred to as "the global consumer culture debate" (Merz et al., 2008; Shaw & Clarke, 1998). On one side of the globalization debate we find scholars who argue for an emerging global consumer culture (GCC). It is argued that these trends lead to the uniformity of customer needs and wishes and hence to the homogenization of global demand because consumers relate and compare themselves not only to their own culture but also to other cultures (e.g. Alden et al., 1999). On the other side of the debate are proponents of local consumer culture (LCC). These scholars hypothesize that distinctive local consumption cultures are resilient against globalization (Jackson, 2004). Between these two extremes, we find advocates of "glocal" consumer culture (GLCC), who argue that consumers often "draw from all available global and local, new and old sources as they use products to position themselves in the local age, gender, social class, religion and ethnic hierarchies" (Ger & Belk, 1996, p. 294).

The work of identifying the most valuable elements from cultural research and integrating them into DfSB will be extensive and is not within the scope of this chapter. However, to illustrate the potential, an example will be given of the application of one tool from cultural research applied in a DfSB context. This example illustrates the implications of applying "Dimensions of National Culture" by Hofstede et al. (2010) to a design targeting the U.S. and Chinese markets.

Example: dimensions of national culture

"Dimensions of National Culture" is a tool to structure and compare national cultures. Hofstede and his research team have investigated variations in national and regional cultures and the effect these variations have on society and organizations. Through analysing studies conducted in a large number of countries, Hofstede et al. developed a scoring system in which numerous national cultures are compared along six dimensions:

1 *Power Distance Index* (PDI) shows the extent to which the less powerful members of the community accept and expect that power will be distributed unequally.
2 *Individualism versus Collectivism* (IDV) represents the degree to which you are expected to take care of yourself and your immediate family, or whether a larger group will look after you.
3 *Masculinity versus Femininity* (MAS) represents the degree to which society focuses on achievement, heroism, assertiveness and material rewards for success as opposed to cooperation, modesty, caring for the weak and quality of life.
4 *Uncertainty Avoidance Index* (UAI) shows the society's tolerance for uncertainty and ambiguity.
5 *Long Term Orientation versus Short Term Normative Orientation* (LTO) deals with the degree to which the society prefers to maintain time-honoured

traditions and norms while viewing societal change with suspicion as opposed to taking a more pragmatic approach that encourages thrift and efforts in modern education as a way to prepare for the future.

6   *Indulgence versus Restraint* (IND) is based on the degree to which people indulge in free gratification of basic and natural human drives related to enjoying life and having fun.

When comparing the scores of the United States and China for the six categories, it becomes apparent that the two countries' scores are relatively similar for MAS and UAI, but quite different for PDI, IDV, LTO and IND. Based on the analysis presented by Hofstede et al., it is possible to draw a number of indicators from this comparison:

- People in both China and the United States are focused on heroism, achievements, assertiveness and material awards. The populations in both countries are willing to take risks, claim ethical considerations for consumption and accept new technology quickly.
- The Chinese population tends to be more willing than the U.S. population to accept unequal distribution of power and, for instance, to do what they are told without being given any justification.
- In the United States, people are more individualistic and expect to take care of themselves, whereas the Chinese population depends more strongly on others.
- The Chinese population is more pragmatic and more focused on saving, learning from others and working hard, whereas the U.S. population is more prone to believe in luck and is prouder of family and country.
- In the United States, people have a stronger tendency to allow free gratification of basic and natural human desires to enjoy life and have fun, whereas in China, such gratification tends to be more strongly curbed by social norms.

Based on this insight, it seems likely that particular design principles may be more successful for use in one country than in the other. For instance, the Chinese tendency to trust authorities and do what they are told without needing justification makes information from authorities more likely to be accepted in China than in the United States, and more likely to result in the desired behaviour change. The stronger collective feeling and social norms in China also make principles building upon others opinions more promising for the Chinese market than the U.S. market. In contrast, promises of immediate hedonic gratification may be more effective in the U.S. market. Such insight may be useful in combination with various DfSB tools, for instance in selecting particular principles for the "Design with Intent" tool or in positioning the design in "Dimensions of Behaviour Change".

Naturally, one should be cautious when applying tools such as "Dimensions of National Culture". The statements cannot be considered absolute, and one should be very cautious about how categorically the statements are allowed to dictate decisions. However, they provide an indication of a tendency, which may prove a valuable starting point for a design. The importance or validity of the various points could then be investigated through more traditional user research. Similarly, other perspectives, tools or approaches from cultural research may prove valuable as alternatives or supplements to "Dimensions of National Culture". In addition, several other forms of culture may be equally important, determined by age, geography, religion, social settings, etc. A thorough investigation into the various relevant aspects of cultural research may prove a valuable contribution to DfSB research and may potentially benefit the development of cultural research as well.

Conclusion

Until now, DfSB research has almost entirely ignored the cultural influence on people's behaviour and their responsiveness to behavioural interventions. This is a serious shortcoming, as there are several reasons to believe this may affect the design's ability to successfully affect the behaviour of the target group and the target group's acceptance of it. Depending on the culture of the target group, particular behaviour-changing interventions may prove successful or may result in utter rejection of the entire design. Cultural insight may thus provide a valuable source of information for making informed decisions about the types of behavioural principles to apply and how they should be applied. Particular characteristics of a culture may enhance the potential value of some principles and disqualify others. Including these considerations in DfSB research and in the design of products or systems aimed at affecting the behaviour of the target group is thus crucial. It is very difficult to design interventions that will successfully affect consumers' behaviour globally, and almost impossible if the various cultural influences are not taken into consideration. Integrating cultural considerations into product and system designs is probably one of the keys to increase the likelihood of designers influencing consumer behaviour on a global scale.

References

Akrich, M. (1992). The de-scription of technical objects. In W. E. Bijker & J. Law (eds), *Shaping technology/building society: Studies in sociotechnical change* (pp. 205–224). Cambridge, MA: MIT Press.
Alden, D. L., Steenkamp, J.-B. E. M. & Batra, R. (1999). Brand positioning through advertising in Asia, North America, and Europe: The role of global consumer culture. *Journal of Marketing, 63*(1), 75. http://doi.org/10.2307/1252002
Bhamra, T. A. (2004). Ecodesign: The search for new strategies in product development. *Proceedings of the Institution of Mechanical Engineers, Part B: Journal of Engineering Manufacture, 218*(5), 557–569.
Brislin, R. W. (1993). *Understanding culture's influence on behavior.* San Diego, CA: Harcourt Brace Jovanovich College Publishers.

Daae, J. (2014, April 29). *Informing design for sustainable behaviour.* (Doctoral Thesis). Norwegian University of Science and Technology, Trondheim, Norway.

Daae, J. & Boks, C. (2014). Dimensions of behaviour change. *Journal of Design Research, 12*(3), 145–172.

de Jong, A. & Mazé, R. (2010). Cultures of sustainability: "Ways of doing" cooking. *Proceedings of Knowledge Collaboration & Learning for Sustainable Innovation ERSCP-EMSU Conference, Delft, the Netherlands, October 25–29, 2010,* 1–25.

Design Council (2002). UK Design Council Annual Review, London.

Dietz, T., Gardner, G., Gilligan, J., Stern, P. & Vandenbergh, M. (2009). Household actions can provide a behavioral wedge to rapidly reduce US carbon emissions. *Proceedings of the National Academy of Sciences, 106*(44), 18452.

Fullerton, S., Kerch, K. B. & Dodge, H. R. (1996). Consumer ethics: An assessment of individual behavior in the market place. *Journal of Business Ethics, 15*(7), 805–814. http://doi.org/10.1007/BF00381744

Ger, G. L. & Belk, R. W. (1996). I'd like to buy the world a Coke: Konsumpano-ramen in weniger entwickelten Gesellschaften [Consumer perspectives in less developed societies]. *Journal of Consumer Policy, 19*(3), 271–304. http://doi.org/10.1007/BF00411411

Hofstede, G., Hofstede, G. J. & Minkov, M. (2010). *Cultures and organizations: Software of the mind* (3rd edn). New York: McGraw-Hill.

House of Lords, Science and Technology Select Committee (2011). 2nd Report of Session 2010–12; Behavior change. (HL Papser 179). London: The Stationery Office Limited.

IPCC. (2007). *Climate change 2007 – Mitigation of climate change: Working group III contribution to the fourth assessment report of the IPCC.* Cambridge: Cambridge University Press.

Jackson, P. (2004). Local consumption cultures in a globalizing world. *Transactions of the Institute of British Geographers, 29*(2), 165–178. http://doi.org/10.1111/j.0020-2754.2004.00123.x

Jackson, T. (2005). *Motivating sustainable consumption: A report to the Sustainable Development Research Network.* Guildford: University of Surrey.

Jelsma, J. (1997). Philosophy meets design. *Shortened Version of a Paper for Presentation at the Annual Meeting of the Society for Social Studies of Science, Tucson, Arizona, 23–26 October,* 1–14.

Kannengiesser, U. & Gero, J. S. (2012). A process framework of affordances in design. *Design Issues, 28*(1), 50–62. http://doi.org/10.1162/DESI_a_00123

Klöckner, C. & Blöbaum, A. (2010). A comprehensive action determination model. *Journal of Environmental Psychology, 30*(4), 574–586.

Kuijer, L. (2014, January 21). *Implications of social practice theory for sustainable design.* (Doctoral Thesis). TUDelft, The Netherlands.

Lilley, D. (2007). *Designing for behavioural change: Reducing the social impacts of product use through design.* (Doctoral Thesis). Loughborough University, UK.

Linton, R. (1947). *The cultural background of personality.* London: Kegan Paul.

Lockton, D. (2013). *Design with intent.* (Doctoral Thesis). Brunel University, UK.

Lockton, D., Harrison, D. & Stanton, N. (2010). *Design with intent: 101 patterns for influencing behaviour through design.* Windsor, UK: Equifine.

Matsuhashi, N., Kuijer, L. & de Jong, A. (2009). A culture-inspired approach to gaining insights for designing sustainable practices. *The EcoDesign 2009 Conference,* December 7–9, Sapporo, Japan.

Merz, M. A., He, Y. & Alden, D. L. (2008). A categorization approach to analyzing the global consumer culture debate. *International Marketing Review*, 25(2), 166–182. http://doi.org/10.1108/02651330810866263

Moray, N. (2004). 2. Culture, context and performance. *Advances in Human Performance and Cognitive Engineering Research*, 4, 31–59.

Norman, D. & Draper, S. (1986). *User centered system design: New perspectives on human–computer interaction*. New York: Lawrence Erlbaum Associates.

Norman, D. A. (1988). *The design of everyday things*. London: First MIT Press.

Pettersen, I. N. (2013). *Changing practices*. (Doctoral Thesis). Norwegian University of Science and Technology, Trondheim, Norway.

Pettersen, I. & Boks, C. (2009). The future of design for sustainable behaviour. *The EcoDesign 2009 Conference*, December 7–9, Sapporo, Japan.

Rodriguez, E. & Boks, C. (2005). How design of products affects user behaviour and vice versa: The environmental implications. *Proceedings of EcoDesign 2005. Tokyo: Union of Ecodesigners*, 1–8.

Shaw, D. S. & Clarke, I. (1998). Culture, consumption and choice: Towards a conceptual relationship. *Journal of Consumer Studies and Home Economics*, 22(3), 163–168.

Spencer-Oatey, H. (2000). *Culturally speaking: Managing rapport through talk across cultures*. London: Continuum.

Tang, T. & Bhamra, T. (2012). Putting consumers first in design for sustainable behaviour: A case study of reducing environmental impacts of cold appliance use. *International Journal of Sustainable Engineering*, 5(4), 1–16. http://doi.org/10.1080/19 397038.2012.685900

Taylor, E. B. (1871). *Primitive culture: Researches into the development of mythology, philosophy, religion, art and custom* (vol. 1). London: John Murray, Albemarle Street.

Tomkins, C. (1966, January 8). In the outlaw area. *The New Yorker*, 1–41.

Van Hemel, C. & Brezet, J. C. (1997). Ecodesign: A promising approach to sustainable production and consumption. *United Nations Environment Programme, Industry and Environment*. New York: United Nations Publishing.

Wever, R., van Kuijk, J. & Boks, C. (2008). User-centred design for sustainable behaviour. *International Journal of Sustainable Engineering*, 1(1), 9–20.

9 The social construction of child consumers

Transmedia toys in light of Slavoj Žižek's notions of pleasure and enjoyment

Tore Gulden

One strategy that is often utilised by the global toy industry is the creation of an environment in which customers are motivated to keep up with the latest releases and to continually plan for their next purchase. The design and marketing platform known as transmedia storytelling (TS) has proven to be successful in providing such a context (Heljakka, 2013; Jenkins, 2010; Kinder, 1991; Pietschmannet al., 2014). TS builds on a main narrative that is presented through multiple media platforms such as cartoons, games, and action figures; via these platforms, children learn about the toy and are familiarised with potential play activities (Heljakka, 2013; Jenkins, 2010; Kinder, 1991). Each type of media reveals certain pieces of information and experiences, thus contributing to an overall toy environment. As the story of develops within the transmedia toy, new figures and objects emerge. These new items are in turn made available as digital and tangible toys, which the children already know by name or function – and which they have understandably been longing to have or are planning to buy. Thus, when a figure in a Lego narrative – the *Chima*, for example – uses a new weapon in the cartoon, that weapon may subsequently appear as a special piece in an ordinary Lego set. The child comes to want to play with this new feature and consequently desires the Lego set due to this change in the narrative. Toy industry designers have thus created a system of craving within the context of a transmedia storytelling platform that instils in children the concept that habitual consumption is required for one to play and experience pleasure. When children learn that such consumption is necessary in order to feel pleasure, they may develop unsustainable behavioural habits (Bhamra et al., 2011; Shove, 2003; Zachrisson & Boks, 2012). It is this repeated craving–purchasing–playing pattern and the related experiences that exist within such a framework that establishes these habits (Ajzen, 1991; Dahlstrand & Biel, 1997; Grankvist & Biel, 2007; Verplanken et al., 2008; Zachrisson & Boks, 2012). In short, children learn that frequent purchases are a vital part of being able to play, to play in groups, and/or to be socially accepted and are therefore likely to continue their consumption patterns.

The ethics and consequences of targeting children have been discussed; for example, in *No Logo* and *Born to Bye* (Klein, 2000; Schor, 2004), the authors express alarm over the increasingly efficient marketing strategies that are used to reach children (Buckingham, 2007). However, explorations of the ways in which these strategies influence play and purchase behaviour – and subsequently the environment – are lacking. Hence, this chapter seeks to explore the role of transmedia toy design in relation to how children desire and perceive pleasure and enjoyment through play and strives to examine how such feelings can influence purchase behaviour. Through this exploration, this chapter seeks to position child consumerism as an important axis within cultural sustainability.

Method

This study is based on a theoretical analysis of transmedia toy design and the behaviours it motivates in light of the various theories on gamification, desire, pleasure, and enjoyment put forth by Slavoj Žižek. Additionally, the concept of transmedia toys is explored though an examination of research on media, including the work of Jenkins (2010), who explores TS in light of development strategies and culture, and Marsha Kinder (1991), who touches on the possible adverse functions of the transmedia storytelling concept. This study also examines the market and brand oriented research of Scolari (2009) and Pietschmann et al. (2014) regarding how the different stages of children's cognitive development are affected by transmedia toys. Furthermore, this study includes two visualisations of transmedia toys which allow us to analyse the systems behind the toys in light of Slavoj Žižek's work in an effort to explore how they influence children's play experience, behaviour, and subsequent desire for toys.

Transmedia storytelling

Toy manufacturers have found that toys linked to media often sell better than toys without such links (Heljakka, 2013, p. 28; Levin, 2010, p. 16). Early mass-produced toys typically emerged based on children's interest in topics such as firefighting, motherhood, war, and fairy tales; however, toys can also develop from popular culture, as is the case with toys inspired by comic books like *Superman* (Heljakka, 2013, p. 19). In this context, Superman cartoons offer children suggestions regarding *how* they might play with an action figure while also serving as market channels *for* those action figures. The potential market success that can be achieved by presenting a toy that is connected to a narrative, as in this example, has led to the creation of a development strategy that begins with the creation of a narrative and is followed by the development of digital and tangible toys – a system that represents a strong context of influence (Shove, 2003). The movie *Toy Story* is one example of such a process, wherein the movie "actors" are in fact toys that are, in turn, sold as real toys (Figure 9.2). The development of toys that perform across multiple media platforms has led to the creation of *supersystems* in which tangible toys comprise a mere part of the entire toy concept. This system is explained by Kinder (1991) as follows:

> In order to be a supersystem, the network must cut across several modes of image productions; must appeal to diverse generations, classes, and ethnic subcultures; ... must foster "collectability" through a proliferation of related products; and must undergo a sudden increase in commodification, the success of which reflexively becomes a "media event".
>
> (p. 123)

In other words, the advertisement of toys has shifted; where once information regarding a new toy was announced on various media platforms, toys have now become an inextricable part of games, cartoons, the Internet, tangible objects, and films. Each type of media presents a different set of challenges and introduces new ways to play, thus revealing different pieces of information about the narrative that together form the overall plot. The various interests that the numerous media forms promote serve as entry points for different target groups. If one enjoys cognitive challenges, then games might serve as an entry point, whereas an interest in collecting things could translate into an appreciation for figure tangibles. Marsha Kinder (1991, p. 38) coined the term *transmedia intertextuality* to explain this division between the supplementary dimensions of a toy that enhance the play experience and the toy's market potential. Henry Jenkins (2003) later introduced the term *transmedia storytelling* to further explain this concept (Heljakka, 2013).

Transmedia toy systems

There is abundant research on designing within the sphere of TS (Heljakka, 2013; Jenkins, 2003, 2010; Pietschmann et al., 2014; Scolari, 2009). The system of experience that TS creates and supports is considered to be the primary function of a toy's branding. As Scolari (2009) observes, "Economic subjects no longer try to sell a product or service by means of persuasive advertising. Now the objectives are much more ambitious; they aim to create a symbolic universe endowed with meaning."

Pietschmann (2014) presents a case study of the universe of Disney's *Cars* to "show the possibilities and limitations of transmedia franchises for children" in order to evaluate their narrative strategies and cognitive requirements. The study is based on Jenkins's seven principles of efficient TS: spreadability and drillability; immersion and extractability; world building; continuity and multiplicity; seriality; subjectivity; and performance or interaction. This mapping of the *Cars* universe reveals that the transmedia franchise began with a feature film "and expanded on that" (Pietschmann et al., 2014) through a storybook, TV series, and website, among other media (see Figure

9.1). According to this study, the TV series, video games, interactive website, and theme park attractions serve to expand this moment in time; that is, such supplementary media were implemented in order to maintain children's interest during the time between the two feature films' release (*Cars* and *Cars 2*) and to expand the main narrative (backstory) during the launch of the toy (see Figure 9.1).

Thus, transmedia toys form comprehensive systems in time and experience. The experiences that the possession of a transmedia toy offers are consciously overlapped in time in such a way that the consumer is given the opportunity to constantly upgrade the toy.

Accordingly, through the introduction of feature films, TV series, and additional videogames, new characters and occurrences enrich the backstory of the toy as time goes on.

While the systems of transmedia toys differ, their main functions are often similar. The transmedia system used to promote the *Toy Story* universe was built on a premise similar to that used in the *Cars* domain; however, the visualisation of *Toy Story* was more comprehensive (see Figure 9.2). Furthermore, *Toy Story* placed a greater emphasis on the promotion of tangible characters in an effort to inspire children's engagement over time (during the period between film releases) through play; as such, in order to support the toys' backstory, toys were made available not only in toy stores but also through agents such as Burger King.

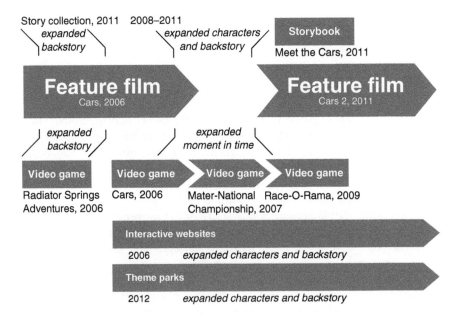

Figure 9.1 Narrative extensions of the *Cars* transmedia franchise.

Source: Pietschmann et al. (2014).

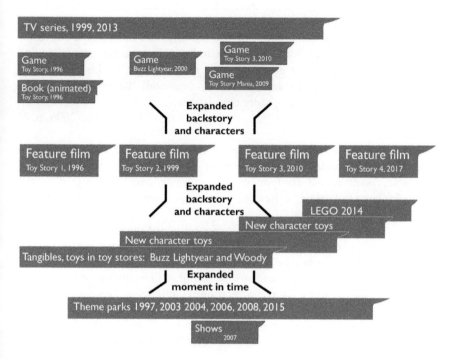

Figure 9.2 Narrative extensions of *Toy Story*.

Games as an element of transmedia toys

Apart from feature films and cartoons, wherein a toy's backstory is clearly explained, games serve as an important factor of spreadability, immersion, and performance or interaction. Games stimulate an emotional engagement in the play experience that emerges from the rules and engendered experiences that this form of media encourages. In games, rules are an essential factor of activation, and one might argue that they serve to get people engaged with "un-necessary obstacles" (Suits, as cited in Perinbanayagam, 2006, p. 3). The happenings, goals, and actions that form the constraints of a game thus motivate people to engage more actively, and the game player subsequently finds him- or herself emotionally involved. As noted by Jasper Juul, "A game is a rule-based formal system with a variable quantified outcome, where different outcomes are assigned different values; the player extends effort in order to influence the outcome and the player feels attached to the outcome" (as cited in Perinbanayagam, 2006, p. 2).

Thus, Juul connects the degree of effort spent in a game to the degree of one's feelings of attachment towards the outcome and, accordingly, towards a product. Perinbanayagam has a similar understanding of games but emphasises that these feelings of attachment not only involve the outcome of the game but also the participants:

The playing of games then are … acts that human agents undertake, as players or spectators, to achieve cognitive involvement and emotional engagement with the other. The playing of games is, in fact, a conversation, a dialogic activity that systematically involves other agents, a continuation of the other processes of everyday life. It is also a means by which a human agent achieves intercourse with the other by using a range of symbols that is broader than language.

(Perinbanayagam, 2006, p. 3)

Games typically establish a certain set of rules within which users have the opportunity to decide on how they want to influence the outcome. Thus, games represent a vital component of transmedia toys with regard to the establishment of a strong context of influence on experience and behaviour (Shove, 2003).

However, the emphasis placed on various types of media can vary, such as in the case of Pokémon. With the release of Pokémon Go in 2016, the games within the transmedia toy have become increasingly important. Niantic, the creator of Pokémon Go, has managed to stimulate behaviour in various ways, encouraging such activities as walking, running, biking, and driving via game-play mechanics; Niantic has thereby achieved a high degree of activation, which serves to create memories and feelings of attachment to the toy (Gulden, 2013; Perinbanayagam, 2006; Schifferstein & Zwartkruis-Pelgrim, 2008). Moreover, the product serves to reinforce memories of prior salient experiences with the product and therefore provides meaning for the user or owner (Schifferstein & Zwartkruis-Pelgrim, 2008). Thus, experiences or feelings towards the toy are not necessarily elicited directly by the product itself; rather, they may be connected to the product because it has encouraged situations that lead to experiences and, subsequently, to feelings towards it.

Games as gamification

The inclusion of games as part of a transmedia toy system serves to inform play. The games that are promoted through TS are often low threshold games that have an easily accessible entry point. That is, these games are easily grasped, and the core of the game is often about performing behaviours that allow the user to earn points, stars, medals, badges, or to reach new levels, all of which serve as part of a reward system (Whaley, 2011 in Deterding et al., 2011). Pokémon Go, which is merely one small component of the Pokémon toy line, is a good example of such a game; in this game, the main goal is collection, an activity that offers the player the opportunity to receive a variety of rewards.

In principle, games, as part of a transmedia toy system, cannot be regarded as gamification. That is, gamification is often regarded as "the use of game design elements in non-game contexts" (Deterding et al., 2011). However, within the context of transmedia toys, where the intention of a game is to inspire engagement with the whole toy (feature films, games, tangibles, etc.) for marketing purposes, games certainly serve to gamify users' behaviour (Deterding et al., 2011; Whaley, 2011). Thus, games serve to please and engage but also to increase sales, which represents a non-game context.

Need and drive as facets of the quality of play

People have the propensity to favour new things and to make purchases based on the urge to generate positive emotions (Chapman, 2005; Dahlen et al., 2010; Nicole van Nes, 2006; Schifferstein & Desmet, 2010). The upgrade process (purchases) of a transmedia toy is thus a stimulating process in itself. Additionally, play among children who have the same toys stimulates the emergence of social systems of interaction (Luhmann & Gilgen, 2012; Tangen, 2004). Subsequently, children look to each other within the system and become inspired to constantly purchase additional elements in order to take part in play that falls within the theme presented by the transmedia toy system (Kinder, 1991).

Accordingly, the collection of items, such as purchasing Premiere League cards or locating creatures in Pokémon Go, may be seen as an upgrade activity. Hence, transmedia toys may become *purposive* in that one can become a social actor and an expert simply by having many collectibles; or become *skilful* in games of competition by getting updated figures with improved or better characteristics. It should be noted that the purposive motivation has different dimensions. To this end, Lacan divided purpose into a biological component – which establishes a need and a goal that is possible to satisfy – and a drive component – which introduces an aim that cannot be fulfilled. He stated that "the purpose of a drive is not to reach its goal but to circle around it" (Lacan in Kreft, 2015). Furthermore, he argued that "[w]hen you entrust someone with a mission, the aim is not what he brings back, but the itinerary (journey) he must take. The aim is the way taken" (Lacan in Kreft, 2015). Taking such a view, one might say that the result is secondary to the quality of the experience that is afforded the player. Accordingly, within a biological purpose, a player's goals or needs (to win, collect, etc.) are easily satisfied, while his or her drive or aim, which are related to the experience, are not. In order to explore how such experiences elicited by aims may be valued as well as created or designed, we turn to John Dewey (1934), who has a similar conception of aesthetic experiences: when the process of experiencing is complex and demanding in such a way that is similar to the experience of the creator, the journey that enabled the production of content is regarded as high-quality and serves to elicit enjoyment.

Access to enjoyment

A player's needs and drives stimulate his or her behaviour and affect the perceived quality of play. Any game can be boring to watch or even play. In football, for example, when two nervous teams simply defend their respective goalposts for 90 minutes due to a fear of losing (or a need to win), the result is often a game without any scoring opportunities and a 0–0 score. Accordingly, the social prohibition of failure and the crowd's expectation of a good and entertaining match lead to a lack of enjoyment on the part of the spectator and perhaps even the players (Žižek, 2014b). However, anxious attitudes (or any other attitude for that matter) on the part of the players do not always result in the desired outcomes. This randomness enables both boring and exciting matches as well as both expected and surprising results. Moreover, when a person has watched five tiresome matches in a row, a mediocre-quality game is more likely to be regarded as exciting due to the contrast of experiences (Cialdini, 2009; Kahneman, 1992, 2011). Accordingly, a "direct injunction [to] 'enjoy!' is a much more effective way to hinder the subject's access to enjoyment than [is] the explicit prohibition which sustains the space for its transgression" (Žižek, 1997). Hence, when access to guaranteed enjoyment is not provided, the probability of enjoyment is greater. Direct access to enjoyment thus illustrates the opposite of a situation wherein *drive* is the motivator of play with a transmedia toy; such a transmedia system may describe play that allegedly provides direct access to enjoyment. Thus, an emphasis on need fulfilment may actually result in dissatisfaction when the child realises that the newly-acquired toy has failed to elicit the promised feelings.

Transmedia toys in light of Slavoj Žižek's notions of pleasure and enjoyment

Slavoj Žižek (2014b) separates the functions of pleasure and enjoyment in a manner similar to the aforementioned division of need and drive. Pleasure is something that one can feel or experience as an immediate phenomenon, something that possibly fulfils a need; in contrast, enjoyment is determined by a drive that must be "learned by imitation" (Žižek, 2014b, p. 72). One example of this separation can be seen when comparing the consumption of juice or chocolate to the consumption of wine. While juice and chocolate elicit instant pleasure, the richness of the wine-drinking experience must be learned. In fact, most people dislike wine upon their first encounter with the beverage (Žižek, 2014b). Applying this idea to the concept of games such as football, it can be argued that goals provide instant pleasure whereas learning how to enjoy playing football requires practice and time. Thus, enjoyment represents a situation wherein a certain amount of effort is demanded, while an immediate feeling of pleasure can be elicited without such a barrier. Effort is connected to the degree of attachment one feels to the outcome of play, as described in Juul's definition of games (Perinbanayagam, 2006). Thus, when considering the specifics of transmedia toys, it is interesting to determine whether the new product elicits only pleasure or both pleasure and enjoyment; this allows us to properly evaluate the quality of the transmedia toy, the game, and the play experience.

However, a game will be ruined if the player does not possess a serious intention (Gadamer, 2004); one must accept or believe in the system that a game promotes in order for such effort and enjoyment to be properly motivated (Gadamer & Holm-Hansen, 2010). Žižek describes such belief in a system in the following way: when others (children) believe in a system, they believe for you, and therefore we believe too (Žižek, 2014a). Thus, the system supports functions of inter-passivity, a term coined by Robert Pfaller to represent something that is the opposite of manipulation but is still a function of influence, in which "we transpose over to the other, our passive reaction – others are passive for us" (Žižek, 1997). When playing a game or when playing with a transmedia toy, such passivity may relate not only to the acceptance of rules or to a lack of transgressive thoughts regarding those rules but also to the acceptance of certain behaviours; for example, it may refer to aggressiveness that can only be expressed on the field, track, or while roleplaying during a board game – and not in society in general. For instance, a normal tackle in football, which merely results in a free kick during a game, would serve as a reason for imprisonment off field, outside the frame of the game (Goffman, 1961). Thus, when every individual within a system or a game "presupposes another agency to believe, then belief functions, [and] the whole system of believe functions" (Žižek, 1997). In short, the expectations of others make the system of belief work. Systems that function in this way – transmedia toy systems, for example – thus have a strong influence on behaviour.

Niklas Luhmann links meaning to expectation in a manner that is similar to the way in which desire is linked to various known and fantasised-about possibilities, thus serving as a connection between the actual and the possible. It could be argued that if one does not expect anything to happen, there is no need to put any effort into achieving (or avoiding) something. Therefore, desire can be linked to expectation and the pursuit of enjoyment and pleasure. According to Žižek, people "never simply [have] the desire for a certain thing. It's always also the desire for desire itself [and] a desire to continue to desire"; moreover, "melancholy is the loss of desire" (Jeff, 2014). Žižek suggests that the Kinder Surprise Egg is an apt example of a toy that meets people's need for desire. Although most people often find the content of this treat – the yolk, which represents the object of desire – to be disappointing, they continue to purchase the eggs (Jeff, 2014). Thus, the need for desire, and the possibility of feeling pleasure, comes before the pursuit of value or a quality experience.

Borrowing a word from Plato and Lacan, Žižek proposed the term *agalma* to describe this inestimable object of desire, defining it as follows:

> agalma ... are not the works of any given subjectivity ... their very structure has much to do with fantasy, the affects they generate (love, fascination, idealization, and the like) do not proceed from an auto-affective process of the psyche.
>
> (Jeff, 2014; Johnston & Malabou, 2013, p. 70)

Based on the above argument, one can claim that the fulfilment of needs via, for example, the making of purchases or perceived outer geometry at point of purchase elicits auto-affective processes or mental shortcuts that may in turn incite acts rather than feelings (Cialdini, 2009; Kahneman, 1992). Accordingly, the desired effects are not dependent on the direct experiences that the product engenders; rather, they are contingent on the possible physical and cognitive events that the product or game motivates.

Nevertheless, if a toy or game designer aims to create a function of agalma – an elicited impact that is achieved by playing with the toy or game – the pleasure related to the perception of "the surface" will also be strengthened (Jeff, 2014). For example, a person who enjoys the complexity of (playing) football will have considerable knowledge about the sport, and perhaps will therefore enjoy the *surface of football* (the collection of cards or special effects on the tip of a football shoe, for example) differently and more profoundly than those who do not play football. Accordingly, it is the subjective effort and the experience that football elicits that enables feelings of enjoyment, not the product itself – unless that product is a part of the larger play experience. Thus, if a play activity's content is easy to predict, play will not facilitate love, fascination, creation, or idealisation. The simple, prescribed, or given uses of objects do not stimulate such feelings or acts when these factors alone comprise a product; this argument is in line with the work of Huizinga (2004), who proposes that "as the opposite of aesthetics is not ugliness but apathy, the opposite to play is not seriousness but the automatic" (Mandoki, 2007, p. 93). Thus, automatic behaviour is not play and does not stimulate enjoyment.

Pleasure as a driver of consumption

Transmedia toys, which base activities of play on the incitement of pleasure and desire, may not provoke a drive in people and thus may not result in subsequent feelings of enjoyment. Accordingly, when only short-lived feelings of pleasure are elicited by transmedia toys, children experience a desire to attain additional pleasure. To this end, transmedia toys are designed to provide such pleasure via new purchases. Therefore, transmedia toys teach children that there is a need for pleasure and that such a need can be purchased. Accordingly, children learn that a high consumption rate (or consumption in general) leads to feelings of pleasure. In regard to sustainable culture, one might contend that by establishing such consumption behaviours, society is reinforcing a culture of unsustainable action and actors.

References

Ajzen, I. (1991). The theory of planned behavior. *Organizational Behavior and Human Decision Processes, 50*(2), 179–211. doi: http://dx.doi.org/10.1016/0749-5978 (91)90020-T
Bhamra, T., Lilley, D., & Tang, T. (2011). Design for sustainable behaviour: Using products to change consumer behaviour. *The Design Journal, 14*(4), 427–445.

Buckingham, D. (2007). Selling childhood? *Journal of Children and Media, 1*(1), 15–24. doi: 10.1080/17482790601005017.

Chapman, J. (2005). *Emotionally durable design: Objects, experiences and empathy.* London: Earthscan.

Cialdini, R. B. (2009). *Influence: Science and practice* (5th edn). Boston, MA: Pearson/ Allyn and Bacon.

Dahlen, M., Lange, F., & Smith, T. (2010). *Marketing communications: A brand narrative approach.* London: John Wiley & Sons.

Dahlstrand, U., & Biel, A. (1997). Pro-environmental habits: Propensity levels in behavioral change. *Journal of Applied Social Psychology, 27*(7), 588–601. doi: 10.1111/j.1559-1816.1997.tb00650.x.

Deterding, S., Dixon, D., Khaled, R., & Nacke, L. (2011). *From game design elements to gamefulness: Defining "gamification".* Paper presented at the Proceedings of the 15th International Academic MindTrek Conference: Envisioning Future Media Environments, Tampere, Finland.

Dewey, J. (1934). *Art as experience.* New York: Minton.

Gadamer, H.-G. (2004). *Truth and method.* London: Continuum International Publishing.

Gadamer, H.-G., & Holm-Hansen, L. (2010). *Sannhet og metode: grunntrekk i en filosofisk hermeneutikk.* Oslo: Pax.

Goffman, E. (1961). *Encounters: Two studies in the sociology of interaction (vol. 1).* Indianapolis, NY: Bobbs-Merrill.

Grankvist, G., & Biel, A. (2007). Predictors of purchase of eco-labelled food products: A panel study. *Food Quality and Preference, 18*(4), 701–708. doi: 10.1016/j. foodqual.2006.11.002.

Gulden, T. (2013). *Modelling memories through design.* Paper presented at the International conference on engineering and product design education, Dublin, Ireland.

Heljakka, K. (2013). *Principles of adult play(fulness) in contemporary toy cultures, From wow to flow to glow.* (Aalto University publication series Doctoral Dissertations), Aalto University, Helsinki. Retrieved from http://urn.fi/URN:ISBN: 978-952-60-5144-4.

Jeff, T. D. (2014). The pervert's guide to ideology. *Library Journal, 139*(11), 58.

Jenkins, H. (2003). Transmedia storytelling. *MIT Technology Review.*

Jenkins, H. (2010). Transmedia storytelling and entertainment: An annotated syllabus. *Continuum, 24*(6), 943–958. doi: 10.1080/10304312.2010.510599.

Kahneman, D. (1992). Reference points, anchors, norms, and mixed feelings. *Organizational Behavior and Human Decision Processes, 51*(2), 296–312. doi: 10.1016/0749-5978(92)90015-y.

Kahneman, D. (2011). *Thinking, fast and slow.* New York: Farrar, Straus and Giroux.

Kinder, M. (1991). *Playing with power in movies, television, and video games: from Muppet Babies to Teenage Mutant Ninja Turtles.* Berkeley, CA: University of California Press.

Klein, N. (2000). *No logo.* London: Flamingo.

Kreft, L. (2015). Aesthetic imagination in football. *Sport, Ethics and Philosophy, 9*(2), 124–139. doi: 10.1080/17511321.2015.1048821.

Luhmann, N., & Gilgen, P. (2012). *Introduction to systems theory.* New York: Wiley.

Nicole van Nes, J. C. (2006). Product lifetime optimization: A challenging strategy towards more sustainable consumption patterns. *Journal of Cleaner Production, 14.*

Perinbanayagam, R. (2006). *Games and sport in everyday life, dialogues and narratives of the self.* Boulder, CO: Paradigm.

Pietschmann, D., Völkel, S., & Ohler, P. (2014). Transmedia critical limitations of transmedia storytelling for children: A cognitive developmental analysis. *International Journal of Communication, 8,* 2259–2282.

Schifferstein, H. N. J., & Desmet, P. M. A. (2010). Hedonic asymmetry in emotional responses to consumer products. *Food Quality and Preference, 21*(8), 1100–1104. doi: 10.1016/j.foodqual.2010.07.004.

Schifferstein, H. N., & Zwartkruis-Pelgrim. (2008). Consumer–product attachment: Measurement and design implications. *International Journal of Design, 2*(3). Retrieved from www.ijdesign.org/ojs/index.php/IJDesign/article/viewFile/325/205.

Schor, J. (2004). *Born to buy: The commercialized child and the new consumer culture.* New York: Scribner.

Scolari, C. A. (2009). Transmedia storytelling: Implicit consumers, narrative worlds, and branding in contemporary media production. *International Journal of Communication, 3,* 586–606.

Shove, E. (2003). Converging conventions of comfort, cleanliness and convenience. *Journal of Consumer Policy, 26*(4), 395–418. doi: 10.1023/A:1026362829781.

Tangen, J. (2004). "Making the space": A sociological perspective on sport and its facilities. *Sport in Society, 7*(1), 25–48. doi: 10.1080/1461098042000220173.

Verplanken, B., Walker, I., Davis, A., & Jurasek, M. (2008). Context change and travel mode choice: Combining the habit discontinuity and self-activation hypotheses. *Journal of Environmental Psychology, 28*(2), 121–127. doi: 10.1016/j.jenvp. 2007.10.005.

Whaley, M. (2011). Game frame: Using games as a strategy for success (book review). *The Booklist, 107*(13), 4.

Zachrisson, J., & Boks, C. (2012). Exploring behavioural psychology to support design for sustainable behaviour research. *Journal of Design Research, 10*(1), 50–66.

Žižek, S. (1997). The big other doesn't exist. *Journal of European Psychoanalysis.* Spring-Fall.

Žižek, S. (2014a). *The interpassive subject.* Retrieved from www.egs.edu/faculty/slavoj-Žižek/articles/the-interpassive-subject/

Žižek, S. (2014b). *Trouble in paradise. From the end of history to the end of capitalism.* London: Allen Lane.

10 Contemporary vernacular Inuit clothing as sustainable fashion

Janne Beate Reitan

Introduction

In recent years, many studies have considered fashion and clothing in terms of sustainability (e.g. Black, 2012; Busch, 2008; Chapman, 2015; Clark, 2009; Fletcher & Grose, 2012; Fletcher & Tham, 2014; Gordon & Hill, 2015; Gwilt & Rissanen, 2012; Niinimäki, 2013; Walker & Giard, 2013). However, to my knowledge, no research has investigated the possibility of simply changing part of a garment in order to contribute to sustainability. Most writers discuss various ways that professional designers can contribute to a more sustainable fashion industry. Such research lacks a focus on the unique idea emerging from the contemporary vernacular outer garment designed and made by the Inuit (Eskimo) women of North Alaska – the Iñupiaq. They simply change the garment's cover – the outer layer – to create a new one.

The concept of *vernacular design* allows for an understanding and appreciation of designs created without access to institutional qualifications. Christopher Alexander (1964) writes about design in "unselfconscious cultures". To avoid the ambiguous and problematic terms *unselfconscious* and *self-conscious*, I use the more neutral term *vernacular design*. This usage takes inspiration from the term *vernacular architecture* (Rudofsky, 1964; Rapoport, 1969, p. 5) to refer to unselfconscious cultures. For self-conscious cultures, I adopt the corresponding term, *academic design*. This chapter is based upon a study undertaken in the *Iñupiaq* village of Kaktovik on the North Slope of Alaska. These people also are known as the North Alaska Inuit (Eskimos). The study analysed how Iñupiaq women practice and learn design as they make present-day vernacular clothing. The methodology included observations, interviews with seamstresses, and authorial participation in designing and sewing in conformity with Iñupiaq tradition. It also included a literature review of former research on Iñupiaq clothing (Reitan, 2007).

This chapter focuses on how the vernacular clothing designed and made by Iñupiaq women can be seen as a form of sustainable fashion. The study takes as its foundation a review of design research according to both vernacular and contemporary clothing design and making (Reitan, 2007). An important part of the investigation has been the cultural context: the people, the place, and the case – the Iñupiaq, the village of Kaktovik and the nature and social significance of Iñupiaq clothing.

Kaktovik (North Slope Borough, 2016) is one of the most remote villages in Alaska. The nearest neighbouring settlement is the oil field of Prudhoe Bay, about 200 km to the west. The nearest village is the Canadian village of Aklavik 200 km to the east, and the nearest city is Fairbanks in the middle of Alaska, 170 km south. The long distances and lack of road links to the outside world might make it seem that the inhabitants of Kaktovik are very isolated; however, despite the remote location, they travel a great deal. The Iñupiaq traditionally lived as nomads until they moved to Kaktovik and other villages to find employment with the US Army and Air Force after the Second World War; as such, travel forms a part of their culture.

The people of Kaktovik have all the facilities common in Western societies, including contemporary frame houses, cars, satellite TV, electronic goods, stores, a post office, community house, and Western style clothing. They also have a kindergarten, a lower and secondary school for their children. In earlier periods of their history, the people of Kaktovik travelled with dogsled teams over vast distances. Today, they usually use ATVs – all terrain vehicles with four wheels – for local transport in the summertime and snowmobiles in the wintertime. For sea travel, they use small boats. When travelling longer distances, or transporting goods, they usually go by airplane using the village airport.

The vernacular Iñupiaq garments, *atigi* and *atikłuk*

Today, there are two primary Iñupiaq vernacular garments: the cloth or fabric *atigi* for outdoor use, which is a kind of parka; and the *atikłuk* for indoor use, which is a kind of dress for women and shirt for men. The Iñupiaq culture is an adoptive and adaptive culture; they adapt to the recourses available in time and space. Before the white people came to Alaska at the end of the nineteenth century, they made their clothing from fur, mostly from caribou (wild reindeer) or from waterproof seal for boots. The atikłuk – the inner garment – had the hair of the fur facing inwards and the atigi – the outer garment – had the hair facing outwards.

At the turn of the nineteenth century, the first white people to arrive were the whalers, bringing with them bags of flour. These bags were made of white cotton fabric that was adopted by the Iñupiaq and adapted as a cover for their fur garments; the fabric held the snow away from the fur. Underneath the fur atigi, the women wore a Western style of clothing, a condition forced by the missionaries and Christian teachers who came to save them from their 'savage' lifestyle. These Westerners sought to civilise them and make them decent people – the split on the hips was too high, so the women were forced to hide under Mother Hubbard gowns (Cunningham, 2003, p. 10). During this time period, the Iñupiaq women wore a Western style of dress *under* the fur atigi (Figure 10.1). Today, it is the other way around, as

Figure 10.1 Western style of dress, worn under a fur atigi.

Source: © Lomen Collection, # 72-71-847, Archives, Alaska and Polar Regions Collections, Rasmuson Library, University of Alaska Fairbanks. Copyright 1903, "Eskimo Belles, Nome, Alaska".

shown by my 'gatekeeper' during my fieldwork in Kaktovik – my sister-in-law Evelyn Anguyak Reitan. She wears a contemporary style of Iñupiaq clothing with a fabric cover – developed from the Mother Hubbard gowns – outside the thick insulating lining (Figure 10.2). Pictures from the 1940s to the 1960s show Iñupiaq women dressed in clothing made of the same fabric as Euro-American women, often striped or chequered patterns. The shape of this clothing followed an original Victorian style but was considerably shorter (Reitan, 2007, p. 106). The Iñupiaq adopted the Victorian style of dress – more or less voluntary – and then adapted it to their particular Iñupiaq style of clothing. This tradition remains today.

Today the fur has been replaced with a lining of a thick, high-quality synthetic quilted lining similar to that used by polar explorers or bought sheepskin. The latter is used for travel and protects children – especially in cold weather. Just outside the warm lining, there is a cover of thin cotton fabric. I once followed one of my informants as she purchased materials for new atigi and atikłuk in Fairbanks, and we went to large fabric stores for *patchwork*,[1]

Figure 10.2 My "gatekeeper" Evelyn Anguyak Reitan in her contemporary style
of Iñupiaq clothing, with the kind of Western style of dress outside
the thick insolation lining, the reversal of how it used to be when
they started wearing fabric clothing.

Source: © photo Galleri Galaaen, Røros.

which is big business all over North America. As opposed to fabric for ordinary dresses, there is a great assortment of patterns, colours and tapes for traditional attire. This contrast exists because white women rarely make their own dresses today. If Iñupiaq women remained dependent on dress material, they would be unable to continue to make their clothing. Therefore, they adopted the patchwork materials and adapted them to their particular style. People from Kaktovik shop in Fairbanks, 700 km away, a city with three or four big fabric stores for patchwork. These stores display rolls of fabrics from wall to wall, floor to ceiling, in different styles and colours, most of them floral-patterned in different sizes. While white women buy small pieces of the fabrics for patchwork, the Iñupiaq seamstresses purchase yards and yards for atigis and atikłuks. This large amount suffices for the whole family until the next visit to Fairbanks or another city. These visits tend to occur annually (or even less often) due to the expense of flying, the only way of travelling from Kaktovik to surrounding areas.

The aesthetic aspects of the vernacular garments are important as well. Because the atigi has an almost loose cover, it is easy to change the outer part of the garment. The expensive lining lasts for many seasons, but it is common to make a new cover annually for Christmas, allowing a new look for the outer garment every year. The covers are smart-looking with a *qupak* trim around the hips, more exciting than most ready-made jackets. Without too much money or labour, the women can change the appearance of the atigi by changing the thin outer cover – the atikłuk – outside the more expensive lining. The atigi has a hood trimmed with a big "sunshine" ruff, preferably made of wolverine or wolf fur. The atigi also usually has fur on the edge underneath and on the wrists.

These features allow the atigi to be a warm, practical garment. The covers include a qupak trim around the hips, built up by numerous rows of bias tape in various colours and widths in addition to one or several rows of rickracks. This trim is composed of small bits of bias tapes in colours that contrast with those of the bottom tapes, which are intermixed using a truly special technique. Clearly, this practical material object – the atigi parka – also functions in a somewhat social arena, creating an aesthetic impression.

Iñupiaq clothing often reflects ethnicity as well. The Iñupiat's trim – the qupak – remains unique so far as I can tell; they also share commonalities that make them Iñupiaq. However, it remains unclear how conscious they are of the ethnic aspects of their everyday clothing; for them, the clothing seems to be more about pride and custom. Clothing as a sign of ethnicity (Martin, 2001; Eicher, 1995) is perhaps more important in connection with Iñupiaq festivities and celebrations, such as Thanksgiving, Christmas and New Year's Eve as well as *Nalukatak* (the whaling festival) and the World Eskimo Indian Olympics (WEIO), particularly during the Eskimo dance. It seems that people are not quite comfortable at the Eskimo dance without their vernacular clothing; indeed, at the WEIO, all Iñupiat who perform wear vernacular clothing. On other festive occasions, Iñupiaq clothing is common but not essential.

This focus on vernacular clothing can be seen as a kind of local production (Fletcher & Grose, 2012, pp. 106–114). Individuals often use local materials, design for local culture and work with local artisans. All of the atigis and atikłuks worn in Katovik are designed and sewn by the women from the village.

Sewing season

With the passage of time, some traditions and customs have changed in terms of when and where Iñupiaq women can make clothing. In the 1800s and perhaps earlier, there was a sewing season at a specific site once a year, and there was a strict taboo against making clothes at other times or places (Burch 1998, p. 106). This sewing season – or clothes-making festival – had to align with other necessities, such as the semi-nomadic travelling necessary for hunting, fishing and other subsistence activities. During this season, the women had to sew a year's worth of clothing and other items for the entire family. Iñupiaq elders confirmed that this season fell on Kaivirvik, which is now Christmas, or actually solstice (North Slope Borough School District, 1994). Before Kaivirvik, the women would make every effort to finish the clothing they would wear during Kaivirvik. This time of year also was characterized by days without daylight up north; thus, they would count their months by the moons. When the clothing-making season ended, it was the month of Suliiqsaunik; they have finished. Then they would play games during the month of Kaivirvik, the month with no daylight. Based upon this description, Rachael Nanginaaq Sakeak believes that they must have finished making clothing in November and played games in December (Edwardsen, 1983, p. 24).

Later, the sewing period began to change along with new subsistence and income conditions. When people moved to Kaktovik and other villages to find employment with the US Army and Air Force after the Second World War, only a few families continued to provide for their families with full-time hunting and fishing. The Iñupiaq's nomadic lifestyle transformed into a more sedentary residential way of life, and their sewing traditions changed as well. After about 1870, the Iñupiaq started to make fabric clothing, at first sewn by hand but later sewn with sewing machines. By 1933, at least some of the women had sewing machines in Kaktovik (Hutchison, 1934, p. 166). After settling down, they could sew at any time during the year; they no longer had to wait for time between travels to hunting or fishing grounds. However, they continued the tradition of a fixed sewing season. Even though they had settled down and most were employed, the Iñupiaq people continued their traditions of hunting, fishing and even whaling. During their spare time in the spring, summer and winter seasons, most people from Kaktovik go camping in the wilderness while they hunt and fish. They often travel by snowmobile in springtime before the snow melts, or by small boat after the ocean-ice has broken up. The extended family travels together, from great-grandmother to new-born baby, often travelling and camping together at permanent cabins or tents. During these times, nobody seems to have much time for sewing. During the winter, though, it is dark due to the polar night, making hunting and fishing difficult. Then, the women of Kaktovik take the time to make new clothing for the year. When I was there, they still made most of their clothing during the sewing season between Thanksgiving and Christmas. Some women started to sew before Thanksgiving in order to have new clothing for that celebration, a feast of traditional Iñupiaq food for everybody in the village held at the Community House. However, few could sew during this time because the whaling season finishes between the end of October and Thanksgiving. The whalers' wives and other women tended to be busy processing the meat and *maktak* – the blubber – from the whale catch, leaving little time for sewing before Thanksgiving.

When Thanksgiving concluded, the sewing season started. The women designed and made all the atigis (outdoor garments) and atikłuks (indoor garments) they needed for the whole year between Thanksgiving and Christmas. Sometimes, they also made male atigi during other seasons of the year, because the men did not change their atigi covers every year for Christmas. Some changed every third year or even more rarely. The men did not use the traditional atigi as often as the women did; many only used them for special dress-up occasions. Therefore, they did not wear out their atigis as fast. The less frequent change might also result from the fact that the trim on the male atigi is much more complicated and time-consuming to make. Because the women did not make male atigi as often, they tended to spend more time on each garment. The women also sometimes made atigi for children outside the main sewing season due to the relatively small amount of labour and time involved. Children use their atigi for everyday life and for playing, so the garments sometimes do not last a whole year. Thus, the mother or grandmother often makes two or three covers for the children in a single year.

The origin of contemporary Iñupiaq clothing

Designed and made by the women of Kaktovik, vernacular Iñupiaq clothing differs from all other clothes I have seen. Each garment is unique but related to all others – a kind of improvisation within tradition. Building on others' work is the rule, and it is not seen as cheating. One of their informal rules is never to copy, neither themselves nor others. All participants learn from each other all the time, a true community of practice (Wenger, 1998).

A Dane and former whaler, Christian Klegenberg had a store on the southwest shores of Victoria Island in Northwest Canada (Oakes, 1991, p. 24). His Iñupiaq wife Qimniq (from Wainwright Inlet) and their daughter Edna taught Copper Inuit seamstresses to make "Mother Hubbard style" garments (Ray, 1977; Issenman, 1997, p. 117). The origin of this garment, a tent-like gown with a wide bottom ruffle, is uncertain. Hawaiian missionaries could have adapted it from the "Mother Hubbard", which was apparently first illustrated in 1765 in Mother Goose's Melody, Dorothy (Ray, 1977, p. 52). After a fire in his boat, Klegenberg recounts the following:

> The fire and the water between them had done some damage to my own calicoes, which I intended for trade along the Siberian coast. You may ask, why calicoes in the Arctic? Because Eskimos are proud of their best clothes, and in the summer time, they protect them by covering them with a calico slip, just as some people cover their best upholstered furniture that way in the summer. The Eskimo women will make smocks for their men, and Mother Hubbard gowns for themselves. Speaking of clothes in the Arctic, I may as well mention here that our form of clothing, made of woollen and cotton materials, including socks and underwear, will serve very well in the Arctic during the summer. But in the winter, the Eskimo skin garments are warmer, lighter, and more comfortable, especially the style of them prevailing in Alaska, Mackenzie River District, and on Victoria Island. Farther to the east the clothing made is more clumsy, and the caribou skins are not so well prepared.
>
> (MacInnes, 1932, p. 142)

In those days, they used the term *calicoes* to refer to both the plain-woven cotton fabric and the atigi covers and atikłuks made of it.

The desire for novelty

Here, one may ask the following question: is the desire for novelty and creativity a threat to sustainability? Iñupiaq women want a new look for their atigi parka every year. They seek this annual transformation as a way of recreating themselves; however, it is also a matter of pragmatics: the thin cotton fabric cover wears out after a year of use. Still, the question remains: is this a desire inflicted by modern society? As Captain Christian Klegenberg asserts, the desire for novelty is perhaps not new:

> The girls came in their best clothes; all made of skins which they had laboured over and sewn during the summer for the winter styles. Of course, the general shape of their garments in the Arctic does not change, but the trimmings and the color of the ornamental furs and the ways these are attached and the fancy work which goes with them do change quite a bit from winter to winter, and the women seem to know through the summer just what the most fetching mode will be for the next winter. I was made to know somewhat about these things after I began to have daughters in the Arctic coming into their teens and dancing through the season of the long night. One year the girls will be waiting [*sic*] still-born caribou calf that looks like seal but is darker. Another year all their trimmings must be ermine, and the next dark wolf, and the next red fox, and so on, even if their poor father must reach down so far south

as Great Slave Lake to get what they want. Skin clothes will take all of a summer to make daintily, what with tanning, and selecting trimmings to match for mukluks and mittens and parka.

(MacInnes, 1932, p. 74)

Klegenberg had to travel about 1,500–2,000 km into Canada to obtain the materials his daughter desired, indicating a great effort to satisfy a daughter's desire for novelty.

The potential of sustainability by changing parts of garments for novelty

I see great and unexploited potential in the idea of changing a single part of garments as the Iñupiaq do when changing the covers of their garments. Klegenberg mentioned "their best upholstered furniture" as it is more common to change furniture covers, either using a professional upholsterer or following a DIY (do it yourself) mindset. Some furniture manufacturers also sell covers for such changes, either because the old ones wear out or because the owners are seeking novelty. The best known example is perhaps the Klippan sofa from IKEA (n.d.). Another example is the 1972 Ekstrem chair design by the Norwegian designer Terje Ekstrøm, manufactured by Varier Furniture (n.d.).

Italian researcher Marina Bianchi sees the consumer as an active producer (1998, 2002). She stresses that "there are both cognitive and utility incentives to produce novelty and variety in consumption" (Bianchi, 2002, p. 6). In this case of changing just part of a garment, the outer layer or cover, I see the consumer as an active producer buying only the part that is worn out while keeping the part that lasts longer.

It seems to me that there is another important aspect: the ease with which women could create and change their self-presentation with the help of atigi covers. The garment is a material object functioning in the social arena to make an aesthetic impression, offering the opportunity to create a new look by choosing a new fabric and a matching qupak trim. This function perhaps also holds true for those who do not design and make their own atigi, but only wear the garments. I have not seen this idea for a more sustainable fashion anywhere else, and I think it is a worthwhile lesson from the Iñupiaq: one can have a new look by simply changing the cover, the outer layer of the winter jacket, more often. This concept can be viewed as a kind of "slow fashion" or "slow design". One can keep the lining for years but change the cover once a year, allowing for greater longevity in total. This longevity is essential in achieving sustainability:

> The fast pace of novelty – frequent new styles – is a key result of pressures for economic growth. Slow and long design responds by attaching novelty to the deeper meaning of consumption, for example through

connections to nature or to the wider community. This type of design also addresses infrastructure that makes it easier to shift our long-term commitments.

(Thorpe, 2014, p. 69)

I recently bought a winter jacket from Patagonia (2016). It consists of two jackets zipped together: one warm down jacket and one water and windproof jacket. They can be worn together when it is wet, cold and windy. Alternatively, they can be worn separately. I might wear the down jacket if it is just cold but not windy, and I might wear the water and windproof jacket if it is wet and windy but warm. Unfortunately, I had to buy both jackets together, but I would encourage Patagonia to sell the jackets separately. I probably will wear the water and windproof jacket more often than the down jacket because wet and windy weather is more common during the year than cold weather. Therefore, the water and windproof jacket will likely wear out before the down jacket. At that time, it would be ideal to replace only the water and windproof jacket, keeping the down jacket to zip them together again when necessary due to weather conditions. Do you hear me, Patagonia?

In her *Local Wisdom* project, Kate Fletcher (2011) states that our "technology bias overlooks the power and agency that culturally embedded practices like low energy use, garment refashioning and novel ways of clothes' wearing have in influencing sustainability" (p. 171). I see the Inupiaq way of making a new winter jacket by just changing the outer layer as a part of these culturally embedded practices. Before accessing textile fabrics, the Iñupiaq wore atigis made of caribou fur every day for a whole year, wearing them out before obtaining a new garment at the sewing festival in the dark season of winter, when the sun did not rise north of the Polar circle at the North Slope of Alaska. The Inupiat maintain this sewing season in the dark season, now during the weeks between Thanksgiving at the end of November and Christmas at the end of December. Today, however, they do not have to change the whole garment, but only the outer cover, keeping the expensive inner lining for years and even decades. This custom actually results from economic necessity: the lining is very expensive. Nonetheless, it also leads to ecological advantages, forming a small piece of the big picture needed for sustainability.

Sustainable fashion is a conglomerate of many different actions – from designers, producers and consumers in the general public. All of us have to do our part if we desire a more sustainable future. It can be as simple as changing a cover instead of buying a whole new garment when only the outer layer is worn out.

Note

1 To sew together small pieces of fabric in particular patterns, often geometric, to make blankets, pillow covers, duvet and quilt covers or other items.

References

Alexander, C. (1964). *Notes on the synthesis of form*. Cambridge, MA: Harvard University Press.

Bianchi, M. (ed.). (1998). *The active consumer: Novelty and surprise in consumer choice*. London: Routledge.

Bianchi, M. (2002). Novelty, preferences, and fashion: When goods are unsettling. *Journal of Economic Behavior & Organization*, 47(1), 1–18.

Black, S. (2012). *The sustainable fashion handbook*. London: Thames & Hudson.

Burch, E. S., Jr. (1998). *The Inupiaq Eskimo Nations of Northwest Alaska*. Fairbanks, AK: University of Alaska Press.

Busch, O. (2008). *Fashion-able. Hacktivism and engaged fashion design*. University of Gothenburg. Retrieved from https://gupea.ub.gu.se/bitstream/2077/17941/3/gupea_2077_17941_3.pdf

Chapman, J. (2015). *Emotionally durable design: Objects, experiences and empathy* (2nd edn). London: Routledge.

Clark, H. (2009). Slow + fashion. *Fashion Theory*, 12(4), 427–446.

Cunningham, P. A. (2003). *Reforming women's fashion, 1850–1920: Politics, health, and art*. Kent, OH: The Kent State University Press.

Edwardsen, D. P. (ed.) (1983). *Uqaluktuat 1980, elders' conference, womens session*. Barrow, AK: North Slope Borough, Commission on Inupiat History, Language and Culture.

Eicher, J. B. (ed.). (1995). *Dress and ethnicity*. Oxford: Berg.

Fletcher, K. (2011). 4.4 Post-growth fashion and the craft of users. In A. Gwilt & T. Rissanen (eds), *Shaping sustainable fashion. Changing the way we make and use clothes* (pp. 165–175). London: Taylor and Francis.

Fletcher, K. & Grose, L. (2012). *Fashion & sustainability: Design for change*. London: Laurence King.

Fletcher, K. & Tham, M. (2014). *Routledge handbook of sustainability and fashion*. London: Routledge.

Gordon, J. F. & Hill, C. (2015). *Sustainable fashion: Past, present, and future*. London: Bloomsbury.

Gwilt, A. & Rissanen, T. (2012). *Shaping sustainable fashion: Changing the way we make and use clothes*. New York: Taylor and Francis.

Hutchison, I. W. (1934). *North to the rime-ringed sun. Being the record of an Alaskan-Canadian journey made in 1933–34*. London: Blackie & Son Limited.

IKEA. (n.d.). KLIPPAN cover two-seat sofa. Retrieved from www.ikea.com/gb/en/products/sofas-armchairs/leather-sofas/klippan-two-seat-sofa-kimstad-white-art-20306293/

Issenman, B. K. (1997). *Sinews of survival. The living tentlike legacy of Inuit clothing*. Vancouver: UBC Press.

MacInnes, T. (1932). *Klegenberg of the Arctic*. Toronto: Jonathan Cape.

Martin, C. B. (2001). Mediated identity and negotiated tradition. The Inupiaq Atigi 1850–2000. PhD diss., University of Alaska, Fairbanks, AK.

Niinimäki, K. (2013). *Sustainable fashion: New approaches*. Helsinki: Aalto University.

North Slope Borough. (2016). *Kaktovik*. Retrieved from www.north-slope.org/our-communities/kaktovik

North Slope Borough School District. (1994). *Kaivirvik. Winter solstice*. Retrieved from www.google.no/url?sa=t&rct=j&q=&esrc=s&source=web&cd=2&cad=rja&

uact=8&ved=0ahUKEwiM5OfvuYPQAhWBHywKHXNeCusQFgghMAE&url=
http%3A%2F%2Fnsbsdearlylearning.wikispaces.com%2Ffile%2Fview%2FKaivirvik_
WinterSolstice.docx&usg=AFQjCNEZ90VwTq6iNzKWhd3KIr3j55fkmg&sig2=
EbzwvCbRpGzohxAvzqiuoQ

Oakes, J. E. (1991). *Copper and caribou Inuit skin clothing production.* Canadian
Ethnology Service Mercury Series Paper. Hull, Quebec: Canadian Museum of
Civilization.

Patagonia. (2016). *Patagonia women's tres 3-in-1 parka.* Retrieved from http://eu.
patagonia.com/enNO/product/womens-tres-3-in-1-parka?p=28407-0

Rapoport, A. (1969). *House form and culture.* Englewood Cliffs, NJ: Prentice Hall.

Ray, D. J. (1977). *Eskimo art. Tradition and innovation in North Alaska.* Seattle: University of Washington Press.

Rudofsky, B. (1964). *Architecture without architects. An introduction to non-pedigreed architecture.* New York: The Museum of Modern Art.

Thorpe, A. (2014). Economic growth and the shape of sustainable fashion. In Kate
Fletcher & Mathilda Tham (eds), *Routledge handbook of sustainability and fashion*
(pp. 64–73). London: Routledge.

Varier. (n.d.). Ekstrem chair. Retrieved from www.varierfurniture.com/en_no/
Movement-Chairs/Ekstrem/Variations-Ekstrem/Ekstrem_Black_KNI009

Walker, S. & Giard, J. (2013). *The handbook of design for sustainability.* London:
Bloomsbury.

Wenger, E. (1998). *Communities of practice. Learning, meaning, and identity.* Cambridge:
Cambridge University Press.

11 Fit in ready-to-wear clothing

Why people dispose garments before they are worn out

Veronika Glitsch

Since I began to teach clothing design and tailoring with an emphasis on redesign and alteration tailoring, I have worked with hundreds of students and workshop participants to fit clothes for their bodies. Most of my students were not able to tell exactly what was wrong with the clothing items they had bought, but they just preferred not to wear them. They stand in front of the mirror, fidgeting, and tell me that they have put on this particular clothing item many times but always take it off again. They bought the clothing as they liked the fabric or the cut, but something happens when they put it on. They seek explanations of why they do not wear it and talk about the colour and patterning. Often, though, I can see at a glance that the cut is wrong for their body shape, and we do a fitting and make the necessary changes to make the clothing fit their body. Then, as the students stand in front of the mirror, I can see their happiness that the clothing now truly fits their body, and they can finally enjoy wearing that particular item. These experiences tell me that fit is important with regard to whether clothing is worn or not. They show that those unskilled in the tailoring discipline cannot necessarily put their finger on what is wrong with the fit of a garment in relation to their body shape.

In this initial example I establish a link between ill-fitting clothing and the fact that clothing items are seldom used until they are worn out. After having reviewed what previous research says about why individuals dispose of clothes before they are worn out, I shall investigate whether there is a connection between fit and disposal of clothing. In reviewing studies investigating why people stop wearing their clothes, I focus on why the rate of clothing disposal is so high in Norway, the United Kingdom and comparable countries: 30 kg annually per UK inhabitant (Allwood et al., 2006) and 24 kg annually per Norwegian. By studying the factors leading to clothing disposal, I hope to discuss what clothing designers and tailors working in ready-to-wear clothing production can do in their practices to maximise the user period.

Life cycle assessment (LCA) studies show that the use phase, as measured by the average usage time, has the greatest environmental impact during the life cycle of a garment. We use clothes too little and wash them too often at too high temperatures (Laitala & Boks, 2012, p. 124). To reduce the environmental impacts of clothing consumption, it is important to discuss what changes can lead people to wear their clothes for longer. It might seem that the actual production of clothes causes the greatest environment impacts, but these LCA studies point to the importance of the user period.

My starting point for this study is this question: what qualities of clothing make people wear out their clothes or stop wearing them before they are worn out? Seeking answers to this question, I focus on fit in clothing with the practice of pattern construction in mind.

Problems with fit as a reason for clothing disposal

While the literature reviewed here considers many aspects of clothing and clothing production, I focus on the findings relevant to the main topic of *fit of clothing*. In "Consumer reuse and recycling of post-consumer textile waste", Domina and Koch (1999) report the results from a survey on the reasons for the disposal of clothing (see Table 11.1). Of the 396 respondents, 88 per cent were women, and the average age was 38 years old. The respondents could select multiple reasons for disposing clothing over the past year and indicated whether they chose to give the clothing to various organisations, pass it on to others or use it as rags. Therefore, the total percentages exceed 100 per cent. Table 11.1 shows that one of the most frequently mentioned reasons was that a garment did not fit. As well, respondents did not want to waste garments. The most frequently selected reasons for discarding clothing show that the respondents aimed to find ways to reuse or recycle discarded clothing (Domina & Koch, 1999, p. 351).

Table 11.1 Methods of disposal of textiles and reasons for disposal

	Methods of textile disposal[a]						
Reasons for discard	C %	SA %	RO %	GS %	PO %	R %	MR %
Not wasted	69	78	78	82	70	64	69
Did not fit	71	75	64	87	82	28	49
Valuable	75	–[b]	41	76	76	–	35
Convenience	45	65	–	63	37	34	–
Out of style	50	57	41	–	–	28	41
Tired/bored	–	–	–	62	32	–	–
Damaged	–	–	–	–	–	91	46
Helps needy	–	86	86	–	–	–	–

Source: Domina and Koch, 1999.

Notes
a C = consignment; SA = Salvation Army; RO = religious organisation; GS = garage sales; PO = passed on; R = rags; MR = modified and reused.
b (–) = not applicable.

I assume that behind the wish to not waste useable clothing lie the reasons why the respondents did not want to wear the clothing themselves. Here there could be hidden reasons about poor fit that the respondent might not be able to formulate.

Klepp (2001) conducted a study, reported in "Hvorfor går klær ut av bruk? Avhending sett i forhold til kvinners klesvaner [Why do clothes go out of use? Disposal in relation to women's dress habits]", on the relation of clothing disposal to women's dress habits, focusing on fashion and wear-and-tear as reasons for clothing disposal. Klepp (2001) interviewed 24 Norwegian women aged around 40 years old about their clothing habits. The informants were asked to collect clothes they no longer used or wanted to get rid of. Six months later, these clothes were documented, and the reasons respondents gave for no longer using them were recorded. Table 11.2 shows the results for the respondents' reasons for clothing disposal, organised into six categories: (1) situational obsolescence; (2) functional obsolescence; (3) quality (technical) obsolescence; (4) psychological obsolescence; (5) not used; and (6) preservation.

Klepp (2001) does not put special emphasis on issues with fit as a reason for disposal, but in reviewing the report, I extracted the most relevant examples related to issues with fit. Problems with fit might lie behind other reasons

Table 11.2 Reason for disposal as a percentage of the number of reasons and as percentage of the amount of clothing

	Type of obsolescence	*Percentage of total number of registered reasons*
1	Situational (the owner has developed new consumer needs, such as changed body size, has other similar clothes or clothes have too narrow use area)	19
2	Functional (new and better products have come to the market)	1
3	Technical or quality-related (the product is worn out, ruined or is uncomfortable in use)	35
4	Psychological (the owner is tired of the product and wants something new, does not use that style anymore or clothes that seem outdated)	31
5	Never used (product not suitable for purpose. Often bought on impulse or received as present.)	13
6	Museal (the owner takes the product out of use and keeps it for other purpose, does not want to use it in order to not to ruin it)	1
Total		100

Source: Klepp (2001) English version sourced from Laitala and Boks (2012, p. 126).

for disposal. For example, Klepp (2001) describes a yellow trouser suit which has had several owners but has been worn by none of them. The respondent could not tell what was wrong with the suit. Its fashion could have been outdated as it has not been worn for many years, but why did its first owner not wear it? SIFO, an unbiased Norwegian governmental institute that conducts consumer research, tested the suit and concluded that the jacket was too narrow through the shoulders and consequently uncomfortable in use. Klepp (2001) defines this as a technical error, and I assume that the lack of a good fit led the first owner of the yellow trouser suit to not wear it. Such fit problems could arise from the quality of the pattern construction or a lack of fit between the proportions of the garment and the body shape of the first owner.

Klepp (2001) mentions several aspects of fit related to body shape. First, Klepp (2001) claims that the user period becomes shorter for clothes that have a low tolerance for changes in body shape. A garment that does not fit properly catches the user's attention, and a garment that needs to be corrected feels uncomfortable when used. Obvious corrections are needed when a skirt is too tight for walking, a blouse slips out of trousers, or straps fall down from the shoulders (Klepp, 2001, p. 133). Klepp (2001) concludes that there is a need for more technically oriented textile research focused on the body's interaction with clothing. In previous research, the body has attracted little attention, even though, as this study shows, it plays a significant role in both wear-and-tear and changes in body shape as reasons for disposal (Klepp, 2001, p. 174).

An interesting result of Klepp's (2001) study counters a commonly claimed reason for disposal: that clothes go out of use due to changes in fashion. Klepp (2001) shows that clothes disposed due to outdated fashion were older (8.05 years) than clothes disposed due to wear and tear (7.5 years). This finding means that, if actively worn, clothes wear out before fashion has changed so much that their owners discard them as outdated fashion. This pattern could result from the fact that garments are sometimes left unused for years and then discarded due to being outdated (Klepp, 2001, p. 162). My assumption is that fit issues are a major reason that clothes are kept but unused for many years. Even if outdated fashion is the reason for disposing of clothing lying unused in the wardrobe, the reason for not wearing the garment when it was in fashion might be a lack of good fit.

Four articles (Laitala, 2010, 2014; Laitala & Boks, 2010, 2012) on sustainable clothing design through social and technical durability report the results of a survey asking respondents about garments they no longer wear. In 2010, the questionnaire was sent to 1,300 households in Norway and received 546 responses, of which 77 per cent came from women (Laitala & Boks, 2012, p. 128). The survey focused on consumers' experiences and opinions about their clothing habits, particularly their maintenance routines, disposal and environmental initiatives. Respondents were asked what they wanted to be different to encourage them to use their clothes several times (Laitala & Boks, 2012).

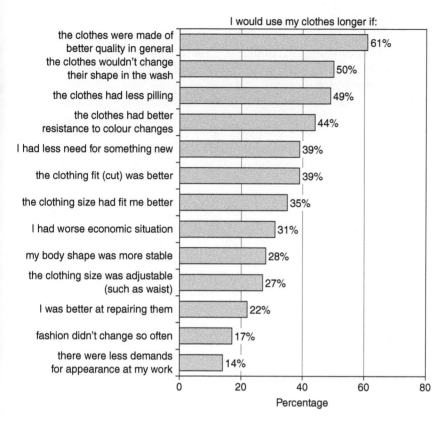

Figure 11.1 Percentage of respondents agreeing to each statement as the second part of the sentence 'I would use my clothes longer if…'.

Source: Laitala and Boks (2012).

Certain reasons for disposal are interesting in relation to fit issues: the clothing fit (cut) was better (39 per cent); the clothing size had fit me better (35 per cent); my body shape was more stable (28 per cent); and the clothing size was adjustable (such as waist) (27 per cent). Here, as in Klepp (2001) survey, a large percentage of the reasons could be associated with fit issues related to respondents' experiences with ready-to-wear clothing (Laitala & Boks, 2012, p. 130).

The research also included a qualitative study in which members of 16 households were interviewed about their reasons for disposing of clothing. The households collected garments that went out of use over a period of six months and listed their clothing acquisitions. The respondents were then interviewed about why the garments went out of use. In total, 619 garments were disposed of, and respondents gave up to five different reasons why a garment was no longer used. These reasons were categorised into 63 sub-categories, which were then grouped into seven main categories:

1   Size and fit issues (too large or small, outgrown, fit at specific areas, etc.): 19%
2   Changes in the garment (e.g. abrasions, colour changes, broken zipper or soiling that cannot be cleaned): 49%
3   Fashion or style changes (either general fashion or individual style changed): 5%
4   Functional shortcomings (e.g. unpractical, electrostatic, too cold to use in the area): 6%
5   Situational (does not fit with other clothes, no occasions to use it, have several similar or better garments): 8%
6   Taste-related unsuitability (e.g. dislike of style, colour or design): 11%
7   Other or unknown: 2%

(Laitala & Boks, 2012, p. 130)

Women and men had relatively similar reasons for disposal, except for fit issues, which women mentioned more than twice as often as men (Laitala & Boks, 2012). In qualitative interviews, the respondents from 16 households had difficulties putting into words why garments that were not worn out had gone out of use. This finding clearly parallels the previously described survey by Klepp (2001). Respondents (Laitala & Boks, 2012, p. 131) often state that they simply did not wear the garment or did not like it. When urged to elaborate, the respondents gave varied answers: some said that the garment did not suit them, that it was difficult to combine with other clothes, that it felt outdated or that they did not like the colour or pattern (Laitala & Boks, 2012, p. 131). These responses, in my experience of customising clothing by body shape for customers and students, often hide fit issues which are not apparent to those unskilled in tailoring who consequently use other expressions. The survey also showed that 18 per cent of the clothes out of use had never been used or had been used only once or twice (Laitala & Boks, 2012, p. 131). My assumption is that the reasons for a garment never being used or used only a few times could relate to a lack of good fit for the respondent.

Laitala and Boks (2012) conclude that women's clothing presents a major design challenge: the adaptation of clothing to different body shapes. Not many ready-to-wear garments in the market today fit well on different bodies or are flexible enough for continued use when weight and body shape change. Laitala and Boks (2012) claim that a greater focus on this issue by designers and clothing manufacturers could enable the production of clothing that could be used for longer. Laitala and Boks (2012) refer to studies on clothing size and fit that show that patternmakers usually make a small prototype to use for grading into larger sizes. However, it has also been shown that women who wear large sizes have greater variations in body shape and that it is this group that reports the most problems with fit (Laitala & Boks, 2010, p. 12).

In these surveys, fit issues are mentioned quite frequently as reasons for the disposal of clothing. As I argue, fit issues might lie behind an even larger proportion of the reasons for disposal. It seems that the sizing system used in the production of ready-to-wear clothing does not correspond with the sizes and body shapes of representative target populations. To investigate this issue, I explore the origin of sizing systems and how grading practices and the application of ease to patterns affect the fit of clothing. The study aim is to determine whether certain changes to these practices can make it more likely that more people will find well-fitting garments among ready-to-wear clothing. This, I assume will affect whether and how long a garment is used in the long term.

Sizing systems, grading practice and ease

The industrial revolution led to the first mass production of clothes. This created a need for profitable industrial systems to produce well-fitting clothes for a population with large variations in size and body shape. Variations in body shape consist of different proportions and body postures that affect how clothing fits the bodies. The complexity of dress sizes is greater than that of other products related to body size, such as furniture and bikes that ergonomically fit a wider range of users (Ashdown, 2007, p. xvii).

Current practices in the production of ready-to-wear clothing use sizing systems developed by individual companies based on individual choice and grading practices. These sizes are not standard or designed using the average measurements of a target group in a current population area. Clothing manufacturers want to provide a range of sizes but also to avoid confusion among consumers looking for an appropriate size. Consumers might perceive clothing negatively if they have to try on many different sizes to find one that fits. This is often cited as the reason why manufacturers usually have a small range of sizes. However, too few sizes can also lead to dissatisfaction as consumers cannot find clothes that fit them. The challenge is to develop a sizing system that does not have too many sizes or too few (Petrova, 2007).

Manufacturers usually copy existing size tables or use size tables they have developed based on the desired target group. Size tables are often adjusted through trial and error, but the size designation (i.e. small, medium, large) remains the same. This pattern leads to mismatches between the size designations of different manufacturers. It is also unclear whether size designations refer to a body measurement or a measure from the garment; for instance, whether waist size is the size of the garment at the waist or the size of the consumer's waist. Companies might prefer to use their own size tables over standardised sizing systems as they fear losing their signature if they use the same size table as other manufacturers. The amount of design ease, or the ease added to a pattern to alter its silhouette or general shape, which a designer chooses to put into a garment does not affect the body measurements for which the garment is made. Here, manufacturers can show their individuality, even if they use the same sizing systems as other companies (Petrova, 2007, pp. 60–61).

However, poor equivalence of sizing systems is not the only reason clothes do not fit the target group; it could also be due to inadequate pattern construction. How a garment fits the body depends on how and where wearing ease is placed in the garment. Ease should not be the same for all sizes but should be customised for different sizes. However, it is not a common practice for manufacturers to use a fit model for each size. Usually, one fit model is used to fit a prototype of the base garment and then changes are made to the pattern before it is graded. Consequently, ease and garment fit to the body shape are not adjusted for different body shapes and sizes (Petrova, 2007, pp. 81–82).

The term *standard sizes* is often used to refer to sizing tables not developed according to a standard. To qualify as a standard, a sizing system must be published by a governing organisation that works with standards. The two leading organisations active in the development of standards for clothing sizing tables are ASTM International (founded in 1898, known as the American Society for Testing and Materials until 2001) and the International Organization for Standards (ISO, founded in 1947) (LaBat, 2007, pp. 88, 92). Since body shapes and sizes vary so much among population groups, it would be useless to create standard size charts for the entire world population. When a standard sizing system is developed for a particular population, it is important that proper measurements be taken from a representative sample of the population. LaBat (2007) claims that most available standard size tables are based on measurements not representative of relevant population groups. The common practice in the production of ready-to-wear clothing is to start with a garment's key dimension, such as bust width. Then anthropometric measurements of the bust width of the actual target group are taken, and the range of bust widths is divided into ten sizes spaced at similar intervals. This practice, though, has nothing to do with developing a sizing system based on the anthropometric measurements of a target population by size (Gupta, 2014). Gupta (2014) claims that this process of developing sizing systems leads to satisfactory fit for only 20 per cent of target groups.

That most sizing systems used by manufacturers of ready-to-wear clothing are not representative of actual populations (Ashdown et al., 2007, p. 370) creates a situation in which many people cannot find appropriate clothing for their body shape and size in ready-to-wear clothing stores. Laitala et al. (2011) and Laitala et al. (2009) conducted a study on clothing sizes and size labelling in Norway, Sweden and Finland. Their research questions were which consumer group has the greatest difficulty finding clothes that fit their bodies and preferences and the implications of current sizing systems for consumers (Laitala et al., 2011). The topics of the survey questions included the respondents' experiences with and opinions about dress sizes and experience of their own bodies. Of the 2,834 people who responded to the Internet survey (1,958 Finns, 497 Norwegians, 331 Swedes and 48 of other nationalities), 81 per cent were female. In addition to the quantitative survey, qualitative in-depth interviews were conducted in Norway with 8 people, 3 men and 5 women (Laitala et al., 2009, p. 47). The aim was to interview people who had atypical body types according to the sizing systems used for ready-to-wear clothing. The respondents were asked which dress size they normally used and were requested to describe their physique, weight and height. They were then asked whether they found it easy to find clothes that fit their style, size and body shape (see Figure 11.2). Respondents who felt that it was difficult to find clothes that fit their body shape were divided into groups by gender and size/body shape, as shown in Figure 11.3 (Laitala et al., 2011).

As Figure 11.3 shows, women had greater difficulty finding suitable clothes than men. Men of normal height and weight and thin women of average height found it easiest to find clothes that fit them. Women with a round or large body shape and thin, short men had trouble finding clothes that fit. The groups of respondents who found it difficult to find clothes of appropriate sizes also reported that they rarely or never found appropriately sized clothing in styles that met their preferences. For example, a large, young woman could feel that she had to dress like an old lady, and a big man might be able to find only formal black suits that fit him (Laitala et al., 2011, p. 32).

Laitala et al. (2011, p. 35) observed that the women who found it easiest to find clothes that fit their body weighed less than the average weight of women. Men in the average weight group also found it easier to find clothes. This pattern is consistent with contemporary beauty ideals for men and women. Laitala et al. (2011) refer to studies showing that tall males and short females are preferred partners. Short men are seen as less attractive and have lower status,

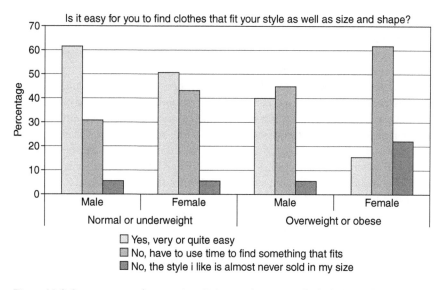

Figure 11.2 Responses to the question 'Is it easy for you to find clothing that fits your style, size and body shape?'.

Source: Laitala et al. (2011, p. 30).

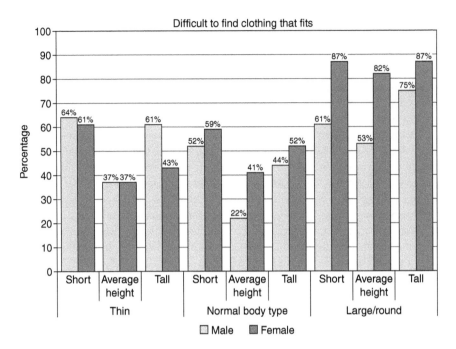

Figure 11.3 Percentage of respondents who had difficulties finding clothing that fits.
Source: Laitala et al. (2011, p. 30).

while the ideal man weighs a normal amount and is toned. Laitala et al. (2011) suggest that consumers closest to the leading body ideals found it easiest to find suitable clothes for their bodies (Laitala et al., 2011, p. 35).

To determine whether specific body parts were the most problematic to fit in mass-produced, ready-to-wear clothing, respondents were asked to describe their arms, legs, chest, waist, hip circumference, shoulders and the ratio of their upper and lower body (Laitala et al., 2009). The results showed that respondents whose body parts deviated from what was considered to be the norm or ideal had trouble finding clothes that fit. Of the 81 per cent of male respondents who had difficulty finding suitable clothes for their body shape, 71 per cent described their arms and back as short, 68 per cent their shoulders as narrow, 67 per cent their hip measurements as large and 65 per cent their chest as large. Of the women who experienced difficulty finding clothes that fit their body shape, 85 per cent described themselves as having a big belly or waist, 80 per cent a large bust, 79 per cent short arms, 78 per cent large hip measurements and 75 per cent broad shoulders (Laitala et al., 2009).

How a garment fits the body is connected to satisfaction and well-being. Satisfaction with how a garment fits the body contributes to mental and social well-being (Alexander et al., 2005). How a garment fits the body and which cuts are favoured are individual and subjective. Alexander et al. (2005, p. 57) distributed a survey to 232 female students at a university in the United States and collected 223 responses. Using drawings, respondents selected from three options for preferences of how different types of garments fit their body. They also indicated what body shape they thought they had from the options of rectangular, pear-shaped, inverted triangle and hourglass figure. They were also asked whether they were satisfied with the shape and size of various parts of their body. Nearly 64 per cent of respondents replied that they often had to alter ready-to-wear garments to make them fit. Another 54 per cent of respondents were somewhat satisfied or mostly dissatisfied with how ready-to-wear garments fit their body (Alexander et al., 2005, p. 59). Informants grouped by body shape reported fit issues involving different body parts. The groups of respondents with rectangular, pear-shaped and hourglass figures reported fit problems with the bust more often than the group with an inverted-triangle figure. The pear-shaped and hourglass figure groups reported more fit issues at the waist, hips and thighs and in dress and pant length than groups with rectangular and inverted-triangle body shapes. The group with the inverted-triangle body shape was the most satisfied with the fit of ready-to-wear clothing (Alexander et al., 2005, p. 59).

Schofield and LaBat (2005) discussed the relationships between grading, sizing and anthropometric data, examining how the grading of various sizing systems affects the size fit for different body shapes and sizes. Women often blamed themselves if they had trouble finding clothes that fit them. When they found that ready-to-wear garments did not fit them, they blamed perceived flaws and deficiencies in their own body shape and size instead of the sizing system (LaBat, 1990). Large-scale anthropometric studies have been conducted in attempts to improve the sizes of ready-to-wear clothing fit for the US population. Schofield and LaBat (2005), though, believe that these efforts cannot provide a general solution to fit issues in relation to standard sizes. To develop a standard sizing system that fits the current population, body measurements and the measurements that underlie grading of different sizes should be based on anthropometric data from large-scale studies.

The findings of Schofield and LaBat (2005, p. 14), who studied 40 measurement tables from 1873 to 2000 and compared the upper body measurements and the grading in different sizing systems, indicate a reduction in fit for different body shapes, alongside higher efficiency in grading sizes and a more streamlined system rather than fitting to anthropometric measurements. If standard sizes are to fit a large group of women, then the grading should follow women's body dimensions (Schofield & LaBat, 2005). This is possible, but it requires changing grading practices and grading each size separately. Today's software can handle grading even without constant, linear or proportional rules (Schofield, 2007, p. 190). Individually grading for each size based on anthropometric measurements would make it possible to produce garments that fit equally well on bodies of all sizes. This, however, is not the case in today's practice (Schofield, 2007, p. 193). The results of research surveys on different aspects of the fit of clothing, such as sizing systems, grading and ease, point to possible changes in tailoring practices for the mass production of ready-to-wear clothing. Changes can be made to achieve a better fit for the majority of particular target groups.

Summing up

The quantity of textiles discarded every year indicates that clothing is not worn out before disposal. LCA studies counting the number of times a garment has been worn show that discarded clothing is not often worn out. Reasons why garments come out of use have been suggested in studies as respondents explained why they stopped using garments. Studies from several countries identify the same two main reasons why women's garments come out of use:

1   The garment does not fit the user's body in the way the user desires.
2   The quality of the material is unsatisfactory (bumps, stretch, holes).

The current practice of manufacturers of ready-to-wear clothing is as follows. Various international standards organisations (ISO, ASTM) have developed tables of measurements to standardise sizing, but these standards are only partly based on anthropometric measurements. The anthropometric measurements used in the standards might be old and not representative of actual populations. Manufacturers often prefer to use their own sizing systems and tables of measurements instead of standard sizes as they fear being too similar to other manufacturers (LaBat, 2007, pp. 102–103). Tables of measurements and size tables tend to not include anthropometric measurements from representative populations. A prototype is designed and tested on a fit model whose body shape represents the image the company wants to present to its audience. This model is usually slim and not representative of the average woman in the manufacturer's target group. Changes are made to the prototype pattern pieces after modifications made during fitting, and the pattern is then sent for grading. The practice of grading does not use measurements, proportions or scales that follow representative anthropometric measurements. Pattern makers who do grading usually follow systems which systematise and simplify body sizes, allowing pattern pieces to be adjusted to the sewing process. For example, side and shoulder seams have the same angle, so the parts to be sewn together have the same grain direction, and the front and back pieces of a block pattern have a similar height and width (from waist to shoulder and from waist to the side seams). Anthropometric measurements from representative population groups, though, show that actual increases in body size and shape are not as linear and systematic as those used in traditional grading practices. Given that the sizing tables, patterns and grading of ready-to-wear clothing consistently deviate from anthropometric measurements of representative populations, it is unsurprising that many consumers have difficulty finding well-fitting clothes in ready-to-wear clothing stores.

Dissatisfaction with the fit of ready-to-wear clothing is pervasive. Developing standards based on anthropometric measurements from different population groups to make existing standard sizing systems more realistic would be a significant contribution to improving sizing systems (LaBat, 2007, p. 89). To enable as many people as possible to find suitable garments in ready-to-wear clothing stores, grading practices should be improved by working with individual measurements for each size. This could be possible by using advanced computer software to do grading rather than relying on manual grading systems. The ease in the garment could be adjusted separately for sizes so that the garment would appear similar in different sizes. Finally, the cut could be adapted to the typical body shapes for different sizes, optimising how the garment fits different body shapes. The most significant factors that affect clothing fit based on the research discussed can be summarised as follows:

1   Measurements and proportions underlying the sizing systems used by patternmakers to make block patterns.
2   Grading practice (i.e. increases and reductions to create different sizes) and how and with which measurements the sizes increase and decrease.
3   Extent of wearing ease and design ease and how and where ease is applied to a pattern, affecting how tightly or loosely different parts of the garment fit the body.
4   Pattern construction and cut of the garment and how these can be adjusted to make all the sizes in a size range appear the same, as is not the case with most of today's mass-produced ready-to-wear clothing.

Previous research has been done on the first three factors (sizing systems, grading and ease). I have not found previous research on the fourth: how pattern construction and cut can be adapted among sizes to provide the majority of a target group with well-fitting clothing. This is a gap in the field that I hope to address in my future research.

References

Alexander, M., Connell, L. J. & Presley, A. B. (2005). Clothing fit preferences of young female adult consumers. *International Journal of Clothing Science and Technology*, 17(1), 52–64.
Allwood, J. M., Laursen, S. E., Malvido de Rodríguez, C. & Bocken, N. M. P. (2006). *Well dressed? The present and future sustainability of clothing and textiles in the United Kingdom*. Retrieved from www.ifm.eng.cam.ac.uk/uploads/Resources/Other_Reports/UK_textiles.pdf
Ashdown, S. P. (2007). *Sizing in clothing*. Cambridge: Woodhead Publishing.
Ashdown, S. P., Lyman-Clarke, L. M., Smith, J. & Loker, S. (2007). Production systems, garment specification and sizing. In S. P. Ashdown (ed.), *Sizing in clothing* (pp. 348–375). Cambridge: Woodhead Publishing.
Domina, T. & Koch, K. (1999). Consumer reuse and recycling of post-consumer textile waste. *Journal of Fashion Marketing and Management*, 3(4), 346–359.

Gupta, D. (2014). Anthropometry and the design and production of apparel: An overview. In D. Gupta & N. Zakaria (eds), *Anthropometry, apparel sizing and design* (pp. 34–66). Cambridge: Woodhead Publishing.

Klepp, I. G. (2001). *Hvorfor går klær ut av bruk? Avhending sett i forhold til kvinners klesvaner (Rapport nr. 3/2001) [Why do clothes come out of use? Disposal in relation to women's dress habits (Report no. 3/2001)]*. Retrieved from www.sifo.no/files/file48469_rapport2001-03web.pdf

LaBat, K. L. (2007). Sizing standardization. In S. P. Ashdown (ed.), *Sizing in clothing*. Cambridge: Woodhead Publishing.

Laitala, K. (2010). *Sustainable clothing design-Information from use as a basis for innovative design*. Paper presented at the Nordcode seminar, Akershus.

Laitala, K. (2014). *Clothing consumption: An interdisciplinary approach to design for environmental improvement*. Trondheim: Norwegian University of Science and Technology.

Laitala, K. & Boks, C. (2010). *Clothing design for sustainable use: Social and technical durability*. Paper presented at the Knowledge Collaboration & Learning for Sustainable Innovation ERSCP-EMSU conference, Delft, The Netherlands.

Laitala, K. & Boks, C. (2012). Sustainable clothing design: Use matters. *Journal of Design Research, 10*(1/2), 121–139. doi: 10.1504/JDR.2012.046142.

Laitala, K., Hauge, B. & Klepp, I. G. (2009). *Large?: Clothing sizes and size labelling*. Copenhagen: Nordic Council of Ministers.

Laitala, K., Klepp, I. G. & Hauge, B. (2011). Materialised ideals: Sizes and beauty. *Culture Unbound: Journal of Current Cultural Research, 3*(1), 19–41.

Petrova, A. (2007). Creating sizing systems. In S. P. Ashdown (ed.), *Sizing in clothing* (pp. 57–87). Cambridge: Woodhead Publishing.

Schofield, N. A. (2007). Pattern grading. In S. P. Ashdown (ed.), *Sizing in clothing* (pp. 52–201). Cambridge: Woodhead Publishing.

Schofield, N. A. & LaBat, K. L. (2005). Exploring the relationships of grading, sizing, and anthropometric data. *Clothing and Textiles Research Journal, 23*(1), 13–27.

Part IV

Design education for citizenship

12 Developing holistic understanding in design education for sustainability

Ingvill Gjerdrum Maus

Sustainable development through design education for young people

Striving towards sustainable cultures is part of the sustainable development that global societies have agreed on (World Commission on Environment and Development, 1987), and in which education is assigned a key role (United Nations Conference on Environment and Development, 1992, §25.14 d and §36). One initiative, led by the United Nations, was to declare 2005–2014 *The Decade of Education for Sustainable Development.* The United Nations Educational, Scientific and Cultural Organization's (UNESCO) final report states that education shall provide learners with knowledge, skills and values to discover solutions to today's sustainability challenges (2014, p. 3). UNESCO's final report note that sustainability is now included in the general goals of education in many countries, but they need to reorient their teacher education towards relevant academic content and learning methods (2014, pp. 30–31).

Norway had already introduced sustainability in its core curriculum for education at all levels in 1993. This was followed by introducing environmental concerns in handcrafting in 1997 (Royal Ministry of Education, Research and Church Affairs, 1999, pp. 9, 51–54, 203–217) and sustainability in products life cycles in 2006 in the curriculum for Arts and Crafts (*Kunst og håndverk* in Norwegian) (Ministry of Education and Research, 2006) – a school subject that comprises art, design, architecture and visual communication at primary and lower secondary level. The environmental issues are not remote to the school subject's tradition of engaging with handcraft by using materials from nature (Nielsen, 2009, pp. 109–112). Though, new is the emphasis on reflection on the relations between products and environmental sustainability.

Design education for sustainability

However, there are areas for lower secondary education to draw on in development of their educational practice. The field of professional design education has discussed products and environmental sustainability sporadically since the mid-twentieth century and more systematically since the 1980s. The scope of topics in product design innovation has evolved from the reduction of environmental impact from product qualities and from products' life-cycles with the extraction of raw material, production, use and disposal to design for material recycling in biological and technological loops, emotionally durable design, sustainable behaviour and poverty reduction. Nonetheless, broadening the scope of design for sustainability (DfS) has not reduced the importance of designing each product with the minimum environmental impact (Ceschin & Gaziulusoy, 2016). Through this focus, environmental impact has become a quality criterion in design and it has brought forward various strategies in DfS. Minimising the damage of bad design does not immediately make a product sustainable, but design strategies clarify what to expect from the design (McDonough & Braungart, 2013, pp 13, 29). The professional field of design argues for a sharing of this design knowledge, both through product design that encourages participation and competence among the users (Stegall, 2006) and through design learning for all in education (European Design Leadership Board, 2012, pp. 66–71). Even though the perspectives and practices in design education for sustainability are developed to comply with the needs of professional design, they are also relevant to education at lower secondary level.

Professional design education for sustainability is described as education *for* sustainability, not *about* sustainability. Sustainability refers here to the sustainable societies that we aim to achieve through design education. Design refers to development where design is perceived as part of both the problems and the solutions to the over-consumption of resources in the production of goods and in everyday behaviour in societies with unsustainable practices. Education refers to the development of understanding through design work in the studio (Clune, 2010). Clune describes two approaches to design education for sustainability. The first is a master-and-apprentice model that focuses on how to design. The second is a student-centred model where the students are less dependent on the teacher. This model also engages in the definition of problems and what to design and is open to problems to which the teacher does not know the solutions (Clune 2010). Design education at the lower secondary level (13–16-year-old students) has similarities to the master-and-apprentice model, with the focus on *how* to design. Nonetheless, the inclusion of the issues of *what* to design, and of unsolved problems, is essential for their future in a world that is in need of change. The contribution of the students' design education to the development of sustainable societies is substantial. It has the potential of empowering ordinary young citizens for skilled, democratic participation in practical problem solving in their everyday living, studies and future working lives.

Students' points of view as the basis for educational change

The political intentions of education for sustainable development are formalised in the Arts and Crafts curriculum (Ministry of Education and Research, 2006) and practices in design and design education for sustainability are available to draw on. However, changes in education do not only depend on implementation at the ideological level of political intentions and the formal level of the curricula, but also on changes in the perceived and operationalised level among teachers and school leaders, as well as in the experienced level among students (Goodlad et al., 1979, pp. 58–65; Nielsen, 2009, pp. 27–31). UNESCO points to the present needs for development in teacher education (2014, pp. 30–31). This chapter focuses on students' perspectives as the basis for changes in educational practice to enhance understanding in design for sustainability. The starting points for this study are two diverging viewpoints among students on whether the topic of environmental concerns serves the purpose of learning creative and practical work in Arts and Crafts classes.

Students' perspectives

This is a study of students' perspectives on environmental concerns in product design as an educational topic in the school subject of Arts and Crafts. Semi-structured group interviews (Fontana & Frey, 2008) were conducted among seven 10th-grade students (aged 15–16) in a Norwegian lower secondary school in the spring of 2015. The interviews were held with two groups: the first with two female students and the second with three female and two male students. The interviews were part of the preparations for an action research project on the above-mentioned educational topic. The interviews were intended to identify the potential and possible challenges that should be prepared for in the educational activities in the action research. The research project's focus was rooted in studies on designing for sustainability (Stegall, 2006), with a particular emphasis on design for increased product life spans (Cooper, 2005) and design for the circular use of resources (McDonough & Braungart, 2009, 2013). A school that organised its Arts and Crafts education to facilitate the project and provide guidance for students was recruited to participate in the project as a case study. This school organised Arts and Crafts classes in groups comprised of half the size of the classes in most of the other school subjects. The classes were led by teachers with subject specialisations and held in equipped studios. Several of the Arts and Crafts projects were comprehensive and lasted for a full semester. However, the interviewed students had little or no experience with sustainability and environmental concerns as topics in the school subject. Nonetheless, they expressed interest and relevant knowledge on environmental impacts of products and product use during the collaborative reflections on the prepared and the elaborated interview questions. Their reflections comprised the knowledge they acquired through formal education in Arts and Crafts and other school subjects, as well as through experiences in everyday living and complementary information by other channels. UNESCO defines two categories of other channels for education: unformal education by educators at museums and non-formal education by other channels such as media (UNESCO, 2014, pp. 20, 30–31). In design education for sustainability this distinction is useful because actors have different bases for the information they provide. Interest in promoting a sustainable image that is difficult to fulfil is known to generate misleading information on environmental concerns, known as 'greenwashing' (Boehnert, 2013, pp. 447 and 452; 2015, p. 7).

Two perspectives

The first group of student interviewees had a positive attitude towards learning about environmental concerns in relation to product design in Arts and Crafts. They said that talking about the topic helped their understanding, and they reasoned that their knowledge of it would be useful for both their practical design and handcraft work in school and in their everyday lives. The second group expressed a negative attitude. They reasoned that it was a theoretical topic with key answers, which would disrupt the school subject's purpose of engaging in creative processes and practical design and handcraft work, as well as shift the practice in classes from practical to theoretical work. They trusted in their teacher to make environmentally safe choices on behalf of their design and handcraft projects. They explained their perspectives on students' need for variation in work methods throughout their schooldays, the needs of students who struggle with theoretical work and the needs of students aiming at future professions in handcrafts.

Without delving into the sources to their development of points of view, this chapter will concentrate on a key issue for the operationalisation of design education for sustainability, to clarify how the students' perspectives coincide with the essential elements in educational practice on DfS. To examine this, the study uses the concepts from the German pedagogue Wolfgang Klafki's (1959/2001, 1985/2001) theory of *kategorialen Bildung* as analytical lenses.

Klafki's theory of *kategorialen Bildung*

The close relation between the purposes of education and the selection of educational topics stands as a core topic of discussion in German and Nordic education's theoretical tradition of *Didaktik* [*didaktikk* in Norwegian]. *Didaktik* is a term that originates from the Greek *didaskein*, meaning "to teach", "to be a teacher" or "to educate". The German and the Nordic traditions refer to *Didaktik* as the "art of teaching" or the "study of teaching", which involves a broader discussion than the English term *didactics*, referring to "curriculum and methods" or "curriculum and instruction" (Hopmann & Riquarts, 2000).

In the *Didaktik* tradition, educational topics respond to the purpose of education. This point is particularly made by Klafki, who elaborates that the relation between education's purpose and topics must be perceived not only by the teacher but also by the students (Klafki, 1959/2001, p. 194). This is fundamental for the students' ability to develop through education, a development called *Bildung [formation* in English, *danning* in Norwegian] in the German tradition of *Didaktik*. The term *Bildung* has its origin in *Bild* (image), which holds the double meaning of representing both what *is* and what *might be*, thus the idea of transformation (Kouppanou, 2016). *Bildung* refers to students' development in order to participate in the ongoing development of both education and society in general.

Kategorialen Bildung

Within this tradition of *Didaktik* and *Bildung*, Klafki (1959/2001) developed his theory of *kategorialen Bildung*, a foundation for his later works (1985/2001) and an influential concept in the field of *Didaktik* (Hohr, 2011, p. 164). Klafki built his theory on a critique of single-sided views on the purpose of education as either learning of educational content or development of the student. Klafki offers a more holistic view of the purpose of education. He argues that the students' learning of educational content and their development depend on each other and evolve together in educational practice. Therefore, they cannot be considered two separate purposes of education. Rather, the purpose of education is to prepare students to develop in their encounters with educational content. Klafki explains this development as a phenomenon, an experience of the student. It occurs when his or her subjective conditions – such as critical thinking, judgement, will and imagination – unite with objects that culturally represent the world, such as classical culture and scientific knowledge. In this way, understanding constitutes a higher unity than a synthesis of subjective and objective conditions: a holistic understanding. Understanding evolves through engagement with the object. The engagement process opens the subject's general insights and experiences, while the objective opens its general content, clarifying categories as understandable for the subject. Klafki calls this process a double-sided opening, and the experienced phenomenon is *kategorialen Bildung*. *Kategorialen* does not refer to categories for discrimination between alternatives (*differentis specifica*) but to the phenomenon experienced by a student when his or her understanding opens and evolves as categories for him or her (Klafki, 1959/2001).

The purpose of topics

The holistic understanding that evolves when the students' subjective conditions engage with the object of the educational content leads Klafki to argue that the purpose of the educational topics must be grounded in both subjective and objective terms. The students' opening up to the educational topics depends on their understanding of the topics' significance in their past, present and future lives. However, their perspectives of relevance spring from their horizons of experience. The role of teachers is not only to understand the students' perspectives but also to challenge and expand their points of view and to build bridges between their perspectives on their past, present and future (Hohr, 2011, p. 167; Klafki, 1959/2001, p. 194).

Klafki's perspective is that educational topics of relevance to the students' present and future lives prepare them for participation in society and in its development. These are topics that enhance autonomy in terms of self-determination, co-determination and solidarity. Furthermore, these are topics that enhance *Bildung* for all with the starting point in their horizons of understanding, topics with core contents on key contemporary problems such as sustainability and social justice, and topics that develop broad interests and skills (Hohr, 2011, pp. 167–169; Klafki, 1985/2001, p. 176).

Exemplification of subjective and objective terms

Educational topics must be exemplified by educational materials where the topic is visible in the situation, incident or item. The exemplary value of the material comprises both the subjective and the objective aspects and must therefore be both elementary to open the students' understanding and fundamental to open the general idea of the topic (Klafki, 1959/2001). The thought of the exemplary is rooted in Aristotle's thought of general ideas as present and possible to experience in the perceptible, as opposed to the thought of Aristotle's teacher Plato who argued that the perceptible is unreal and a shadow of an underlying general idea (Hohr, 2011, pp. 167–169). Klafki himself questions in his later works whether 'elementary' and 'fundamental' are relevant terms for describing exemplification. Exemplary value comprises scientific knowledge but cannot be derived from science because it also constitutes the subjects' contemporary understandings (Klafki, 1985/2001, pp. 174–175).

Klafki's perspectives on students' development through engagement with educational materials provide us with lenses to examine how the students' perspectives coincide with the essential elements in educational practice on DfS.

Designing for sustainability opens understanding on the influence between products and potential environmental impacts

Klafki's theory of *kategorialen Bildung* provides the essential knowledge for the operationalisation of educational topics in educational practice. This case study uses three fundamental ideas from Klafki's theory as analytical lenses to examine the students' perspectives, as well as the objects and the exemplification of these in the DfS process. First, the experience of understanding (described by Klafki as *kategorialen Bildung*) evolves in the encounter between a subject and an object, a human and the culturally represented world, and in school between a student and the educational material that exemplifies the educational topic. Second, the students' development of understanding starts in their points of view on the purpose of the educational topic in their past, present and future lives. From these perspectives, the teacher must prepare for a broadening of their horizons and enhance autonomy in terms of self-determination, co-determination and solidarity. The student groups' two perspectives on environmental concerns in product design as an educational topic identified in the interview data are as follows: (a) it is useful for both practical design and handcraft work in school and in everyday consumption; and (b) it is a theoretical topic with key answers, which will disrupt the school subject's purpose of engaging in creative processes and practical design and handcraft work, as well as shift the practice in classes from practical to theoretical work. Third, the development of understanding depends on the exemplification of the topic. The objects of educational materials exemplify the educational topic's DfS when they visualise the general ideas of DfS in the situation, incident or item and, at the same time, comprise the students' subjective conditions of critical thinking, judgement, will and imagination. An analysis of the educational practice in DfS and the students' perspectives through the lenses of Klafki's theory clarifies fundamental issues in the preparation for the development of understanding on DfS among students.

Clarifying educational practice in designing for sustainability

The overall purpose of DfS equals the purpose of education for sustainable development – to develop sustainable societies in sustainable environments. The DfS topic engages in practical approaches for this development. It comprises the bidirectional influence between products and environments, where both affect each other. Products influence ecological, social and economic environments. They draw from natural resources, alter landscapes, reduce biodiversity, pollute the environment and generate waste during their entire lifecycle, from material excavation, development, use and disposal to material reuse. Environments also influence the design of products. Environments provide natural resources for materials and energy for the production and use of products and set limits for resource extraction. With the appreciation of low negative impacts and high positive impacts on environments presented in current design theories (Cooper, 2005; McDonough & Braungart, 2009, 2013; Stegall, 2006), it is fair to say that environmental concerns have become quality criteria for product design. With the purpose and general idea of DfS in place, an analysis of this topic through the lenses of Klafki's theory will locate the objects in an educational situation in DfS.

As the educational topic comprises DfS, two subtopics need exemplifying in the objects of educational materials: one involves design products and the other relates to potential environmental impacts from products. The different characteristics of these objects set the premises for the students' methods of engaging with them. Design products can be exemplified with a *design product (present object)* that is present in the school studio and experienced through practice in the design and handcrafting process, with the potential of opening the understanding about the product's qualities. The potential *environmental impacts (absent object)* of this product are absent from the school studio and must be exemplified with information and knowledge and be experienced through reflection, with the potential of opening the understanding about environmental impacts. Experience of the design product and reflection on the information on the knowledge about potential environmental impacts engage the students in the DfS process. In DfS, their reflections on the bidirectional influence between the product and the environment are used in the process of designing and handcrafting the product. This process exemplifies the DfS topic and is therefore also an object in the educational practice in DfS. Klafki defines the situations, incidents and items that exemplify the educational topics as objects (Figure 12.1).

Students' standpoints for development of understanding

This model clarifies educational practice in designing for sustainability. Additionally it can help us clarify the differences between the students' perspectives on the educational topic of environmental concerns in product design.

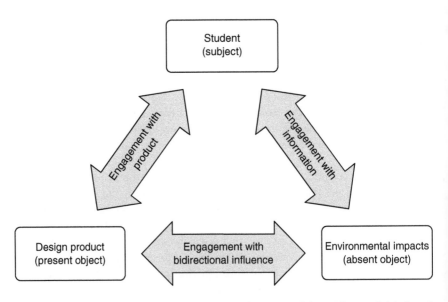

Figure 12.1 Educational practice in designing for sustainability. The model is based on Wolfgang Klafki's (1959/2001) theory of *kategorialen Bildung*.

The first perspective is of the topic as useful for practical design and handcraft work in school and in everyday living. This refers to engagement with the bidirectional influence between the design product and the potential environmental impacts in design projects. The second perspective is that the topic is theoretical and holds key answers, which will disrupt the school subject's purpose of engaging in creative processes and practical design and handcraft work, as well as shift the practice in classes from practical to theoretical work. This perspective mainly refers to the engagement with the information on potential environmental impacts as an additional topic to the engagement with the product and the design process. Environmental concerns become a topic to learn about rather than to use in the design process. This causes worries, which the students who relate environmental concerns to the design process do not express. However, the students agree that the main purpose of the education is to engage in the design process of making a product. To follow Klafki's (1959/2001; 1985/2001) idea, it is from this point of view that the students' development of understanding starts and from this standpoint that the teacher must prepare for broadening their horizons towards a holistic understanding of DfS.

Development of understanding through examples

The standpoint for the students' development of understanding is the design process and it is here the topic of DfS must be exemplified. According to the theory of Klafki, the exemplification both represents the general idea of the topic and opens the students' understanding (1959/2001; 1985/2001, pp. 15–20). This comprises in the topic of DfS exemplification of the design product, the potential environmental impacts and the bidirectional influence between the two in the design process.

In the design product (present object) that is present in the school studio, the product's qualities that cause the environmental impacts can be exemplified, perceived, experienced and altered as they are developed during the design and handcrafting process. These are qualities with direct environmental impacts, such as the selection of materials from renewable resources and design for material recycling when the product is no longer used (McDonough & Braungart, 2009, 2013). Additionally, these are qualities that reduce consumption through an increase in the products' life spans. Examples of these qualities are high quality materials, quality handcrafting and durable, maintainable and mendable constructions (Cooper, 2005, p. 61). These can also be characteristics that enhance emotional product attachment, such as scarce products and products intended as gifts (Gulden et al., 2010). The possibility of experiencing the qualities and their relation to oneself in the school studio makes them perceptible examples of product qualities. However, the environmental impacts that the product and its use impose cannot be perceived or exemplified in the product.

The information about potential environmental impacts (absent object) is absent from the school studio. This includes limits on how much resource excavation, material production, emissions and waste are tolerated by nature, limits on human exposure to toxic substances, and lower limits on production costs without dropping to poverty-level wages for production workers and without exploiting nature. It also consists of positive impacts such as fertile soil from the compost of biodegradable products (McDonough & Braungart, 2009, 2013). A common characteristic of these aspects is that they are not present in space and time to be perceived and experienced in the school studio while designing a product. They accumulate over time, when the resources are extracted, the emissions occur, the waste is disposed, and the production workers are exploited. Precautionary details on how to avoid causing environmental damage can be found in product information. Additionally, examples of long-term consequences of violations of environmental limits are accessible through sources such as the Internet. These examples are essential to understanding the general issue in DfS.

It is primarily in the DfS process that the knowledge about products' potential environmental impacts relates to objects of perception in space and time in the school studio. Here, the potential environmental impacts can be reflected on, as well as altered and become practical implementations of importance to sustainability in the students' products. The knowledge informs students about the strategies to design for sustainability. Examples on these are the negotiations between designing for resource-efficient or durable products (Cooper, 2005). It offers knowledge about the engagement with design and handcraft for increased product life spans (Cooper, 2005). It explains about designing for emotional product attachment (Gulden et al., 2010). It teaches students about safety in products and production (McDonough & Braungart, 2009, 2013) with the use of protective equipment in material handling, according to health, environment and safety information (HES).

The design process of creative problem solving and the performance of handcraft engage the students' subjective conditions, critical thinking, judgement, will and imagination with scientific knowledge on the topic. The examples of the product and the potential environmental impacts inform each other by providing design issues that students should be critical and creative about, as well as for the thorough execution of the handcrafting. This meaning reaches beyond the students' relation to the product and beyond the present time of this particular school project. The design process grounds their understanding of the concept of the product qualities' direct or indirect influence on sustainability in practical, empirical experiences with the product they are designing. This grounding of concepts in experiences is in line with the core characteristics of the *Didaktik* tradition (Gudmundsdottir et al., 2000, p. 321). The DfS process has the potential of exemplifying the development towards sustainability as not only understandable, but also relevant because it offers influential engagement. DfS brings purpose to the educational topic of environmental concerns in design.

Understanding design problems and design solutions enhances societal change

Education for sustainable development, high on the international agenda and of relevance to students, comprises the long-term goal of sustainability in ecological, social and economic environments, along with the developmental steps to achieve it. These are vast topics that can seem incomprehensible. Both students and teachers can feel powerless in encountering issues that need new solutions in the near future. Exemplification in practical design and handcraft work breaks down the topics into manageable sizes and brings these into the classroom as perceptible in practical work. Nonetheless, DfS's immanent idea that design is part of both the problem and the solution to environmental unsustainability is challenging. Whether the examples should represent design problems, design solutions or both is a relevant question. The selection of examples can be challenging in the education of young people. Nonetheless, Klafki reminds us that the purpose of education is to empower students for democratic participation in societal development with autonomy in and through self-determination, co-determination and solidarity (Klafki, 1985/2001, p. 176).

Exemplifying environmental concerns in design education might seem as risky as opening Pandora's box: once the reflections have begun, it generates many complicated problems. First, it opens up a massive critique of our present educational practice, as well as of our everyday living. Most of today's products, both commercial and those we design and make in school, raise some sort of environmental concern. Second, revealing these concerns about design makes the products we design, as well as consume, examples of unsustainable design practices rather than the sustainable solutions we aim to achieve. Third, these examples of unsustainable products can bring up questions of how to solve problems to which the teacher does not have answers, either because the teacher's knowledge on the issue is limited or the solutions are yet to be found. To reduce the issues with teachers avoiding unsolved problems, decreasing the students' dependence on teachers has been suggested in professional design education (Clune, 2010).

Exemplifying sustainable solutions demonstrates what we aim to achieve and possible paths to reach our goal, but it brings up other issues. First, it excludes most of our everyday products, as well as the products we design in school, and exemplifies DfS as a niche for a handful of products. Second, broadening the scope by including products with fairly good solutions could be done by focusing on sustainable details while disregarding unsustainable ones although this would provide misleading information on environmental concerns, in terms of "greenwashing". Greenwashing educational practice is incompatible with the idea of education for sustainable development. Rather, the role of formal education is to empower students to recognise when greenwashing occurs in the formal, unformal or non-formal education. Sustainable development requires information and honesty about what the problems are and what direction development should be heading in.

Exemplification of problems without solutions has the potential of generating despair. Will it leave the students only with the hope that the solutions will emerge sometime in the near future? However, solutions are not things that emerge or develop by themselves; neither do sustainable societies develop by themselves in the future. Teenagers are already participating in societal development and will continue to do so during their entire lives. They consume products and engage in democratic processes and will soon vote in elections and join the work force as employees and entrepreneurs. Education's goal is that they participate in societal development in a sustainable direction to secure fruitful lives for themselves, their children and the generations to come. Education's responsibility is to empower young people to do so. Reflection on what needs to be changed is fundamental to the idea of development, whether it involves unsustainable products or the unsustainable practices that we engage in when using these products. The idea of development is the idea of design (Clune, 2010). The variety of design strategies in DfS helps us clarify what to expect from design and therefore also what is exemplified in educational practice. Design education for sustainability clarifies challenges and solutions towards sustainable development and makes it relevant for the young.

Designing for sustainability – a holistic approach

The starting point for this study has been the set of initiatives for the development of sustainable societies through design education. Against the background of Klafki's fundamental idea that students' development of understanding starts from their points of view, two groups of students were asked about their opinions on the new educational topic. An analysis was laid out on the central element of Klafki's theory of *kategorialen Bildung* and the theory of DfS. This indicates that the students who consider environmental concerns as an additional topic to learn about rather than to use in the design process express a negative attitude towards the topic, which the students who relate environmental concerns to the design process do not express. Furthermore, the study has discussed how environmental concerns have the potential of being resources rather than obstacles in creative and practical work, as long as they exemplify how potential environmental impacts and design products influence each other and can be altered. The students favouring creative and practical work form the heart of DfS; it is a most beneficial starting point for broadening their horizons on the relevant role that their interest in practical and creative work plays in the development of sustainable societies. Such a role includes the ability to develop solutions that involve environmental awareness. This brings up the complexity of environmental concerns and design solutions as educational topics at the lower secondary level.

References

Boehnert, J. (2013). Ecological literacy in design education: A foundation for sustainable design. In J. B. Reitan, P. Lloyd, E. Bohemia, L. M. Nielsen, I. Digranes & E. Lutnæs (eds), *Design learning for tomorrow. Design education from Kindergarten to PhD. Proceedings from the 2nd International Conference for Design Education researchers, 14–17 May 2013, Oslo, Norway* (Vol. 1, pp. 442–457). Oslo: ABM-media.

Boehnert, J. (2015). Ecological literacy in design education: A theoretical introduction. *FORMakademisk*, *8*(1), 1–11. doi: http://dx.doi.org/10.7577/formaka demisk.1405

Ceschina, F. & Gaziulusoy, I. (2016). Design for sustainability: An evolutionary review. Paper presented at the Design Research Society's 50th Anniversary Conference, Brighton, UK. Retrieved from www.drs2016.org/059/

Clune, S. (2010). Deep learning and industrial design education for sustainability. Paper presented at Connected 2010–2nd International Conference on Design Education, University of New South Wales, Sydney, Australia.

Cooper, T. (2005). Slower consumption: Reflections on product life spans and the "throwaway society". *Journal of Industrial Ecology*, *9*(1–2), 51–67.

European Design Leadership Board (2012). *Design for growth & prosperity*. Retrieved from http://europeandesigninnovation.eu/wp-content/uploads/2012/09/Design_ for_Growth_and_Prosperity_.pdf

Fontana, A. & Frey, J. H. (2008). The interview: From neutral stance to political involvement. In N. K. Denzin & Y. S. Lincoln (eds), *Collecting and interpreting qualitative materials* (pp. 115–159). London: Sage.

Goodlad, J. I., Klein, M. F. & Tye, K. A. (1979). The domains of curriculum and their study. In J. I. Goodlad (ed.), *Curriculum inquiry: The study of curriculum practice* (pp. 43–76). New York: McGraw-Hill Book Company.

Gudmundsdottir, S., Reinertsen, A. & Nordtømme, N. P. (2000). Klafki's Didaktik analysis as a conceptual framework for research on teaching. In I. Westbury, S. Hopmann & K. Riquarts (eds), *Teaching as a reflective practice. The German Didaktik tradition* (pp. 319–334). London: Routledge.

Gulden, T., Moestue, C. & Berg, A. (2010). Psychology-based design approach (PSYDA): A pedagogical concept. Paper presented at the International Conference on Engineering and Product Design Education, Norwegian University of Science and Technology, Trondheim, Norway. Retrieved from www.academia. edu/990718/Psychology_Based_Design_Approach_PSYDA_-A_Pedagogical_ Concept

Hohr, H. (2011). Kategorial danning og kritisk-konstruktiv didaktikk – den didaktiske tilnærmingen hos Wolfgang Klafki [Kategorialen Bildung and critical-constructive Didaktik – The Didaktik approach of Wolfgang Klafki]. In K. Steinsholt & S. Dobson (eds), *Dannelse: Introduksjon til et ullent pedagogisk landskap [Bildung: Introduction to a unclear pedagogical landscape]*. Trondheim: Tapir Akademisk Forlag.

Hopmann, S. & Riquarts, K. (2000). Starting a dialogue: A beginning conversation between Didaktik and the curriculum traditions. In I. Westbury, S. Hopmann & K. Riquarts (eds), *Teaching as a reflective practice: The German Didaktik tradition* (pp. 3–11). New Jersey: Lawrence Erlbaum Associates Inc.

Klafki, W. (1959/2001). Kategorial dannelse: Bidrag til en dannelsesteoretisk fortolkning av moderne didaktikk [Kategorialen Bildung: A contribution to a Bildung

170   *I. G. Maus*

theoretical interpretation of modern Didaktik] (A. Gylland, Trans.). In E. L. Dale (ed.), *Om utdanning [About education]* (pp. 167–203) (1st edn). Oslo: Gyldendal.

Klafki, W. (1985/2001). *Didaktikk og dannelsesteori – Nye studier [Didaktik and Bildung theory – new studies]* (B. Christensen, Trans.). Århus: Forlaget Klim.

Kouppanou, A. (2016). Imagining imagination and Bildung in the age of the digitized world picture. In A. Fulford & N. Hodgson (eds), *Philosophy and theory in educational research: Writing in the margin* (pp. 121–128). Oxford: Routledge.

McDonough, W. & Braungart, M. (2009). *Cradle to cradle: Remaking the way we make things.* London: Vintage Books.

McDonough, W. & Braungart, M. (2013). *The upcycle: Beyond sustainability – designing for abundance.* New York: Melcher Media.

Ministry of Education and Research. (2006). *Arts and crafts subject curriculum.* Retrieved from www.udir.no/upload/larerplaner/Fastsatte_lareplaner_for_Kunnskapsloeftet/english/Arts_and_crafts_subject_curriculum.rtf.

Nielsen, L. M. (2009). *Fagdidaktikk for kunst og håndverk: i går, i dag, i morgen [Art and crafts education: yesterday, today, tomorrow].* Oslo: Universitetsforlaget.

Royal Ministry of Education, Research and Church Affairs. (1997). *Core curriculum for primary, secondary and adult education in Norway.* Oslo: Royal Ministry of Education, Research and Church Affairs.

Royal Ministry of Education, Research and Church Affairs. (1999). *The Curriculum for the 10-year compulsory school in Norway Oslo: National Centre for Educational Resources.* Retrieved from http://urn.nb.no/URN:NBN:no-nb_digibok_2010032503005.

Stegall, N. (2006). Designing for Sustainability: A Philosophy or Ecologically Intentional Design *Design Issues, 22*(2), 56–63.

United Nations Educational, Scientific and Cultural Organization. (2014). Shaping the future we want: UN Decade of Education for Sustainable Development (2005–2014). (Final report). Retrieved from http://unesdoc.unesco.org/images/0023/002301/230171e.pdf

World Commission on Environment and Development. (1987). *Our common future.* Retrieved from www.un-documents.net/ocf-02.htm

13 Rethinking consumption culture

Educating the reflective citizen

Eva Lutnæs

Educating for denial

Despite a growing number of climate change mitigation policies, the annual emission of greenhouse gases has grown more quickly from 2000–2010 than it has in the three previous decades. This alarming fact, reported by the Intergovernmental Panel on Climate Change (IPCC, 2014, p. 42), conflicts with the substantial emission reduction needed to keep the global mean temperature from rising. We have not been able to successfully integrate large-scale changes into our unsustainable ways of living, and most people act as though the threat of global warming can be ignored (Giddens, 2011; Norgaard, 2011). According to UNESCO (1997), progress depends upon the products of educated minds: research, invention, innovation, and adaptation, and launch educational initiatives to achieve the aforementioned as a powerful tool to change the way people think and act. Stephen Sterling, however, claims that "most education daily reinforces unsustainable values and practices in society. We are educated by large to 'compete and consume' rather than to 'care and conserve'" (Sterling, 2001, p. 21). In his seminal book, *Ecological Literacy*, David W. Orr addresses the need for an epistemological shift: "This crisis cannot be solved by the same kind of education that helped create the problems. Against the test of sustainability, our ideas, theories, sciences, humanities, social sciences, pedagogy, and educational institutions have not measured up" (1992, p. 83).

Education for sustainable consumption (ESC)

Transforming culture is a vital concept of education for sustainable development (ESD): "learn[ing] the values, behavior, and lifestyles required for a sustainable future and for positive societal transformation" (Decade of Education for Sustainable Development, 2008). In this logic, education serves as a site of counterculture, providing experiences that emanate from its distance to the everyday lives of young people (Ziehe, 2000). It is an arena to explore and present alternative ideas, building the capacity to question, rethink, and transform our current knowledge base and cultural practices instead of passively reproducing them. This chapter addresses one subset within the ESD umbrella: education for sustainable consumption (ESC). The subset is advocated as a means of "developing human resources and encouraging reflective, critical and active citizens who are capable of making informed choices" (UNEP, 2010, p. 14). ESC involves knowledge on how students' own patterns of consumption affect the environment and people across the world, but also the courage to care and fundamentally rethink definitions of human needs and desires (UNEP, 2011, p. 8). The favourable outcome of ESC is the critical citizen: "individuals who are self-reflexive – setting themselves and their world in question – and have a deep concern for the lives of others" (Darts & Tavin, 2010, p. 241). However, the transition into a more sustainable model of society depends on citizens that act on their knowledge by designing and implementing large-scale changes that really make a difference. Still, a teacher cannot prescribe changed attitudes, new consumer habits, and political activity amongst his or her students – the idea of influencing people's environmental behaviour in a predetermined way contradicts the essence of education (Wals, 2011, p. 178). Behavioural change as such cannot be the core objective, but it is rather the awareness of how conflicts and inequities embed everyday consumption.

Critical literacy

Critical literacy has been highlighted as a central concept in policy documents originating from the UN Decade on Education for Sustainable Development (UNEP, 2010, pp. 24–25; UNESCO, 2012, p. 2; UNESCO, 2014a, p. 66) and in the research literature (Boehnert, 2015, p. 452; Fallingen, 2014; Sterling, 2010, p. 19). The educational concepts of competence and literacy both involve familiarity with codes within specific fields of knowledge as well as acting in line with expected practices. However, the concept of literacy adds resilience by empowering individuals to challenge established regimes of knowledge and structures in a society (Boehnert, 2015; Stornaiuolo, 2015; Nielsen & Brænne, 2013; Illeris, 2012). There is a notable lack of consensus regarding the definition of critical thinking (Lai & Viering, 2012, p. 11). The myriad of different approaches on what critical thinking implies makes a key concept of ESC – critical literacy – vague and thus difficult to implement in classroom practices.

This chapter explores how education could challenge students to rethink consumption culture and transform deep-rooted structures of society towards ways of living within the capacity of our supporting eco-systems. I turn to three key texts on reflective inquiry – *How We Think?* (Dewey, 1933 [1910]), *The Reflective Practitioner* (Schön, 1983) and *The Pedagogy of the Oppressed* (Freire, 1970) – asking how each one of them informs the education of responsible consumers empowered to make changes in their individual patterns of behaviour and to use their power as citizens to stimulate policy change at the local and global level. This exploration draws upon the work of

Lyons, who gathered the three historical stands into one interpretative frame-work. According to Lyons (2010, p. 1), reflective inquiry is approached by Dewey (1933 [1910]) as a mode of thinking, by Schön as a way of knowing (1983), and by Freire (1970) as critical reflection. The texts on reflective inquiry provide methods for unearthing the current state of practice, but how to get from awareness and criticism to transformation is less elaborated. In order to design learning experiences that foster both knowledge of social inequity and exploitation of nature, as well as skills to rethink and transform unsustainable patterns, this chapter uses reflective inquiry and methods from systems-oriented design (Systems Oriented Design, 2016).

A state of perplexity

First published in 1910, John Dewey's book *How We Think?* remains a standard text in the field of education (Lyons, 2010, p. 13). Dewey defined reflective thinking as a distinctive operation of thought involving "(1) a state of doubt, hesitation, perplexity, mental difficulty, in which thinking originates, and (2), an act of searching, hunting, inquiring, to find material that will resolve the doubt, settle and dispose of the perplexity" (Dewey, 1933 [1910], p. 12). Dewey described reflective thinking as an inquiry into the grounds that support our beliefs – a thorough search for justifying reasons to establish belief upon a firm basis of evidence and rationality in order to transform an unsettled situation into one that is coherent, clear, settled, and harmonious (Dewey, 1933 [1910], pp. 9, 16, 100–101). The goal in making reflective thinking an educational aim, as Dewey (1933 [1910], p. 17) depicted it, was to convert appetitive, blind, and impulsive action into intelligent action; to act in deliberate and intentional fashions to attain future objects; and to command what is now distant or lacking. Dewey's aims are echoed in recent ideals of educating citizens to be able to oppose the "throw-away" society as conscious consumers and responsible decision makers (Nielsen, 2013, p. i). Dewey named a state of doubt or perplexity as the cause of reflective thinking. I find this a viable contribution for educating critical consumers. Drawing upon Dewey, the point of departure for reflective inquiry might be to determine a difficulty that must be surmounted (Dewey, 1933 [1910], p. 14) and that truly challenges the students' habits of mind; it should be designed to put them in a state of doubt and question the grounds that support their own beliefs and consumer practices.

The second step of reflective thinking, persistent inquiry, could make students aware of global inequities and injustices surrounding everyday consumption. However, Dewey's aspirations of a firm basis of evidence to settle the situation are of little use facing the complexities of consumerism. There is no one way to guarantee the most ecologically and socially responsible actions. In "Chocolate, Place, and a Pedagogy of Consumer Privilege", David A. Greenwood (2010) described the dilemmas of buying chocolate. Consumption of chocolate is connected to exploiting lives through slave labour (including child labour) in Ghana and the Ivory Coast; however, it also represents the livelihoods of people that choose to work on the cocoa fields. For them, working offers the opportunity of a better life than that which they could achieve without work. The consumer is left with the paradoxical question of whether to buy more or less chocolate. A similar dilemma faces the consumer buying clothes from multinational companies such as H&M and MANGO. The collapse of Rana Plaza, an eight-story commercial building, on 24 April, 2013 brutally demonstrated the working conditions for garment workers in Bangladesh. Although alarming cracks were discovered the previous day, workers were ordered into the factory building (Al-Mahmood, 2013). This event made Western shoppers question the ethics of fast fashion, long after the pictures of dead workers disappeared from the newspapers. This made customers wonder: what would a surviving Bangladesh woman prefer? That I keep her in work by buying the clothes she makes, or that I make myself feel better by choosing to buy clothes labeled "made in Turkey"? Consumer conscientisation is a learning process that opposes the daily training in economic privilege and ignorance by which consumers learn "the price of everything and the cost of nothing" (Greenwood, 2010, p. 195). Strategies of critical reflection in consumer education ought to involve exploring multiple voices and accepting the continual perplexity involved in unpacking and questioning consumer privilege (Greenwood, 2010, pp. 198–199).

Consumption as reflective practice

Donald Schön (1983) wrote *The Reflective Practitioner: How Professionals Think in Action* to address how professionals gain knowledge through practice and explore the relationship between the kinds of knowledge honoured in academia and the kinds of competence valued in professional practice. Schön aimed to bridge the dualism of theory versus practice, arguing that knowing, learning, and theorising take place while the practitioner makes judgements, frames problems, and designs solutions. Schön's contribution is an epistemology of practice based on his study of how senior practitioners – architects, psychotherapists, engineers, planners, and managers – guide junior practitioners. He identifies the concepts "knowing-in-action", "reflection-on-action", and "reflection-in-action" embraced by many educators of professionals as a new scholarship for teaching. "Knowing-in-action" is a spontaneous and intuitive performance, "reflection-in-action" is reflection in the midst of a performance, and "reflection-on-action" involves reflecting on action and exploring the knowledge that is implicit in the action (Schön, 1983). In order for Schön's concepts to inform the education of critical consumers, one needs to make a leap: the professional practitioner assumes the role of a consumer and the professional practice is staged as the practice of consumption. There are obvious differences between the two roles: whereas the professional practitioner represents and acts according to standards of a community, the consumer represents him or herself and can act upon personal preferences and values. They share, however, the routines of everyday life. I find Schön's

(1983, pp. 49–50) concept of knowing-in-action transferable to how consumers judge the quality of fabrics, the fit of a garment, or pick the perfect gift for a friend. Schön's concept situates consumer judgements as spontaneous and intuitive performances for which they cannot state adequate criteria, rules, or procedures – consumers' knowledge is implicit in their patterns of action. The quest for consumer education is to disrupt this intuitive flow of actions and make them reflective – I explore how to do this by looking into Schön's concepts of reflection-in-action and reflection-on-action.

According to Schön (1983, pp. 50, 56, 63), reflection *in* or *on* action occurs when one is confronted with surprise, value conflicts, uncertainty, dilemmas, or puzzling situations. Schön's description is strikingly similar to the ideas of Dewey, which he has credited as directly influencing his own theory of reflective practice (Schön, 1992). Confrontation is the key to replacing intuition with reflection. This calls for the educator to provoke the student, disrupting the naturalisation of consumer culture (Sandlin, 2010) and challenging the student to "surface and criticize his initial understanding of the phenomenon, construct a new description of it" (Schön, 1983, p. 63). Schön identified multiple objects of reflection:

> the tacit norms and appreciations which underlie a judgment, or on the strategies and theories implicit in a pattern of behavior. He may reflect on the feeling for a situation which has led him to adopt a particular course of action, on the way in which he has framed the problem he is trying to solve, or on the role he has constructed for himself within a larger institutional context.
>
> (Schön, 1983, p. 62)

The above-quoted objects of reflection construct different approaches for educators to design learning experiences that allow students to research their consumer practices. I assumed that pre-reading *The Reflective Practitioner* would frame reflection as a tool to solve problems, but Schön's (1983, p. 48) critique of Herbert Simon's (1969) notion of design as changing existing situations into preferred ones made me reconsider. The artistry of professional practitioners, as Schön (1983, p. 18) puts it, lies in their ability to find the problem, not only to solve it. First, the problem must be constructed through interactively naming what must be addressed and framing the context in which the problem will be dealt with (Schön, 1983, p. 40). Schön labelled this explorative approach "problem setting" and provided a device to manage its complexity, moving from puzzlement and confusion to action in education in order to achieve sustainable consumption.

Transformation of the world

In *The Pedagogy of the Oppressed*, the Brazilian educator Paolo Freire (1970) brought attention to what he framed as the banking concept of education.

Here, students receive, file, and store narrations from the teachers in the empty vaults of their minds. The banking concept of education offers few opportunities for students to analyse how political, cultural, and social contexts shape their lives. Freire (1970, p. 49) wanted to empower people to take action against oppressive powers and perceive a limiting situation not as a static reality, but as transformable. The author launches *critical consciousness* as a key to empowerment: "To surmount the situation of oppression, people must first critically recognize its causes, so that through transforming action they can create a new situation, one which makes possible the pursuit of fuller humanity" (Freire, 1970, p. 47). Freire's alternative to the banking concept of education is the practice of problem-posing education. Here, teachers pose a problem that challenges humans' relations in the world and with the world and facilitate a dialogue of co-investigation with students to unveil oppression and situations as historical realities susceptible to transformation (Freire, 1970, pp. 81, 85). The core of Freire's libertarian and humanist pedagogy is for people to discover themselves as permanent re-creators of the world: "To exist, humanly, is to *name* the world, to change it" (Freire, 1970, p. 88, original emphasis). Freire seeks to enable people to transform the sociocultural realities that shape their lives by the words they choose and how they act.

UNESCO (2014b) describes ESD as a transformative learning process that aims to change the way people interact with the world. According to Mezirow (1990), who draws upon the work of Freire, transformative learning occurs in response to a disorienting dilemma that makes people question the validity of the meaning of the perspectives with which they make sense of the world, and if necessary, to transform them. In the rationale of consumer education, a disorienting dilemma could be to question a taken-for-granted meaning perspective; for example, that to give a present is always a good deed. Although the receiver of a present might feel loved, the praxis drives over-consumption with severe environmental and social costs. To question the validity of meaning perspectives can involve the negation of values that have been very close to the centre of one's self-concept (Mezirow, 1990, p. 12). As a learning experience, ESD could be deeply uncomfortable and provocative. Designed to trigger distortions in habitual thinking, transformative learning is a beehive of constraints, resistance, and emotions. It is an inquiry into students' personal encounters with the world that touches upon their identity, values, and ways of living. Ideology critique (Brookfield, 2010) is a second tradition that draws upon the work of Freire and allows for a shift from individual meaning perspectives to context – questioning what powers and societal structures make us think and act the way we do as consumers and recognising uncritically accepted and unjust dominant ideologies embedded in everyday situations and practices. Ideology critique reveals the normal order of life as a socially constructed reality, and thus, a reality that can be remade by human effort (Brookfield, 2010, p. 221). Ideology critique in the context of consumption culture could arise from a question like the following: Why does the majority of the Western population regard overconsumption as making our lives easier and serving our best interests? Guided through the process, students gain insight into the ethical and environmental implications of different habits of consumption, ideologies such as global capitalism and economic growth, and further concepts to identify and analyse how power permeates consumer choices and hegemonic assumptions. The value of inaugurating teenagers into transformative learning and ideology critique is that it helps them to crack open the reality of consumption as complex, contradictory, and ambiguous.

Shared phases across key texts on reflective inquiry

Lyons (2010, pp. 1, 9) made an innovative move by bringing three major developments of reflective inquiry together as one interpretative framework. The idea of interconnectedness between Dewey, Schön, and Freire is vital to Lyons – still, her template that locates conceptualisations and practices of reflective inquiry relies on individual features. Lyons' interpretative framework reveals three different objectives for teaching or implementing reflective inquiry. I approached the texts with their different agendas in mind, but I discovered unifying ideas in how they describe *reflective inquiry* as a specific operation of thought. Exploring the texts for ideas on ESC, I found a shared structure of four phases across the texts that contribute to the understanding of reflective inquiry beyond my specific topic of concern. The four shared phases are interpreted via the concepts of confrontation, exploration, evaluation, and transformation.

1   Confrontation. The foundation of reflective inquiry is a temporary collapse in the ordinary script of life: a state of perplexity (Dewey), puzzling situations (Schön), and the discovery of oppression (Freire). These distortions challenge one's personal encounters with the world.
2   Exploration. The second phase is explorative: a thorough search for justifying reasons (Dewey), surface initial understanding (Schön), and a dialogue of co-investigation (Freire). This is a process of unmasking the status quo of current sociocultural realities.
3   Evaluation. The third phase is a time of reckoning: rational examination of evidence (Dewey), criticising initial understanding (Schön), and challenging relations (Freire). The idea that unifies the texts is that awareness gained from unmasking reality is the precognition for change.
4   Transformation. The last phase searches for an emancipatory potential or new understanding. From knowing *what the world is*, one can resolve the situation based on a firm basis of evidence (Dewey), construct new descriptions (Schön), and create a new situation (Freire).

Reflective inquiry begins with the experience of confrontation that calls a person's own habitual patterns into question. In the next phase, current sociocultural realities are explored to enhance one's knowledge of the situation.

The information provides a backdrop to reassess prevailing practices and habits of mind in an evaluative phase aiming to gain new understanding. Change is the ultimate goal of the process and occurs when new understanding enables transformed actions and habits of mind.

Reflection or critical reflection

Although the three texts have a shared structure, there is a vital difference between them on whether or not reflection is linked to the prefix "critical". Reflection without this prefix works towards improvements within an established field of practice, the how of the action, whereas critical reflection addresses the fundaments of a practice, the why of the action, and the reasons and consequences of what we do (Mezirow, 1990, p. 13). Critical reflection calls the foundations and imperatives of the system itself into question, assesses their morality, and considers alternatives (Brookfield, 2010, p. 219). The purpose of critical reflection is a profound change in our attitudes and actions. Of the three scholars considered here, Freire promotes the practice of critical reflection, advocating "the very transformation of the world" (Lyons, 2010, p. 16) as the agenda of reflective inquiry. Dewey does not use the term critical in his text, instead arguing that reflection is the thorough search that he recommends in the exploratory phase; he considers it to be existing knowledge. The text by Schön is not so easily located. The reflective practitioners of Schön are considered to improve their practices within the framework of an established system. Fook (2011) even argues that the popularity of Schön's work has conflated "critical reflection" with "reflective practice". In the few sections where Schön (1983, pp. 62–63) does use the term "critical", I found some striking similarities with Mezirow's transformative learning (1990) on surfacing initial understanding as a prerequisite to coping with troublesome situations and framing one's role or a description of a phenomenon differently. Thus, I have chosen to locate Schön in an intermediate position.

Critical literacy and empowerment through ESC

Within the context of ESC, I find a need for both "reflection" and "critical reflection". Reflection promotes vital adjustments of consumption patterns within the framework of the established system – consumers who stop when shopping and ask themselves "Do I really need this?" or "Why do I want to buy this?" Critical reflection is what citizens need to transform the very system of consumption and to change the key cultural beliefs that drive the hazard of current overconsumption.

Moving from awareness to transformation through systems thinking

The texts on reflective inquiry provide descriptions on how to unearth the current state of practice, but how to get from awareness and criticism to transformation (e.g. creating a sustainable future that does not yet exist) is less elaborated. Orr (1992) champions awareness and action, describing prerequisites to ecological literacy: "the study of environmental problems is an exercise in despair unless it is regarded as only a preface to the study, design and implementations of solutions" (p. 94). In order to take action as responsible citizens, awareness of unsustainable consumerism and severe climate change is crucial, but to evoke empowerment, students need to recognise their capacity to transform that reality. The capacity to transcend the known is the expertise of design. In the next section, I turn to designerly ways of thinking (Cross, 2007) in order to unearth methods to explore how things ought to be (Simon, 1969), more specifically, system-oriented design, as it is a designerly approach that can be used to address complexity (Sevaldson, 2013).

Surfacing complexity of consumption culture

Systems thinking is well established within the field of ESD (Cloud, 2005; Martin, 2008; Porter & Cordoba, 2009) and entails a shift in perception from the part to the whole – learning to think in terms of relationships, interdependencies, patterns, and context: "Systems thinking is 'contextual', which is the opposite of analytical thinking. Analysis means taking something apart in order to understand it; systems thinking means putting it into the context of a larger whole" (Capra, 1996, p. 30). Systems thinking comprises an approach to consumer education where students unfold the societal context of their individual patterns of consumption in order to understand connectedness and discern areas of advancement. In Schön's (1983, p. 40) terms, they set the problem. In terms of systems-oriented design, they identify relationships and map complexity through a process of visualisation. The context of individual habits of consumption can be unfolded in a vast collage of images and text, a process called GIGA-mapping. Sevaldson (2011) explains GIGA-maps as trying to grasp, embrace, and mirror the complexity and wickedness of real problems. A GIGA-map is a visual aid to understand relations and structures in a system made by interrelating and systematising knowledge, preconceptions, or speculations of relevance to a certain subject (Romm et al., 2014; Sevaldson, 2013). The process of making a GIGA-map enables students to surface complexity of consumption culture and to become aware of the sociocultural reality that shapes their individual patterns of consumption. The detailed and information-dense map provides a visual aid to conduct reflective inquiry, identify areas of advancement, and derive new modes of production, trade, and consumption.

Systems thinking and the four phases of reflective inquiry

The four phases of reflective inquiry viewed through the methods of systems-oriented design could provide a structure for learning experiences within ESC that foster both knowledge of social inequity and the exploitation of nature and skills to rethink and transform unsustainable patterns of consumption. Based on the structure of the four phases (confrontation, exploration, evaluation, and transformation), I have created two different scenarios (A and B) designed to involve teenagers and young adults in the exploration of solutions that can foster sustainability on a micro level (their everyday habits) and a macro level (economic and social systems). In Phase 1, Confrontation, students are introduced to a disorienting dilemma that challenges their personal encounters within the context of consumption. Phase 2, Exploration, enables students to surface habitual patterns of expectation, dynamics of power, and ethical dilemmas of consumer culture by making GIGA-maps. In Phase 3, Evaluation, students use the GIGA-map as a shared platform to question and evaluate habits of consumption and the system that drives consumption culture. Phase 4, Transformation, challenges students to identify areas of improvement and explore new modes of production, trade, and consumption.

Unmasking and rethinking as a fulcrum of ESC

I explored three key texts on reflective inquiry in order to pinpoint the capacity of critical literacy in ESC. Across the different agendas in the texts of Dewey (1933 [1910]), Freire (1970), and Schön (1983), I identified four shared phases of describing reflective inquiry as a distinctive operation of thought: (1) confrontation, (2) exploration, (3) evaluation, and (4) transformation. This shared structure across the key texts contributes to the understanding of reflective inquiry beyond the specific topic of this chapter (the education of aware, critical, and empowered consumers). The main difference between the texts is whether or not reflection is linked to the prefix "critical". Reflection alone operates towards improvements within the established field of practice, whereas critical reflection addresses the fundaments of a practice – why we think and act the way we do. The purpose of critical reflection is profound change in our attitudes and actions. Within the context of ESC, I find a need for both reflection and critical reflection. Reflection promotes vital adjustments of consumption patterns within the framework of the established system, while critical reflection is what citizens need to transform the system in order to promote large-scale changes in our unsustainable ways of living.

The dual process of unmasking and rethinking makes ESC a fulcrum. Students need to think of themselves as part of the problem: address the loss of ethics, question taken-for-granted assumptions, disrupt the naturalisation of consumer culture, and unveil its dynamics of power. Nevertheless, in order to act as responsible citizens, they also need to think of themselves as part of the solution; recognise their capacity to transform reality; design paradigmatic changes in both their everyday lives as well as political, social, economic, and technological structures of society; embrace transformation via relying on the capacity to construct alternative patterns of consumption; imagine future scenarios; and identify how things ought to be. Thus, designerly ways of

Table 13.1 Two scenarios (A and B) using systems-oriented design and the four phases of reflective inquiry

Phases of reflective inquiry	Scenario A: gift economy – the language of love and (over) consumption	Scenario B: being or having – happiness and the need for newness
PHASE 1 CONFRONTATION	*Disorienting dilemma*: We buy gifts to make the people we love happy, but our practice have environmental and social costs that are not included on the receipt.	*Disorienting dilemma*: The need for newness drives consumerism, but does consumption improve your quality of life?
PHASE 2 EXPLORATION	*GIGA-map*: Unfold the complexity of the gift economy. 1 Make an exploratory collage that maps your habits of mind when buying a gift. 2 Map the stakeholders, sites and use of resources involved. Start with the production of the gift and trace the journey of the gift to the end of its probable lifecycle in a sequential visual structure.	*GIGA-map*: Unfold the complexity of consumerism related to identity construction, desires, market mechanisms and quality of life. 1 Map how consumption relates to your sense of happiness in life. 2 Map mechanisms in consumer culture that makes people want to buy new things in a relational visual structure.
PHASE 3 EVALUATION	*Review*: 1 Who gains and who loses in the gift economy? Attach symbols on the GIGA-map that surface economic, social and environmental implications. 2. Identify and discuss ethical dilemmas involved in the gift economy and relate them to your own patterns of consumption.	*Review*: 1 Identify the core elements that ensure happiness in your life and analyse their connectedness to mechanisms in consumer culture surfaced by the GIGA-map. 2 Discuss the environmental consequences of our need for newness.
PHASE 4 TRANSFORMATION	*Future scenarios*: Mark one aspect of the gift economy on your map to explore further with potential for improvement. Suggest and visualise solutions or interventions that could transform the gift economy towards more socially just and ecologically sustainable practices.	*Future scenarios*: Create future scenarios that replace the need for the new with alternative modes of living and consuming.

thinking make a vital contribution to the field of ESC. This chapter proposes the four phases of reflective inquiry with methods from systems-oriented design and suggests a model that fosters both knowledge of social inequity and exploitation of nature and skills to rethink and transform unsustainable patterns of consumption. Visualising the complexity in consumer culture through a GIGA-map makes connectedness and ethical dilemmas tangible as a shared platform to conduct reflective inquiry. GIGA-maps make the consequences of over-consumption more perceptible and thus less easy to ignore. Confrontation is the first phase of reflective inquiry as well as the process of rethinking consumption culture. Consequences of climate change need to concern people at a personal level if they are to question and transform deep-rooted structures of society towards ways of living within the capacity of our supporting ecosystems.

References

Al-Mahmood, S. Z. (2013, 27 April). Bangladesh factory collapse: Police detain owners, as death toll exceeds 350. *Guardian*. Retrieved from www.theguardian.com/world/2013/apr/27/bangladesh-collapsed-factory-owners-detained

Boehnert, J. (2015). Ecological literacy in design education – a theoretical introduction. *FORMakademisk, 8*(1), 1–11. doi: http://dx.doi.org/10.7577/formakademisk.1405

Brookfield, S. (2010). Critical reflection as an adult learning process. In N. P. Lyons (ed.), *Handbook of reflection and reflective inquiry: Mapping a way of knowing for professional reflective inquiry* (pp. 215–236). New York: Springer.

Capra, F. (1996). *The web of life: A new scientific understanding of living systems*. New York: Anchor Books, Doubleday.

Cloud, J. P. (2005). Some systems thinking concepts for environmental educators during the Decade of Education for Sustainable Development. *Applied Environmental Education & Communication, 4*(3), 225–228. doi: 10.1080/15330150591004625.

Cross, N. (2007). *Designerly ways of knowing*. Basel: Birkhäuser.

Darts, D. & Tavin, K. (2010). Global capitalism and strategic visual pedagogy. In J. A. Sandlin & P. McLaren (eds), *Critical pedagogies of consumption: Living and learning in the shadow of the "shopocalypse"* (pp. 237–248). New York: Routledge.

Decade of Education for Sustainable Development (2008). *About us*. Retrieved from www.desd.org/about.html

Dewey, J. (1933 [1910]). *How we think: A restatement of the relation of reflective thinking to the educative process*. Boston, MA: Houghton Mifflin.

Fallingen, N. (2014). *Business as usual? – How to cultivate ecoliteracy in the subject Art and Crafts*. (Master's dissertation). Oslo: Oslo and Akershus University College of Applied Sciences.

Fook, J. (2011). The development of critical reflection. In G. A. Askeland (ed.), *Kritisk refleksjon i sosialt arbeid* (pp. 13–16). Oslo: Univeritetsforlaget.

Freire, P. (1970). *Pedagogy of the oppressed*. New York: Seabury Press.

Giddens, A. (2011). *The politics of climate change* (2nd edn). Cambridge: Polity.

Greenwood, D. (2010). Chocolate, place, and a pedagogy of consumer privilege. In J. A. Sandlin & P. McLaren (eds), *Critical pedagogies of consumption: Living and learning in the shadow of the "shopocalypse"* (pp. 193–200). New York: Routledge.

Illeris, H. (2012). Nordic contemporary art education and the environment: Construction of an epistemological platform for Art Education for Sustainable Development (AESD). *InFormation: Nordic Journal of Art and Research*, *1*(2), 77–93. doi: http://dx.doi.org/10.7577/information.v1i2.221

IPCC. (2014). *Climate change 2014: Mitigation of climate change contribution of Working Group III to the Fifth Assessment Report of the Intergovernmental Panel on Climate Change*. O. Edenhofer, R. Pichs-Madruga, Y. Sokona, E. Farahani, S. Kadner, K. Seyboth, … J. C. Minx (eds). Retrieved from www.ipcc.ch/pdf/assessment-report/ar5/wg3/ipcc_wg3_ar5_full.pdf

Lai, E. R. & Viering, M. (2012). *Assessing 21st century skills: Integrating research findings*. Retrieved from http://researchnetwork.pearson.com/wp-content/uploads/assessing_21st_century_skills_ncme.pdf

Lyons, N. P. (2010). Reflection and reflective inquiry: Critical issues, evolving conceptualizations, contemporary, claims and future possibilities. In N. P. Lyons (ed.), *Handbook of reflection and reflective inquiry: Mapping a way of knowing for professional reflective inquiry* (pp. 3–22). New York: Springer.

Martin, S. (2008). Sustainable development, systems thinking and professional practice. *Journal of Education for Sustainable Development*, (1), 31–40. doi: 10.1177/097340820800200109.

Mezirow, J. (1990). *Fostering critical reflection in adulthood: A guide to transformative and emancipatory learning*. San Francisco, CA: Jossey-Bass Inc.

Nielsen, L. M. (2013). "Design learning for tomorrow – Design education from kindergarten to PhD". In J. B. Reitan, P. Lloyd, E. Bohemia, L. M. Nielsen, I. Digranes & E. Lutnæs (eds), *Proceedings from the 2nd International Conference for Design Education Researchers (Vols. 1–4)* (pp. i–iii). Oslo: ABM-Media.

Nielsen, L. M. & Brænne, K. (2013). Design literacy for longer lasting products. *Studies in Material Thinking*, *9*(1), 1–9. Retrieved from www.materialthinking.org/papers/125

Norgaard, K. M. (2011). *Living in denial: Climate change, emotions, and everyday life*. Cambridge, MA: MIT Press.

Orr, D. W. (1992). *Ecological literacy: Education and the transition to a postmodern world*. Albany, NY: State University of New York Press.

Porter, T. & Cordoba, J. (2009). Three views of systems theories and their implications for sustainability education. *Journal of Management Education*, *33*(3), 323–347. doi: 10.1177/1052562908323192.

Romm, J., Paulsen, A. & Sevaldson, B. (2014). *Practicing systems oriented design: A guide for businesses and organisations that want to make real changes*. Oslo: The Oslo School of Architecture and Design.

Sandlin, J. A. (2010). Learning to survive the "Shopocalypse": Reverend Billy's anti-consumption "pedagogy of the unknown". *Critical Studies in Education*, *51*(3), 295–311.

Schön, D. A. (1983). *The reflective practitioner: How professionals think in action*. New York: Basic Books.

Schön, D. A. (1992). The theory of inquiry: Dewey's legacy to education. *Curriculum Inquiry*, *22*(2), 119–139. doi: 10.2307/1180029.

Sevaldson, B. (2011). "GIGA-mapping: Visualisation for complexity and systems thinking in design". Paper presented at the MAKING DESIGN MATTER! Proceedings from the *Nordes'11: The 4th Nordic Design Research Conference, Helsinki*. Retrieved from www.nordes.org/opj/index.php/n13/article/view/104

Sevaldson, B. (2013). "Systems oriented design: The emergence and development of a designerly approach to address complexity". In J. B. Reitan, P. Lloyd, E. Bohemia, L. M. Nielsen, I. Digranes & E. Lutnæs (eds), *Proceedings from the 2nd International Conference for Design Education Researchers* (Vol. 4) (pp. 1765–1786). Oslo: ABM-Media.

Simon, H. A. (1969). *The sciences of the artificial (vol. 136)*. Cambridge, MA: MIT Press.

Sterling, S. (2001). *Sustainable education: Re-visioning learning and change (vol. 6)*. Totnes: Green Books for the Schumacher Society.

Sterling, S. (2010). Transformative learning and sustainability: Sketching the conceptual ground. *Learning and Teaching in Higher Education*, (5), 17–33.

Stornaiuolo, A. (2015). Literacy as worldmaking. Multimodality, creativity, cosmopolitanism. In J. Rowsell & K. Pale (eds), *The Routledge handbook of literacy studies* (pp. 561–572). New York: Taylor and Francis.

Systems Oriented Design. (2016). Retrieved from www.systemsorienteddesign.net/

UNEP. (2010). *Here and now! Education for sustainable consumption. Recommendations and guidelines*. V. Thoresen (ed.). Retrieved from www.unep.fr/scp/marrakech/taskforces/pdf/H&NMay2010.pdf

UNEP. (2011). *Visions for change. Recommendations for effective policies on sustainable lifestyles*. Retrieved from www.unep.fr/scp/marrakech/taskforces/pdf/H&NMay2010.pdf

UNESCO. (1997). *A transdisciplinary vision for concerted action*. Retrieved from www.unesco.org/education/tlsf/mods/theme_a/popups/mod01t05s01.html

UNESCO. (2012). *ESD. Building a better, fairer world for the 21st century*. Retrieved from http://unesdoc.unesco.org/images/0021/002166/216673E.pdf

UNESCO. (2014a). *Shaping the future we want. UN Decade of Education for Sustainable Development (2005–2014) Final Report*. Retrieved from http://unesdoc.unesco.org/images/0023/002303/230302e.pdf

UNESCO. (2014b). *Sustainable lifestyles*. Retrieved from www.unesco.org/new/en/education/themes/leading-the-international-agenda/education-for-sustainable-development/sustainable-lifestyles/

Wals, A. E. J. (2011). Learning our way to sustainability. *Journal of Education for Sustainable Development*, (2), 177–186. doi: 10.1177/097340821100500208.

Ziehe, T. (2000). School and youth – A differential relation. Reflections on some blank areas in the current reform discussions. *Young*, 8(1), 54–63.

14 Persuasion and play

Crafting a sustainable culture

Ragnhild Tronstad

The idea that design can fill a rhetorical function and be used in persuasion is not only intriguing but is also increasingly relevant. For example, as the UN reports on climate change have made progressively clear, a drastic cut in unsustainable energy use is our only option to avoid causing an irrevocable climatic catastrophe. In this, each one of us will have to make sacrifices. We can simply not go on living – that is, consuming – the way we are used to. As designer and sustainability strategist Leyla Acaroglu (2013) has convincingly demonstrated, clever design solutions can make some of our sacrifices less painful, correcting our behaviour in ways we are hardly able to notice. This way, design can contribute to making sustainable living less arduous. Another possible way for design to contribute is by making the sustainable option appear more attractive, using strategies of persuasion to make us want to choose sustainability. For one thing is certain: Positive change will not happen by itself and not unless we play along and want to help make it happen.

So, how can design be used rhetorically, in this sense, to persuade? The discourses within design research on persuasive design reveal a range of possible understandings of the term, from the idea that objects may be designed to convey complex arguments to the view that all design is persuasive per se (in that it necessarily, to some degree, influences how we see or interact with our surroundings) (Buchanan, 1985). In this chapter, theories and examples will be discussed in which a rhetorical, persuasive function is articulated in design with the purpose of guiding people to make more sustainable choices. How are the designed artefacts and processes thought to work persuasively? What is their inherent rhetorical function?

The specific focus of the chapter is on how examples and theories of persuasiveness in design connect to concepts of cultural sustainability. As philosopher Rosi Braidotti argues, '[both] the scale and the consequences of climate change are so momentous as to defy representation. Humanities and more specifically cultural research are best suited to fill in this deficit of the social imaginary and help us think the unthinkable' (Braidotti, 2013, p. 160). The recently published report from *COST Action IS1007: Investigating Cultural Sustainability* titled 'Culture *in*, *for* and *as* sustainable development' emphasises the variety of ways in which culture impacts sustainable development. In one perspective, culture complements the conventional three pillars of sustainability (ecology, economy and sociality) as a fourth pillar in its own right (culture *in* sustainable development). Others regard the role of culture in this relationship as that of a mediator, influencing the way we perceive and approach the other three (culture *for* sustainable development). A more foundational view of the role of culture in sustainable development recommends that culture be approached as the very foundation on which a sustainable future must be based (culture *as* sustainable development) (Dessein et al., 2015, pp. 28–29).

A correspondingly broad spectrum of perspectives is reflected in the theoretical discourses on persuasive design that are discussed in this chapter. Interestingly, the first alternative, 'culture *in* sustainable development', where culture is approached as a more or less autonomous, individual pillar, is not as dominant in the design discourses as in other cultural fields. This might be due to the design professions' disposition towards the practically founded and applied in contrast to, for example, the cultural domain of art that historically has valued and strived towards a position of autonomy.

The second perspective, culture *for* sustainable development, is more representative of current trends in persuasive design. However, my main motivation in writing this chapter is to demonstrate how the third perspective, in which culture is regarded as the very foundation for sustainability, is reflected in the cultural phenomenon of play.

In his seminal work *The Ambiguity of Play* (2009 [1997]), Brian Sutton-Smith concludes that the term that most fittingly describes play in its varied and multi-faceted forms is 'variability' (2009 [1997], p. 221). The perspectives from which play has been approached and its nature and possible functions analysed, discussed and theorised in and across a variety of academic disciplines are as numerous as they are heterogenic. In his study, Sutton-Smith unmasks some of the most popular conceptions of play as 'rhetorics of play', representing and promoting specific disciplinary narratives and perspectives. There is no general agreement across disciplines as to what play is or what its function may be, provided that there is a function. We tend to choose the rhetoric of play that best substantiates our argument, writes Sutton-Smith (2009 [1997], pp. 216–217). In order to prevent confusion, therefore, we should acknowledge the existing diversity and be explicit about the particular concept of play to which we subscribe.

In this case, and fundamental to my argument in this chapter, the defining characteristic of play is its structure of intrinsic motivation and reward. In this, I oppose perspectives from which play is seen primarily as a vehicle to achieve some other goal. These perspectives most often ignore what I perceive as the most important aspect of play – 'the simple fact that it is enjoyable in itself' (Csikszentmihalyi, 2014 [1975], p. 136).

With their intrinsic motivational structure, play and games may undoubtedly appear to be apt tools for persuasion, at least at first glance. As we shall see, however, play and game design form a special case in this context and do not conform to the prevailing utilitarian aims of design. On the contrary, laying particular claims to autonomy in being free, disinterested and set apart from 'ordinary' time and space, play and games are phenomena that fundamentally resist being instrumentalised.

Central theories on the ontology of play have pointed to the opposition inherent in all play against having an aim and a purpose to fulfil that is external to play itself, arguing that when play is forced to serve an external purpose, the playful experience is corrupted (Huizinga, 1955 [1938]; Caillois, 1979 [1958]). As a consequence, play and games are not easily utilised as rhetorical tools. As I will argue in this chapter, their persuasive force is intimately connected to our experience of engagement, of being-in-play, which seems to rest upon their being performed for their own sake and not for the sake of obtaining something else. The contested status of the popular marketing strategy of 'gamification' is due partly to this dilemma, as is the problem of using games as a motivational tool in, for example, education. On the positive side, as experienced by Tom Sawyer when contemplating how to escape the paint job his aunt had assigned to him, any boring task can be turned into play provided that we acquire the attitude of doing it *voluntarily* and not because it is demanded or expected of us (Twain, 2010 [1876], pp. 10–16).

The concept of persuasion is itself not straightforward or unambiguous. Its implied meanings span from violent threats to sweet seduction. In the context of this chapter, it is understood in terms of its rhetorical capacities, and while it may border on the manipulative it is never a matter of force.

Persuasive design

Related to the area of product semantics, one understanding of persuasion in design concerns the ability of the designed product to communicate its intended function and area of use to the user. While basic and inherent, this rhetorical performance by artefacts may have wide-reaching implications in terms of scripting and determining the way we behave and interact with our surroundings. Thus already, on this level, design may have a decisive persuasive function, subtly influencing our lives and futures.

Arguing that persuasion in the field of design is not restricted to the communication of designer intent but is an integral part of how we relate to artefacts, design researcher Johan Redström approaches the rhetorical dimension of design from a slightly different angle. He suggests that designers take advantage of the implicit dialogue or negotiation that is always taking place between an object and its user and expose it in order to ask rhetorical questions about the object and its use (Redström, 2006, p. 117). To illustrate his argument, he offers two examples from his own practice – The Energy Curtain and The Erratic Radio – both demanding a sacrifice from the user in order to function properly. The Energy Curtain has a solar panel on its outside and fibre optics woven into the fabric on the inside that can light up the room in the evening, provided that the curtain has been left down to collect energy from the sun during the day. In other words, if the user wants light in the room in the evening, she is not able to enjoy the sunlight lightening up the room during the day. The Erratic Radio is sensitive to energy consumption in its close vicinity and will be 'disturbed' when this reaches too high a level. Therefore, the user needs to be conscious about the other electric appliances in use in order to operate it (ibid., p. 119). The Energy Curtain and the Erratic Radio are examples of objects that persuade the user to act in a certain manner; to do so, they present her with a 'procedural argument' inspiring reflection (see below). In this, they are related to the movement or attitude within design activism identified in Anthony Dunne's *Hertzian Tales* (2008 [1999]) as *critical design* (frequently also referred to as *speculative, conceptual* or *discursive design* or as *design fiction*.) It could be argued that if the purpose of objects like these is to make the user think and reflect rather than to be of any actual use, they should not be considered as examples of persuasive design but rather to belong in the art domain. Dunne and Fiona Raby counter such an assumption in their *Critical Design FAQ*, asserting that

> [Critical Design] is definitely not art. It might borrow heavily from art in terms of methods and approaches but that's it. We expect art to be shocking and extreme. Critical Design needs to be closer to the everyday, that's where its power to disturb comes from.
>
> (Dunne & Raby, 2007)

Similar techniques of estrangement and replacement of everyday situations and objects have, of course, also been widely employed in art contexts throughout the last hundred years within avant-garde art movements that specifically aimed to make art as a category obsolete, integrating it into the practices of everyday life (e.g. Bürger 1984 [1974]). If there is indeed a line to be drawn between art on the one hand and critical or speculative design on the other, it seems to rest on the view of art belonging to a separate, autonomous domain of life, a view to which few today would subscribe. However artificial the difference appears, it may function as a reminder of the important connection to everyday life implied in such critical design practices, grounded as they are in actual use and a fundamental relationship to users rather than audiences.

Persuasive technology

Design with intent (DwI) is an area of persuasive design where design is openly intended to result in certain user behaviour (Lockton et al., 2008). It relates to the field of persuasive technology or *captology* (where 'capt' is an acronym for *computers as persuasive technology*), founded by the social scientist B. J. Fogg in 1998. Fogg defines persuasive technology as 'any interactive computer system designed to change people's attitudes or behaviors' (Fogg,

2002, p. 1) 'without using coercion or deception' (Fogg, 2002, p. 15). He admits, though, that the line between persuasion and coercion is not easily drawn and that there are examples of technological persuasion where the human actor is rather forced to behave in a certain manner in order to be allowed to participate in the interaction at all (Fogg, 2002, p. 21, note 2). In order not to confuse persuasion with coercion, it might be instructive to stress the rhetorical dimension of persuasion as the differentiating factor that distinguishes between the two. Like seduction, persuasion is a rhetorical mode. Coercion, however, is not.

Interactive media and technology have particular advantages over non-interactive media and technology when it comes to persuasion. One advantage is their capacity to continuously evaluate the overall situation, which allows them to adjust their persuasive strategies according to the input and responses of the person with whom they are interacting (Fogg, 2002, p. 6). In this, they have a certain rhetorical flexibility that non-interactive artefacts lack. The ubiquity of mobile media, such as smart phones, adds another advantage in terms of potential persuasive impact. Ubiquitous media provide the opportunity of timing one's messages so that the target can be addressed in the exact moment for persuasion to be successful, a feature that in studies of rhetoric is known as *kairos* (Fogg & Eckles, 2007). Thus, being constantly available to our smartphones makes us more vulnerable to their persuasion than to the persuasion of stationary desktop computers. Through web surfing, shopping and socialising online, we feed our smartphones with personal information. As it is increasingly commonplace to allow our phones to track our physical whereabouts through geo-location technology, this information travels with us as we move about in the physical world bringing our phones with us. Analysing and comparing these data, marketers may use them to target us when we are the most available or vulnerable to persuasion; that is, when the opportunity exists for us to immediately act upon the information we receive.

In interacting with users, critical design and persuasive technology have the capacity to make procedural arguments. This is a term coined to capture the rhetorical structure and affordances of a genre that combines the flexible responsiveness of interactive technology with the cultural consciousness of critical design – *serious games*.

Persuasive games and procedural rhetoric

In his 2007 study *Persuasive Games*, game designer and theorist Ian Bogost examines how persuasion takes place in serious games, that is, computer games that serve a purpose other than pure entertainment. Analysing examples of educational games, advertising games and games designed to support a political cause or campaign, he demonstrates the capacity of digital media to present persuasive arguments in the form of processes and recommends that we approach the technique as a particular type of rhetoric:

> I suggest the name *procedural rhetoric* for the practice of using processes persuasively, just as verbal rhetoric is the practice of using oratory persuasively and visual rhetoric is the practice of using images persuasively.
>
> (Bogost, 2008, p. 125)

According to the philosopher Kenneth Burke, the basic function of rhetoric is 'to form attitudes or to induce actions in other human agents' (Burke, 1969, p. 41). In Burke's theory, language and symbols are sites where identification processes may occur and where attitudes, concepts and beliefs may be negotiated (King, 2010, p. 9). In the procedural rhetoric of video games described by Bogost, the symbolic medium or 'site' for identification and negotiation is made up by game rules, computational procedures and processes.

> Video games represent processes in the material world – war, urban planning, sports, and so forth – and create new possibility spaces for exploring these topics. That representation is composed of the rules themselves. We encounter the meaning of games by exploring their possibility spaces. And we explore their possibility spaces through play.
>
> (Bogost, 2008, p. 121)

In a similar manner, when design researcher Redström, as previously described, introduced a new set of rules to a familiar situation, changing the way we interact with everyday artefacts such as a radio and a curtain, he prescribed them with new possibility spaces for the users to explore. The space was defined by a novel set of affordances and restrictions that the user had to determine to be able to meaningfully interact with the objects. Encountering a familiar artefact under such circumstances, we are forced to reconsider our familiar conception of it. This is a situation in which we are likely to allow the artefact to speak to us. Thus, a new possibility space may function as a facilitator for the object to have rhetorical impact.

In later years, interactive entertainment media, such as computer and video games, have presented us with a medley of new possibility spaces to explore through simulation. The propensity of game worlds to provide alternative possibility spaces for players to discover is a feature with interesting rhetorical potential. Instead of using verbal arguments and reasoning in trying to persuade people to a more sustainable lifestyle and explaining for them the consequences of over-spending the world's resources, game designers may place us within simulations of possible worlds where we experience these consequences as direct responses to our simulated actions in the world.

In the introduction to this chapter, I referred to Acaroglu's inspirational TED talk on how clever design solutions can facilitate sustainable choices in people's everyday lives. One of her main arguments is that the environmental impact of a product often hinges on a complex set of circumstances not always correctly reflected in the popular conceptions or in Acaroglu's terms, 'environmental folklore', dictating which products or behaviour are considered the most 'sustainable'. Evidently, in typical everyday interactions with household goods 'user decisions (or the lack of them) are responsible for a significant proportion of the products' environmental impact' (Lockton et al., 2010, p. 2). To make educated choices, we may have to replace the 'environmental folklore' with a more profound understanding of how our behaviour affects the environment.

The advantage of procedural rhetoric in this respect is its ability to handle complex questions using dynamic, interactive simulations to realistically represent choices, as we may have to deal with them in the physical world. For example, in educational games such as *My Sustainable House* (2006), children may experiment hands-on with basic sustainable living and more advanced principles of sustainability by constructing their own sustainable houses and towns. Similar games exist aimed at professional building planners, providing a simulated work environment in which the knowledge and expertise of all professions involved in constructing a sustainable indoor environment are represented as parameters. Here, a variety of complex building strategies can be tried out and their consequences experienced, almost intuitively and completely free of risk (Bloom et al., 2015). Such simulated computer-generated environments constructed for learning purposes are one strand of the media phenomenon often referred to as *gamification*.

Gamification

Gamification is a contested concept in many respects. It is most widely known as a marketing strategy in which the consumer is awarded points or other symbolic rewards as a means to secure his or her loyalty to the marketed product. Examples are geo-location apps such as Foursquare and Facebook Places that reward their users with points every time they log in to specific venues. Similar strategies are also used outside of commercial marketing. Sometimes called gamification and other times promoted under different labels, these are strategies purporting to adopt the motivational structure of games and to use it in the service of goods such as health or education or to solve complex environmental problems. As game designer, theorist and enthusiast Jane McGonigal argues, cleverly designed game structures may be just what we need to 'fix' a broken reality and change what is wrong in our world (McGonigal, 2011).

As a marketing strategy, gamification has been criticised for misusing the very concept of 'game' when in reality, the reward structures it promotes are but a small and rather insignificant part of the motivational potential inherent in game structures and game design (Deterding, 2010; Robertson, 2010). In a brilliantly illuminating rhetorical analysis of why 'gamification' is such a deceitful concept, Bogost suggests we stop using it altogether and replace it with a term that better describes what it essentially is – *exploitationware* (2011b). Framed as exploitationware, gamification emerges as an embarrassingly frank reminder that the impact of culture on development is not always sustainable (cf. Dessin et al., 2015, p. 52).

On the more sympathetic side, gamification may also be employed as a strategy to serve sustainable causes, for example, helping people to establish a more sustainable lifestyle. Designed to persuade people to act in accordance with principles of sustainability, games like these are seldom very sustainable *games*, though. As I will argue in the following section, games and play are corrupted and stripped of their most characteristic trait when used as a means to obtain an external goal: they cease being playful and fun. In fact, games represent a particularly interesting and instructive case of cultural sustainability, as functional gameplay is by definition sustainable, producing what it consumes in the same interactive move.

Play and intrinsic motivation

Psychologist Mihaly Csikszentmihaly has famously described the autotelic, that is, the intrinsically motivating and rewarding structure of play as a state of 'flow' (2014 [1975]).

> Flow denotes the holistic sensation present when we act with total involvement. It is the kind of feeling after which one nostalgically says: 'that was fun', or 'that was enjoyable'. It is the state in which action follows upon action according to an internal logic which seems to need no conscious intervention on our part. We experience it as a unified flowing from one moment to the next, in which we feel in control of our action, and in which there is little distinction between self and environment; between stimulus and response; or between past, present and future.
>
> (Csikszentmihaly, 2014 [1975], pp. 136–137)

Flow is not restricted to play activities but can occur in any kind of activity with clear and non-contradictory rules 'where one can cope, at least theoretically, with all the demands for action' (2014 [1975], p. 143) The deep involvement that characterises flow relies on a set of circumstances that must be fulfilled, of which the most important is that the challenges posed in the situation are in balance with our skills to handle them. Importantly, this is a subjective *perception* of what the challenges and skills are (2014 [1975], p. 147). Thus the parameters defining the situation may be objectively or subjectively adjusted to enhance the chance of flow to occur, even by changing our attitude to the situation, as we saw in the example paraphrased in the introduction to this chapter from *The Adventures of Tom Sawyer*. Closely related to the concept of flow, in *The Craftsman* (2008), sociologist Richard Sennett investigates craftsmanship as an attitude towards one's occupation that can be acquired by almost anyone through disciplined practice: 'the rhythm of routine in craftsmanship draws on childhood experience of play, and almost all children can play well' (2008, p. 268). For the craftsman, work is experienced as a 'self-motivated, sustained activity' that 'steadily adds value to his life' (2008, pp. 264–265). Connecting craftsmanship to self-governance, Sennett sees in the craftsman an extended capacity to take care of his world and environment. Finally, flow is recreational. In flow, whether it occurs in play or the kind of self-sustainable work situation implied in Sennett's concept of crafting, we are taken out of ourselves, temporarily forgetting our identities and problems (Sennett, 2008, p. 254; Csikszentmihalyi, 2014 [1975], p. 146).

In Bogost's theory of persuasive games, the player may learn to cope with environmental issues through the procedural rhetoric of video games. To Bogost, persuasion is a process that involves reason and dialogue. In his book, Bogost seems more concerned with how to secure rhetorical clarity and impact when designing persuasive games than with the qualitative experience of playing, however. Arguing that a meaningful coherence between message and game rules can only benefit the player's enjoyment of the game, the experienced scholar and game designer appears to ignore a rather significant aspect of what makes play and games into treasured experiences – that they are not founded in or bound by but represent a relief from reason. In an illuminating passage, Bogost asks if it would not be 'better' for a child to learn to discern through gameplay the manipulative techniques that make amusement parks appear magical compared to being manipulated by the same techniques to blindly desire every plush animal that is for sale in the park (Bogost, 2007b, p. 182). From the long-term perspective of an adult engaged in bringing up a responsible citizen, he might be right. A child, however, would likely consider the instant gratification of its desire to have a plush animal to be the better choice.

The conflict of interests between adult and child is one thing, mirroring the lopsided balance between 'useful' and 'fun' that often characterise serious games. The apparent prejudice against the manipulative as something to be avoided in the context of persuasive games is another. Bogost criticises Fogg's captology for seeking to persuade

> without engaging users in a discourse about the behaviour itself or the logics that would recommend such actions or beliefs.... Despite Fogg's suggestion that *captology* acronymizes 'computers as persuasive technologies', the phrase itself conjures the sense of *capture*, of arrest and incarceration by an authority. A better name for Fogg's work would perhaps be *manipulative technology*.
>
> (2007b, pp. 61–62)

To experience play, however, do we not have to let go of control and allow ourselves the risk of being manipulated? Evidently, Bogost's ideal player is not one mindlessly indulging in gameplay, allowing himself to be played but one taking pleasure in discovering and learning about the world in which we live – how it functions or how it ought to function. Bogost's favourite examples of persuasive games are openly didactic games that have a clear and explicit agenda. Not being played for play's own sake, such games are vulnerable to the mechanism described in the introduction to this chapter – that when play is forced to serve an external purpose, the playful experience is corrupted. Such games seldom succeed in giving the player an exhilarating experience of being fully absorbed and totally devoted to the task at hand. However, this is nothing more than we usually expect of a good game.

The well-played game: play as a model for cultural sustainability

Game designer and fun theorist Bernie DeKoven writes: 'When we are playing well, we are at our best. We are fully engaged, totally present, and at the same time, we are only playing' (DeKoven, 2002, p. 3). The double consciousness he describes is key to excellence in play. It is a matter of attitude rather than skills and explains why having an outside purpose may ruin the experience of play. Playing to obtain a goal external to play itself, we are no longer 'only playing'. We are no longer fully contained in play.

Yet the attitude of play also implies that activities primarily performed to fulfil an external purpose, such as ordinary work tasks, can be framed and experienced to be motivating and rewarding in themselves, as described by Sennett in his treatise on crafting. Although the primary purpose of serious games may be educational, this does not exclude the possibility of experiencing flow during play. However, in popular opinion, what defines the value of such games is their educational function rather than their potential to produce flow. By emphasising the autotelic structure of play, my point is that the inherently persuasive structure of intrinsic motivation and reward that games provide has a value of its own. Furthermore, it presents us with a model for sustainable living.

As I have attempted to show in this chapter, play and games perform a variety of functions in regards to cultural sustainability. In contrast to the openly didactic focus of Bogost's persuasive games, the ambition, function and meaning of critical design objects such as Redström's Energy Curtain and Erratic Radio is hardly to instruct users on how to cope with environmental issues. More ambiguously, they direct attention to the topic by engaging the users in play. Here, we experience play *in* sustainable development.

Taking up the utilitarian perspectives of persuasive technology and DwI, persuasive games and gamification are cultural forms that investigate how video games and elements from game design may be employed as media through which to promote, teach and facilitate sustainability in people's everyday lives. When promoting a lifestyle that is careful and conscious about not spending too much of the world's limited resources, this is play *for* sustainable development.

However, play itself is not a limited resource but is in principle infinitely renewable. As Dessein et al. describes the third role of culture in sustainable development, it may thus provide 'a new paradigm to the question of sustainable development' (2015, p. 31). Already in 1975, Csikszentmihalyi connected the intrinsic motivation of play to the question of sustainability. He wrote: 'As long as we continue to motivate people mainly through extrinsic rewards like money and status, we rely on zero-sum payoffs that result in inequalities as well as the depletion of scarce resources' (2014 [1975], p. 150).

Play *as* sustainable development invites us to acknowledge and appreciate its intrinsic value. Allowed to play out in its own right, it offers recreation and rejuvenation. The appreciation of intrinsic motivation and reward that the player and the craftsman have in common is, fundamentally, an aesthetic of sustainment. Therefore, rather than forcing play to act in the service of an external goal we could repurpose its inherent recreational structure as a model for cultural sustainability. Spending nothing but itself, it has, in principle, the capacity to motivate and recreate indefinitely.

References

Acaroglu, L. (2013). *Leyla Acaroglu: Paper beats plastic? How to rethink environmental folklore* [Video file]. Retrieved from www.ted.com/talks/leyla_acaroglu_paper_beats_plastic_how_to_rethink_environmental_folklore?source=facebook#.UvqOA9-cvu4.facebook

Bloom, M. F., Bogost, I. & Dunn, C. P. (2015). Serious games: Crafting sustainable solutions through play. Conference presentation, AIA Convention 2015, May 14–16, Atlanta, GA.

Bogost, I. (2007a). Persuasive games on mobile devices. In B. J. Fogg & D. Eckles (eds), *Mobile persuasion: 20 perspectives on the future of behavior change* (pp. 29–37). Stanford, CA: Stanford Captology Media.

Bogost, I. (2007b). *Persuasive games: The expressive power of videogames.* Cambridge: MIT Press.

Bogost, I. (2008). The rhetoric of video games. In K. Salen (ed.), *The ecology of games: Connecting youth, games, and learning* (pp. 117–140). The John D. and Catherine T. MacArthur Foundation Series on Digital Media and Learning. Cambridge: MIT Press.

Bogost, I. (2011a). Gamification is bullshit. [Web log]. Retrieved from www.bogost.com/blog/gamification_is_bullshit.shtml

Bogost, I. (2011b). Persuasive games: Exploitationware. In *Gamasutra: The art and business of making games.* [Online magazine] Retrieved from www.gamasutra.com/view/feature/134735/persuasive_games_exploitationware.php

Braidotti, R. (2013). *The posthuman.* Cambridge: Polity Press.

Buchanan, R. (1985). Declaration by design: Rhetoric, argument, and demonstration in design practice. *Design Issues, 2*(1), 4–22.

Bürger, P. (1984 [1974]). *Theory of the avant-garde.* Minneapolis: University of Minnesota Press.

Burke, K. (1969). *A rhetoric of motives.* Berkeley and Los Angeles: University of California Press.

Caillois, R. (1979 [1958]). *Man, play, and games* [Les jeux et les hommes], translated by M. Barash. New York: Schocken Books.

Csikszentmihalyi, M. (2014 [1975]). Play and intrinsic rewards. In *Flow and the founda-tions of positive psychology* (pp. 135–151). Dordrecht: Springer Science and Business Media.

DeKoven, B. (2002). *The well-played game. A playful path to wholeness.* Lincoln: Writers Club Press.

Dessein, J., Soini, K., Fairclough, G. & Horlings, L. (2015). *Culture in, for and as sus-tainable development. Conclusions from the Cost Action IS1007 Investigating Cultural Sustainability.* Jyväskylä: University of Jyväskylä, Finland.

Deterding, S. (2010). Pawned. Gamification and its discontents. Presentation at *Playful 2012*, London 24 September 2010. [Slides]. Retrieved from www.slideshare.net/dings/pawned-gamification-and-its-discontents

Dunne, A. (2008 [1999]). *Hertzian tales.* Cambridge: MIT Press.

Dunne A. & Raby, F. (2007). *Critical design FAQ.* Retrieved from www.dunnean-draby.co.uk/content/bydandr/13/0

Fogg, B. J. (2002). *Persuasive technology: Using computers to change what we think and do.* San Francisco: Morgan Kaufmann Publishers.

Fogg, B. J. & Eckles, D. (eds). (2007). *Mobile persuasion: 20 perspectives on the future of behavior change.* Stanford, CA: Stanford Captology Media.

Huizinga, J. (1955 [1938]). *Homo Ludens. A study of the play-element in culture.* Boston: Beacon Press.

King, M. (2010). Procedural rhetorics – rhetoric's procedures: Rhetorical peaks and what it means to win the game. In C. Haynes & J. R. Holmevik (eds), *Currents in electronic literacy, special issue 'Gaming Across the Curriculum'.* Texas: University of Texas at Austin, Digital Writing and Research Lab. Retrieved from http://currents.cwrl.utexas.edu/2010/king_procedural_rhetorics_rhetorics_procedures

Lockton, D., Harrison, D. & Stanton, N. (2008). Design with intent: Persuasive tech-nology in a wider context. In H. Oinas-Kukkonen, P. Hasle, M. Harjumaa, K. Segerståhl & P. Øhrstrøm (eds), *PERSUASIVE 2008, LNCS 5033* (pp. 274–278). Berlin, Heidelberg: Springer-Verlag.

Lockton, D., Harrison, D. & Stanton, N. (2010). Concept generation for persuasive design. Poster Proceedings from PERSUASIVE 2010, 5th International Confer-ence on Persuasive Technology, Copenhagen, June 7–9, Series A Research Papers Vol.A44, June 2010. Retrieved from http://bura.brunel.ac.uk/bit-stream/2438/4679/1/Fulltext.pdf

McGonigal, J. (2011). *Reality is broken. Why games make us better and how they can change the world.* New York: The Penguin Press.

My Sustainable House. (2006). [Computer game]. Sust. Architecture and Design Scot-land/Screenmedia.

Redström, J. (2006). Persuasive design: Fringes and foundations. In W. A. Ijsselsteijn, Y. A. W. de Kort, C. Midden, B. Eggen & E. van den Hoven (eds), *Persuasive 2006, LNCS 3962* (pp. 112–122). Berlin, Heidelberg: Springer-Verlag.

Robertson, M. (2010, October 6). Can't play, won't play. [Web log]. Retrieved from www.hideandseek.net/2010/10/06/cant-play-wont-play//

Sennett, R. (2008). *The craftsman.* New Haven and London: Yale University Press.

Sutton-Smith, B. (2009 [1997]). *The ambiguity of play.* Cambridge: Harvard University Press.

Twain, M. (2010 [1876]). *The adventures of Tom Sawyer.* 135th Anniversary Edition. Berkeley, Los Angeles and London: University of California Press.

15 Teaching cultural sensitivity at architecture schools for more sustainable buildings

Lessons from reconstruction

Sabrina Brenner

Introduction

This chapter addresses and questions what skills architects need to be able to work in changing environments. This is done by having a close look at rebuilding processes in the aftermath of natural disasters. In the case of a disaster, where houses are destroyed, numerous agencies and nongovernmental organisations (NGOs) work together with architects from countries all around the world. They collaborate together to design and build new homes for affected communities. Unfortunately, all too often, this turns into a disaster itself. Why is this? And is there a way to change this situation besides simply halting the creation of buildings in unknown contexts? As this chapter will discuss, there are both benefits and difficulties with having an architect involved in these processes. Critical for the future success of architects involved in unfamiliar contexts is the education provided in our architecture schools. What skills do architects need to work, for example, in a post-disaster reconstruction habitat?

Furthermore, the chapter points out the opportunities that lie in an exchange of knowledge between local communities and architects and the benefits of having both parties integrated into the process of participation from the very beginning. These include, amongst other things, building traditions, building codes, the use of materials (question of local availability), the issue of recycling and reuse and adaptation to current and expected future conditions (climatic, geophysical, hydrologic and meteorological). The strong faith in technology of today's society, according to Frampton (1980), emerges from the common belief of modernity in having the ability to control or master nature. It can lead to the conviction that everything can be solved with technical solutions. For example, the simplicity of cooling and heating air technically has contributed to careless attitudes towards orientation, climate, the building envelope and material performance. This is followed by a huge number of buildings that seem to be designed to exist on any site and thus are appropriate for none (cf. Rifkind, 2013, p. 20). Most certainly there is a reason why some local building traditions have been around for thousands of years without significant changes. Therefore, it is important not to displace these traditions before fully understanding them. This is just one aspect of coping with a design for an unfamiliar context, and future architects need to be prepared for this working environment.

The ability of architects to design for different contexts constitutes an important issue especially in light of the fact that the world is becoming increasingly smaller. First, this means architects are working more and more internationally, and second, it means the effects of architectural projects worldwide – for instance, regarding energy consumption – can be felt anywhere. For example, if people in China adapt their houses to climatic conditions, this could lead to a reduction of the energy used for cooling the buildings, which, in turn, has a positive effect on global warming. One could even take a step further and state that this would consequently also be felt in India, by a reduction in weather-related extreme events. All of these aspects can be considered useful if and when architects engage themselves with this planning environment. As a result, a knowledge exchange between professionals could be formed that could improve the global building technologies and planning culture. 'The ideal vision of a pure and optimized dwelling on an abstract flat ground is transformed into a house that seeks to embrace its climate, its physical setting, its architectural heritage, and its local culture' (Bone, 2013, p. 16).

The context

According to Le Corbusier (1923), 'A house is a machine for living in [Une maison est une machine à habiter]', which means it should be designed to provide everything that defines a 'place to live in'. This includes shelter and safety, just as the creation of an environment that offers the possibility of leading a fulfilling life. Based on this, the efficiency of a design must consider the complete range of programme issues, including cultural, emotional and spiritual. This modern paradigm provides a valuable guide for placing cultural resources into context (cf. Stein, 2013, p. 199). Walter Gropius claimed in 1939 that

> studies in the history of art and architecture, intellectual and analytical in character make the student familiar with the conditions and reasons which have brought about the visual expression of the different periods: i.e. the changes in philosophy, in politics, and in the means of production caused by new inventions.
>
> (Gropius, 1954, p. 62)

Planning in the sense of 'context sensitive building design' features many aspects, including climate and culture. For architects, this approach means designing with a sensitivity to communities' needs. Context-sensitive building design is nothing new. Already at the mid-century period at the turn of the twentieth century in modernism, a startlingly large number of architects were concerned with issues known today as environmental. These topics covered material efficiencies, the relationship between site and climate, or other forms of energy-efficient potential (cf. Barber, 2013, p. 188). The only difference with the approach today is the reasons leading to it. Architects in the twenty-first century have to deal with major topics, such as climate change, energy savings caused by a shortage of fossil fuels, a scarcity of resources and the growing gap between rich and poor both between and within countries. On top of this, we now have the situation where architects work on projects all over the world. Thus, more often than not, they work outside of their own cultural and environmental contexts. Special challenges exist in this field of design and are unfortunately all too often undervalued within the discipline. A good example for pointing out this problem is the field of reconstruction after disasters in developing (low-income) countries. In many of these projects, architects are involved in rebuilding houses in a very sensitive context for vulnerable people who have lost their homes. Sadly, it has to be said that the success of these efforts is often very questionable. Even worse, it is not uncommon for reconstruction projects to put the beneficiaries in a position more severe and vulnerable than where they were before. One reason for this is that architects are not familiar with the contexts of the places for which they design. This includes the culture, building technologies, traditional materials and the local climate. So what lessons can we learn from rebuilding projects as we look into the future? And what are the lessons we need to teach our architecture students so that they are qualified to work in different contexts?

> How exactly can the architect 'add value' to the project? What can a formally trained professional bring, what can he/she do better than the mason who has always built the houses in the village? This is the central question. We architects are outsiders and we may possibly never understand the villagers fully, because we are from a different region and have a different background, but at the same time we have know-how that might be of relevance.
>
> (Wemhöner, as cited in Tauber, 2014, p. 202f.)

Architectural education

There is a certain set of skills that architecture students must have to work in contexts outside of their usual environments, but as a number of representatives in this field have seen, many of these are not adequately taught in classical training at our universities. According to Tauber (2014, p. 217ff.), five assumptions are taught at today's architecture schools both implicitly and explicitly as described below. From these assumptions, Tauber (2014) concluded that architecture students turn into professionals who are not adequately capable of facilitating the realisation of people-oriented and sustainable housing. This is primarily with regards to housing in the rural post-disaster context but presumptively can be expanded to some extent to other areas as well. As a result, these architects are of little use to NGOs working on reconstruction projects. Naturally, these assumptions show a worst-case scenario and do not apply for all architecture students without exception, yet the matter is an issue that needs to be addressed.

(I) Tauber's (2014) first assumption was that architects can hardly learn anything from the past. This approach poses an idea opposite that of traditional building cultures. While the latter is based on the transfer of knowledge and findings from generation to generation as well as the repetition of designs, today's teaching often premises that each problem is new and has to be resolved from scratch. Davis (2006) supported this by stating that the formal education of architects has 'traditionally promoted an attitude toward professional expertise that seems opposed to the idea of shared, embedded knowledge' (p. 231).

(II) The second assumption is that the expertise of the architect is better than that of 'ordinary people'. This is taught rather implicitly and leads to the attitude that architects must maintain control over other participants of a design or building process, such as builders, craftsmen and the clients or communities for which they design. Again this opposes the idea of traditional building cultures, which thrives on the sharing of cultural values and habits. Instead, in a sense, it trains the future architect to decline his or her own culture apart from the effect it might have on his or her dealing with and attitude towards other cultures.

The following two assumptions are closely related to each other and are also linked to the one just described.

(III) In architecture schools, there is often the belief that the architect, as the 'star designer', is more important than other professionals of the built environment, due to curricula that demote most other participants. An aspect of this issue is contained in the statement of Meinhard von Gerkan (as cited in Weiland, 2008; translated from German): 'The enthusiasm for personal fulfilment, setting construction marks that point beyond the own lifespan is probably laid-out in the soul of each architect' (p. 1).

(IV) On top of this, there is the idea that 'object building' is more important and a more dignified design task than the design of a conventional house is. As per Tauber (2014), when looking around in architecture schools, there are scarcely any design projects that deal with ordinary (informal) housing in either a rural or an urban context. Rather, architecture students design huge public buildings often with high symbolic value, such as museums, operas, theatres or stadiums, or they simply pick design projects where they create rather unusual private buildings, such as villas, galleries, artists' studios, luxury boat houses, wineries and holiday chalets. This list could be continued endlessly, but it is enough at this juncture to demonstrate where the preferences of many architecture students as well as project chairs are.

(V) The last assumption is that learning can effectively happen in a studio, away from construction sites, buildings, craftsmen and especially the community.

Usually students sit in workspaces at their schools or universities in front of their computers or drawing boards without even having a look at their own surroundings and the reality that exists just outside the door. Davis (2006) points out that the current living environment and daily reality might be the best teachers for architecture students.

According to Tauber (2014), another distortion within architectural education is that architecture students are mainly taught to improve their visual competences but hardly at all to develop communicative abilities or intercultural awareness. This would be a basic precondition for the ability and willingness to think and work on an interdisciplinary basis within diverse cultural contexts. Thus, architecture as it is taught today does not really provide students with the skills required for a working context where it is essential for them to work closely together with a community. An architect who sees his work as an individual pursuit and as the expression of his design preferences cannot work in a context where the design has a community's ownership of expression (cf. Vivek, as cited in Tauber, 2014). It is crucial for architects to understand that they are not 'experts' who automatically have the right answers for all of the tasks and challenges with which they will be confronted. All of these conclusions are not just true for the context of reconstruction after disasters.

> There are many missing pieces that are not given importance in classical training, even though, I would argue that they are very relevant, not only in a post-disaster project, but also, for example, in a regular housing project in Britain.
>
> (Graham, as cited in Tauber, 2014)

Thus, most of these topics that are not given importance in architectural education are relevant everywhere to every architect or professional working on any project in any possible design context. It is therefore apparent that a strong need exists to revise the current curricula to educate students on context sensitivity regarding culture, tradition or the environment.

Who is involved in reconstruction processes (the architect's role)?

In rural (and urban) environments in developing countries, it is still common that people build their homes without any professionals and above all without architects. In other words, people living in these 'non-Western' countries do have the expertise to build houses. This is contrary to 'Western' societies, where formal professionals usually guide building processes. These opposing approaches can lead to difficulties and raise problems when it comes to reconstruction. This is an important issue that plays a decisive role when answering the question of who should be involved in a planning process for post-disaster housing. Jha et al. (2010) defined five different approaches for reconstruction, namely the 'Cash Approach', 'Owner-Driven Reconstruction', 'Community-Driven Reconstruction', 'Agency-Driven Reconstruction in-Situ' and

'Agency-Driven Reconstruction in Relocated Site' (p. 101). They will not be explained in detail here, but all of these approaches differ primarily regarding the selection of participants. Most projects involve at least three actors: the government, the community or villagers and an NGO. And it depends on these actors whether an architect is involved or not. In a study that Gertrud Tauber and her team conducted in Keezhakazakudy-Tsunami Nagar in India, they found that 80 percent of the villagers they interviewed did not even know what an architect was (cf. Tauber, 2014, p. 175f.). The fact that this was the outcome of field research after a post-disaster housing project including an architect was completed makes this finding even more outstanding, an aspect that will be discussed in more detail below. The question of whether architects are needed in reconstruction processes is widely debated, and a number of researchers and practitioners argue that this depends on the project. In any case, NGOs frequently have difficulties in finding good staff, so architects needed for the planning of these projects often lack the skills they need to work in this specific context. Two main factors that cause problems are inexperience and ignorance, especially towards cultural peculiarities, such as local building cultures. These are both issues that state a problem for any construction project in any corner of the world (cf. Wemhöner, as cited in Tauber, 2014, p. 205), even beyond reconstruction in developing countries.

Another important issue that should be discussed at this point is the relevance of community involvement. The recognition has been made that people's involvement in a project is linked to its success (however defined). This led to the so-called participatory turn in development studies and practice in the 1980s and was the root of community participation in this field (cf. Dodman & Miltin, 2011). Another reason for this big turning point was a 40-year history of development activities following a top-down approach that failed in improving the lives and livelihoods of the world's poor. This was due to the fact that the issue of context specificity or local knowledge was not taken into account. Proof exists

> that people have the capacity to build houses that are more likely to respond to their needs than are houses provided by external agencies if adequate financial and technical support and other enabling conditions (e.g. good supervision, massive training of local masons and access to subsidised construction materials) are provided.
>
> (Duyne Barenstein, 2014, p. 161)

For example, through the use of locally available or recycled construction materials, an owner-driven approach can be more cost effective as well as faster compared to other strategies. However, an owner-driven approach does not necessarily lead to a sustainable built environment and resilient community as has been shown in a huge number of reconstruction projects. This is due to the fact that the application of local knowledge and building technologies may be limited as a result of inadequate building capacity or a lack of information, building codes and guidelines (cf. Duyne Barenstein, 2014). Therefore, as Lizzaralde et al. (2014) stated, the organisational design, defined as the composition of the team that will carry out the projects as well as the appropriate distribution of roles and responsibilities within that process team, 'must embody a proper balance between the technical, social, cultural and administrative issues' (p. 23). This means it is of great relevance who is involved in a reconstruction project, and it is also important for each of these participants to bring the skills that are needed to achieve a good result. The architect is one of these participants who can play an active role in the process.

Reconstruction projects

According to the World Bank and the Global Faculty for Disaster Reduction and Recovery (GFDRR), a number of risks and challenges exist with regards to housing reconstruction (cf. Jha et al., 2010, p. 168). In some cases, a lack of local knowledge exists with regards to both appropriate housing design and current construction practices. This can lead to the use of building technologies that are poorly adapted to changing local risks. On top of this, building technologies that are imported and use materials not locally available often require more energy to produce comfortable indoor conditions. This may cause an increase in costs and have a negative environmental impact. In this case, the design and construction can contribute to local as well as global environmental damage. A shortage in building materials and skilled labour, partly due to imported building technologies, results in poor construction quality in structures that are vulnerable, fragile and expensive to maintain. Thus, beneficiaries are exposed to an even greater risk than before the disaster occurred. Another issue that is connected to all of those previously mentioned is the incompatibility of the housing designs or building technologies with local traditions or with the local community's willingness to change. In the worst case, this results in a loss of cultural identity and heritage while also having negative impacts on people's well-being and quality of life. Sometimes the reasons for this are building codes and regulations, usually set by the government, that prohibit the use of local building technologies or do not adequately incorporate the use of local materials and practices. However, in any case, this depends to a great extent on the people who are involved in the design process and therefore also on the architect involved. Vernacular houses are often well adapted to climate conditions and environmental changes, including extreme events, such as disasters. Therefore, existing local building practices as well as cultural, economic and climatic, geophysical, hydrologic and meteorological conditions should all be taken into consideration while choosing the housing design and building technologies for reconstruction projects.

Houses

A large amount of research work concerning reconstruction projects in the aftermaths of disasters concludes the following: All decisions that have to be made regarding building technologies, and housing design should be made in close collaboration with the affected community. Duyne Barenstein and Pittet (2014) pointed out that, in a perfect world, 'a careful participatory analysis of the local housing culture and of the strengths and weaknesses of communities' building practices would define the reconstruction approach to be adopted and the building technologies to be promoted with the aim to "build back better"' (p. 120). Additionally, communities should be empowered to rebuild their own houses on their own through the provision of the required technical and financial support from, for example, the government or an NGO.

In the reconstruction project described in the following, which was a reaction to the tsunami of December 2004, Duyne Barenstein and Pittet (2014) attempted to follow precisely the principles defined above, unfortunately with little success. In 2006, they carried out a reparability assessment of 1,500 traditional houses in two villages in the Nagapattinam district in Tamil Nadu, India. An NGO intended to replace these houses with contractor-built concrete houses. This assessment proved that most of the houses examined were reparable or undamaged and therefore did not need to be replaced. In addition, they also conducted an analysis of the sustainability of the existing housing typologies with regards to the costs of construction and maintenance, thermal comfort and the ecological impact of the materials used. Their findings showed valid evidence of sustainability, reparability and functionality, beauty and comfort for the existing houses. However, the NGO ignored all of these findings, and as a consequence, 700 intact traditional pre-disaster houses were demolished and instead replaced with concrete houses that were both unsustainable and maladapted to both the cultural and the climatic conditions.

In Tamil Nadu, building a house is a social event in which a number of specialised community members participate. The plan of the house is linked to the horoscope of the oldest woman of the family and is done by a priest. Commonly, the women plan and supervise the house construction process. Further, the design of the house, the size and the materials that are used vary with the socioeconomic status of the house owner, including the person's age, family size or financial resources. The first house of a new married couple, for example, is usually very simple and gets improved over the years. Three roof types are used in the area: thatched roofs, terracotta tile roofs and flat reinforced cement concrete (RCC) roofs. Thatched roofs are relatively inexpensive and provide good thermal comfort. Due to the high maintenance requirements, though, families that can afford it replace the straw or coconut leaves with tiles. Both of these vernacular roof systems work for the local climatic conditions but are considered to be backward, in particular by the government. However, although flat RCC roofs demonstrate wealth and modernity, they also lead to an unbearably hot indoor climate. And, as a consequence, people commonly respond to this by building a thatched roof on top of the flat one, if they can afford to do this. The traditional houses usually have only two or three rooms, comprising one main room, which is mainly used as storage, and a large veranda. This veranda is the most important room, as it is where most activities happen. During the day, people entertain their guests and spend their leisure time in this semi-open area, and at night, the veranda is used as a sleeping area.

In the abovementioned reconstruction project, the NGO followed the government's rules and built all houses with flat RCC roofs. They also did not consider building a veranda, which as described before, has climatic and sociocultural importance in this area. Neither the choice of materials nor the design of the new houses was made according to the local climatic conditions or to the cultural traditions. A study also showed that the material that NGOs used for housing construction had a huge environmental impact and lay far behind that of traditional houses. As an overall result, the coconut- and straw-thatched houses were considered the most sustainable regarding economic viability, environmental impact and climatic comfort. In synergy to this, the RCC houses that NGOs built represented the least sustainable housing type in terms of expense, climatic comfort and environmental impact. Further, the community members who were usually involved in the planning and construction process did not play a role in reconstruction. Even worse, because the NGOs worked with external contractors and used new technologies beyond the traditional ones, they also excluded the local people from future maintenance work. Another aspect that takes this project ad absurdum is the fact that due to the poor quality of the construction, many newly built houses are even less safe than the former pre-tsunami houses.

Surroundings

During reconstruction projects, the focus often lies solely on the houses, but the surrounding space, as well as the vegetation, may be equally important aspects to consider. This topic will now be discussed with another post-tsunami housing project in Tamil Nadu that Jasmin Naimi-Gasser (2013) analysed, with a special focus on its sociocultural impact (pp. 137–155). In this project, the government announced the participation of the local community. However, the community meetings were solely used to present ready plans and models as well as to ask the people about their needs, expectations and ability to take part in the building process. All of the vegetation and houses on the site, whether damaged or not, were cleared to simplify the construction work. The new contractor-driven settlement differs from the pre-disaster one in design, choice of material, location, layout and surroundings, including vegetation. The environment, which people were used to, transformed completely due to the reconstruction process. Most importantly, they lost their trees.

Trees can be the providers of community space and therefore can play an important role in the social life of a community. For the community living in this project area in Tamil Nadu, trees 'are connected to notions of health, protection, beauty, and sacredness' (Naimi-Gasser, 2013, p. 141). In this particular case, people used to spend most of their time outside their houses in the shade of trees. This is where they maintained their social networks, spent their leisure time, stored their nets and found protection from the heat. The lack of trees had a significant effect on the well-being of the people and led to loneliness, boredom, physical and mental health problems, discomfort, tension, alcohol problems and deep sadness. In this particular project, the seemingly simple act of cutting down trees to construct houses destroyed a community by disregarding their culture. Even worse, instead of the familiar surroundings and buildings, people were offered a borrowed culture with borrowed houses and a borrowed way of life. Naimi-Gasser (2013) claimed that if people were

> given the option of rebuilding their houses themselves, with adequate technical and financial assistance, the villagers could have dealt with housing in a more holistic way, paying attention to the home compound, rather than only the house, and making sure that their precious trees were spared.
>
> (p. 154)

Lessons learned

The projects discussed above point out some important aspects of post-disaster housing reconstruction that are also applicable to a wide range of housing design processes. During reconstruction projects, the money of the lender often also comes with its cultural values and development standards (cf. Kessler, 2014, p. 81). The same applies to everyone involved in the design and construction process that is not part of the affected community. The housing options offered should instead depend on the local context, the resources available, the culture and the capacity to implement the new housing solutions. The houses of a community reflect both their history and their cultural identity. Therefore, 'people should be rehabilitated in the same way as they have always lived' (Naimi-Gasser, 2013, p. 154). For the reasons stated above, it is often not appropriate to introduce new technologies and materials. It should rather be a priority to find out if the existing traditional technologies, materials and housing designs are an option. Sometimes they may simply need improvement. In any case, everyone involved in the process should be sensitive to the needs of the people and to the social, economic and cultural significance of their housing as well as of space, the community's spaces and the local vegetation (cf. Naimi-Gasser, 2013, p. 154). Post-disaster reconstruction provides the possibility of contemplating the environmental impact of various building technology options, materials and designs. This could be used to encourage not only a safer but also a more environmentally sound and sustainable built environment. Given this shift in focus, traditionally built houses are often more appropriate than the houses that NGOs or other agencies build. The confrontation of people with an entirely new settlement as a replacement of their old houses and their familiar environment can especially have a dramatic impact on their livelihoods, as this deprives them of their history and cultural identity (cf. Duyne Barenstein & Pittet, 2013, p. 135).

These are not all new issues; they have been discussed since 1962 and are, as yet, basically unchanged. These 'same mistakes have been repeated, time and again, because recovery and development are addressed without a cultural perspective' (Naimi-Gasser, 2013, p. 139). It is time that lessons are finally learned.

Possible benefits of having architects involved in the process

At this point, it is crucial to ask about the appropriate role for an architect in the context of reconstruction projects. Also, what skills and attitudes do architects need to be of practical value? There are a number of examples in disaster-affected areas where the absence of competent decision-makers and designers has led to inappropriate housing solutions, leading to the assumption that architects or designers can play a significant part within adaptation processes. However, proof also exists that architects fail in responding to the fundamental needs of their clients or beneficiaries when they take on the 'classical roles' of planner-designer-manager or planner-designer. So how can architects be beneficial for reconstruction projects? Foremost, this depends to a great extent on the skills and abilities the architect possesses, which are strongly influenced by his or her architectural education. Because each project is different, no single 'best' approach exists for the architect's role (cf. Davidson et al., 2007, p. 113). Therefore, the role of the architect can only be defined from within the specific context, and it is not possible to define a single role for the architect along with his or her necessary skills. Thus, various studies have identified a number of important skills and abilities that could improve the outcomes of reconstruction projects.

Often, NGOs in charge of reconstruction projects have no experience with either construction in general or reconstruction. In this case, they do need architects to support their work. As Schwitter pointed out, especially in the case of large-scale relocation projects, architects are needed because they have the skills needed to create a master plan (cf. Schwitter, as cited in Tauber, 2014, p. 202). Some other researchers and practitioners take this further and claim that the support that the beneficiaries need and expect falls within an architect's classical scope of work.

As discussed in the section of this chapter entitled Reconstruction Projects, traditional houses are often likely to be appropriate for local conditions. However, due to the rapid change that communities experience, triggered by pressure – for example, by climate change (cf. Mercer, 2010, p. 250) – the traditional construction technologies that have been used for generations might still need to be improved. Climate change is not a new issue, and for centuries, people have been adapting their homes to climatic trends and seasonal changes in extreme weather events. However, these changes are now happening more quickly than ever, and stronger and more frequent extreme events are also taking place (cf. Halsnaes & Laursen, 2009, p. 83). Hence, scientific and indigenous knowledge could be integrated to strengthen the ability of vulnerable communities to adapt their homes to current and expected future climate conditions without losing their traditional construction practices. In this instance, the architect can act as a promoter of, and catalyst for, an exchange of knowledge.

What skills does an architect need?

In the mid-twentieth century, climate change, energy shortage and climate adaptation were not on architects' agendas. However, they were still mindful of the climate and 'designed according to climatic regional parameters long before the mechanical systems that inhabit most buildings were understood to be impacting global climatic conditions' (Barber, 2013, p. 189). The strategies modern architects used were intended to offer comfortable living situations in any climate, from the arctic to the desert by, 'allowing the building to collaborate more effectively with its natural surround' (Barber, 2013, p. 188). Already in the eighteenth century, a number of concerned doctors and industrialists had 'a practical understanding of the environmental performance of buildings and they complained that many architects were only interested in academic matters of style and form' (Berman, 2013, p. 204). Even though this sounds a bit harsh, it can be compared to the situation we have today regarding post-disaster housing. A high proportion of architects are working in social, cultural and climatic contexts that they are not used to. At the same time, this environment is often very vulnerable, which makes it crucial for professionals to design with greater sensitivity. However, within this design task, architects are just playing a role alongside numerous other actors, most importantly, as mentioned before, the people affected or the community members. In this context, some go even further and state that the key task of architects and other specialists does not lie in design or construction as might be assumed but rather in the understanding of the roles and capacities of the numerous actors involved. As a consequence, design or building professionals (architects, designers, urban planners, etc.) are responsible for determining the necessary rules for developing sustainable housing solutions that respect culture, society and the environment (cf. Lizarralde et al., 2014).

Because every context is different for an architect entering a new environment, first he/she should access and learn about the local way of living, the local building culture and other important local aspects. In many cases, there is a lot to learn from the local people, and therefore, each project should be developed together with them (cf. Maini, as cited in Tauber, 2014, p. 182).

The architect's way of thinking is different. When you work in this context, when you engage with villagers, you need to 'de-professionalise'. You need to come down to their level, in order to learn. Very often, they give practical ideas we may not even have thought about. If you do the work the way you think it is to be done, you have already failed.

(Rajasingh, as cited in Tauber, 2014, p. 183)

This not only applies to reconstruction projects but also it holds some truth for various projects built in a wide range of different contexts. Often architects think the solution is coming from their own contexts or from their own countries. One possible reason for this might be that these professionals simply are not trained adequately for unfamiliar environments and changing contexts, where, according to Tauber (2014), 'it is necessary to see other worlds as much as possible from inside and develop solutions "from within"' (p. 220). An architect working in this context has to have a profound knowledge of different construction technologies, site supervision and project management, but atop this, a number of other skills are required. As Tauber (cf. 2014) identified, the skills required of architects include knowledge of the people's language, the presence of a keen sense of how and with whom to interact and the expertise to understand which and how themes are discussed within the group of people with whom the architect is working (p. 213). It is also important to ask the right questions of the right addressee. Therefore, the architect needs to comprehend what types of questions may be relevant to ask. Thus, he/she also needs to have the intuition for how to ask the questions, which means being sensitive and empathetic towards the poorer sections of a society and different user groups. The architect often has to work in cooperation with different teams and therefore should be open to reaching out to other necessary knowledge resources for developing and planning houses that respond to the people's aspirations and are, at the same time, rooted in their culture. This sometimes even means the architect must confess that he or she does not have the right answer at hand and needs to ask for guidance.

Based on the villagers' statements, the ideal skills of 'their architect' can be summarised as follows. He speaks their language, is well acquainted with their (building) culture, interacts intensely (individually) and listens intently, asks questions if he does not know something, and only then develops the project. He cooperates closely with them during *all* the stages of the project ... he shows what the house will look like in the end ... he has the ability to build a good-quality house.

(Tauber, 2014, p. 212)

In the best-case scenario, the architect becomes an 'insider', so he/she understands the needs of the community and can develop the housing project from the inside. Formally trained architects do not possess the majority of the skills mentioned above. According to Davis (2006), this is due to many reasons, including the fact that in current architectural education, these skills are rarely considered to be of importance.

Because every project area is unique, it is important to closely engage with the people to find out their peculiarities (cf. Rajasingh, as cited in Tauber, 2014). In numerous cases, existing traditional technologies have proved to be adequate and may only need to be revised (cf. Wemhöner, as cited in Tauber, 2014). In case local knowledge does not meet the current state of building technologies and traditional methods are no longer sufficient, it might be necessary to inform the community members about new solutions.

Consequences for architectural education

As a consequence, a paradigm shift is needed in architectural education that emphasises the attitude that architects are neither central nor the 'expert' in a building process (cf. Tauber, 2014, p. 219). First of all, architecture schools should teach sensitivity towards local building cultures, cultural diversities and traditional construction technologies. Studying traditional building codes and technologies is nothing new and has been done by various architects to find inspirations regarding design tasks and environmental issues. For example, in the 1960s Bernard Rudofsky examined vernacular constructions and traditional building methods with the intent of designing for a more liveable world (cf. Bone, 2013, p. 12). An almost endless number of authors address these aspects along with aspects such as traditional architecture and the history of housing and settlements (Goad, 2000; Hyde, 2000; Konya, 1980; Olgyay, 1963; Oliver, 1978; 2003). These pose examples that should be introduced to architecture schools so that they can be passed on to the next generation of students.

Regarding reconstruction projects, students need to be introduced to 'the political and economic dimensions of post-disaster contexts and these dynamics at a local, national and international level' (Tauber, 2014, p. 219). Furthermore, they should explore development paradigms and the different approaches used in post-disaster reconstruction.

In any case, it is important that architecture students learn to respectfully meet other disciplines and to understand both their methods and their requirements. This is true for all participants of a planning process, including builders, masons or artisans, but it is especially crucial regarding the clients or the community for whom they subsequently work. 'Education should build confidence in developing projects together with many different actors out of a given context rather than imposing one's own will onto a situation' (Tauber, 2014, p. 219).

One step towards reaching this sensitivity is to expose architecture students to real places outside of their studios and to get them to talk to people in the surrounding environment as well as experienced professionals. Furthermore, it is crucial to teach scientific analysis methods to enable them to determine and assess the respective contexts with which they may be confronted.

Conclusion

People working in the context of post-disaster reconstruction claim that a huge need exists for architects, while at the same time, they are constantly confronted with the problem that the qualifications for architects are not adequate (cf. Saunders, as cited in Tauber, 2014, p. 216). As stated above, architects need to develop sensitivity towards people's needs and expectations stemming from their cultural and social backgrounds. This is a condition that is not only true for reconstruction projects but also for any project in which an architect is involved that lies outside of his/her very personal context. It can be argued that this is the case with the majority of projects in which an architect will be involved throughout his/her career. Using reconstruction projects as examples in this chapter was a way of opening up the discussion about the skills and abilities architects need in order to be able to work in changing environments. It also identifies how many of these attributes are not taught in current architectural education. So how is an architect defined? What skills does he/she need, and what is the destination of an architect? As a start, all the lessons learned, including in reconstruction projects at the community level, could be shared and used to develop some standards or a raw concept for teaching. In any case, it has become clear that the knowledge and expertise of the communities architects design for are extremely relevant. As Wemhöfer (as cited in Tauber, 2014, p. 203) stated, 'We architects are outsiders', and this applies to all projects regardless of where they are situated and for whom they are designed. Each context is different in terms of social, cultural, climatic, etc., terms. This is exactly what an architect has to be prepared for, and for which an architect has to be equipped. Who else should prepare him/her if not an architecture school?

References

Barber, D. A. (2013). Lessons from lessons from modernism. In K. Bone, S. Hillyer & S. Joh (eds), *Lessons from modernism* (pp. 188–195). New York: The Monacelli Press.

Berman, A. (2013). The search for a healthy living environment and the roots of modernism. In K. Bone, S. Hillyer & S. Joh (eds), *Lessons from modernism* (pp. 201–206). New York: The Monacelli Press.

Bone, K. (2013). Lessons from modernism. In K. Bone, S. Hillyer & S. Joh (eds), *Lessons from modernism* (pp. 11–16). New York: The Monacelli Press.

Bone, K., Hillyer, S. & Joh, S. (eds). (2013). *Lessons from modernism. Environmental design strategies in architecture 1925–1970.* New York: The Monacelli Press.

Davidson, C., Johnson, C., Lizarralde, G., Dikmen, N. & Sliwinski, A. (2007). Truths and myths about community participation in post-disaster housing projects. *Habitat International, 31*(1), 100–115.

Davis, H. (2006). Architectural education and vernacular building. In L. Asquith & M. Vellinga (eds), *Vernacular architecture in the twenty-first century. Theory, education and practice* (pp. 231–244). London: Taylor and Francis.

Dodman, D. & Mitlin, D. (2013). Challenges for community-based adaptation. Discovering the potential for transformation. *Journal of International Development, 25*(5), 640–659. doi: 10.1002/jid.1772.

Duyne Barenstein, J. (2014). Who governs reconstruction? Changes and continuity in policies, practices and outcomes. In G. Lizarralde, C. Johnson & C. Davidson (eds), *Rebuilding after disasters. From emergency to sustainability* (pp. 149–176). Abingdon: Routledge.

Duyne Barenstein, J. & Leemann, E. (2013). *Post-disaster reconstruction and change. Communities' perspectives*. Boca Raton, FL: Taylor & Francis Group.

Duyne Barenstein, J. & Pittet, D. (2013). A social and environmental assessment of pre- and post-tsunami housing and building processes. In J. Duyne Barenstein & E. Leemann (eds), *Post-disaster reconstruction and change. Communities' perspectives* (pp. 119–136). Boca Raton, FL: Taylor & Francis Group.

Frampton, K. (1980). *Modern architecture: A critical history*. London: Thames and Hudson.

Goad, P. (2000). *Troppo architects*. Sydney: Pesaro Publishing.

Gropius, W. (1954). *Scope of total architecture*. Abingdon: Taylor and Francis.

Halsnaes, K. & Laursen, N. (2009). Climate change vulnerability. A new threat to poverty alleviation in developing countries. In S. Davoudi, J. Crawford & A. Mehmood (eds), *Planning for climate change. Strategies for mitigation and adaptation for spatial planners* (pp. 83–93). London: Earthscan.

Hyde, R. (2000). *Climate responsive design. A study of buildings in moderate and hot humid climates*. London: E&FN Spon.

Jha, A. K., Duyne Barenstein, J., Phelps, P. M., Pittet, D. & Sena, S. (2010). *Safer homes, stronger communities. A handbook for reconstruction after natural disasters*. Washington DC: The International Bank for Reconstruction and Development/The World Bank.

Kessler, E. (2014). The resilience of self-build housing to natural hazards. In J. Bredenoord, P. Van Lindert & P. Smets (eds), *Affordable housing in the urban global South. Seeking sustainable solutions* (pp. 73–86). London: Routledge Taylor & Francis Group.

Konya, A. (1980). *Design primer for hot climates*. London: The Architectural Press.

Le Corbusier, X. (1923). *Vers une architecture*. Paris: Les Editions G. Crès et C.

Lizarralde, G., Johnson, C. & Davidson, C. (eds). (2014). *Rebuilding after disasters. From emergency to sustainability*. Abingdon: Routledge.

Mercer, J. (2010). Policy arena. Disaster risk reduction or climate change adaptation: Are we reinventing the wheel? *Journal of International Development, 22*(2), 247–264. doi: 10.1002/jid.1677.

Naimi-Gasser, J. (2013). The remembered trees. Contractor-driven reconstruction and its consequences on communities' well-being in coastal Tamil Nadu. In J. Duyne Barenstein & E. Leemann (eds), *Post-disaster reconstruction and change. Communities' perspectives* (pp. 137–155). Boca Raton: Taylor & Francis Group.

Olgyay, V. (1963). *Design with climate. Bioclimatic approach to architectural regionalism.* Princeton, NJ: Princeton University Press.

Oliver, P. (1978). *Shelter in Africa*. London: Barrie & Jenkins.

Oliver, P. (2003). *Dwellings: The vernacular house worldwide*. London: Phaidon Press.

Rifkind, D. (2013). Reviewing modernism through the lens of sustainability. In K. Bone, S. Hillyer & S. Joh (eds), *Lessons of modernism* (pp. 17–27). New York: The Monacelli Press.

Stein, C. (2013). Modern legacy/sustainable culture. In K. Bone, S. Hillyer & S. Joh (eds), *Lessons of modernism* (pp. 196–200). New York: The Monacelli Press.

Tauber, G. (2014). *Architects and post-disaster housing. A comparative study in South India.* Bielefeld: Transcript Verlag.

Weiland, S. (2008). Der Speer-Faktor. Retrieved from www.spiegel.de/kultur/ gesellschaft/architektur-der-speer-faktor-a-524081.html

Index

Page numbers in *italics* denote tables, those in **bold** denote figures.

sustainable development *continued*
and design education 157, 159, 163,
167, 168; education for sustainable
development (ESD) 171, 176; and
gender 24; housing 69, 70–1, 84;
modernist agenda 40; pillars 3, 4; and
play 194, 195; research 19, 23, 24; role
of design in 1, 2, 3, 5; and urban
sustainability criteria 70–1; weak
sustainability as 42; *see also* culture
sustainable environment, creating sense
of place for 89–90
Sutton-Smith, Brian 186
Sweden 84n5
systems thinking: as contextual 179; and
ESD 179; and phases of reflective
inquiry 179–80, *181*; transformation
through 178–9

tacit knowledge, design as 25
tailoring practice, mass production 11,
141–54; anthropometric clothing
measurements 152, 153; body shape
144, 149, 150, 151; fit, problems with
as reason for clothing disposal 142–7,
153; grading practices 151, 152, 153;
rates of clothing disposal 141; ready-
to-wear clothing 148, 151, 152, 153;
recycling of clothing 143, 144; sizing
systems 147–51; standard sizes 148;
sustainable clothing design 144; *see also*
body shape and clothing design;
clothing disposal; clothing sizing
tables; vernacular fashion
Tamil Nadu, house building 204, 205,
206
Tauber, Gertrude 199, 200, 201, 202,
209, 211
Taussig, M. 91
Taylor, E. B. 109
technology, persuasive 188–9
terrorism 38
Thackara, J. 51
Thanksgiving 135
Third World 22
Thorpe, A. 137–8
Throsby, D. 46
Tilley, C. Y. 91
Timmer, V. 45
Tomkins, C. 107
toys, transmedia *see* transmedia toys
Toy Story 118–19, **121**
Transition Town 47
transmedia intertextuality 119

transmedia storytelling (TS) 117, 118–24
transmedia toys 117–28; concept 118;
enjoyment 123–6; games as element of
121–2; play, quality of 123–4; pleasure
and enjoyment 124–6; research
method 118; transmedia toy systems
119–20, **121**
Trondheim, Norway 78, 84n2
Tronstad, Ragnhild 12, 185

Uncertainty Avoidance Index (UAI)
112, 113
UN Decade on Education for
Sustainable Development 172
UNESCO (United Nations Educational,
Scientific and Cultural Organization)
157, 160, 171, 176
United Kingdom 93–4, 141
United Nations Conference on
Sustainable Development, Rio de
Janeiro (Rio+20) 3, 71
United Nations Division for Sustainable
Development 3
United Nations Educational, Scientific
and Cultural Organization *see*
UNESCO (United Nations
Educational, Scientific and Cultural
Organization)
United Nations Human Settlements
Program 71
United Nations World Commission on
Environment and Development 3
United States 73, 113
unselfconscious cultures 129
UN World Commission on Culture and
Development (1995) 39, 69
urban development projects 23–4
urbanisation 20
urban sustainability criteria, and
sustainable development 70–1
usability, effect of national culture on
109

Van de Velde, Henry 55
vernacular architecture 129
vernacular design 129
vernacular fashion 129–40; iñupiaq
garments 129, 130–1, **132**, 133–4;
novelty 136–8; parts of garments,
changing 137–8; sewing season
(clothes-making festival) 134–5; *see
also* Iñupiaq (Eskimo of North Alaska),
garments of
vernacular houses 203

Taylor & Francis eBooks

Helping you to choose the right eBooks for your Library

Add Routledge titles to your library's digital collection today. Taylor and Francis ebooks contains over 50,000 titles in the Humanities, Social Sciences, Behavioural Sciences, Built Environment and Law.

Choose from a range of subject packages or create your own!

Benefits for you

» Free MARC records
» COUNTER-compliant usage statistics
» Flexible purchase and pricing options
» All titles DRM-free.

REQUEST YOUR **FREE** INSTITUTIONAL TRIAL TODAY

Free Trials Available
We offer free trials to qualifying academic, corporate and government customers.

Benefits for your user

» Off-site, anytime access via Athens or referring URL
» Print or copy pages or chapters
» Full content search
» Bookmark, highlight and annotate text
» Access to thousands of pages of quality research at the click of a button.

eCollections – Choose from over 30 subject eCollections, including:

Archaeology	Language Learning
Architecture	Law
Asian Studies	Literature
Business & Management	Media & Communication
Classical Studies	Middle East Studies
Construction	Music
Creative & Media Arts	Philosophy
Criminology & Criminal Justice	Planning
Economics	Politics
Education	Psychology & Mental Health
Energy	Religion
Engineering	Security
English Language & Linguistics	Social Work
Environment & Sustainability	Sociology
Geography	Sport
Health Studies	Theatre & Performance
History	Tourism, Hospitality & Events

For more information, pricing enquiries or to order a free trial, please contact your local sales team: www.tandfebooks.com/page/sales

 Routledge
Taylor & Francis Group

The home of
Routledge books

www.tandfebooks.com

For Product Safety Concerns and Information please contact our EU
representative GPSR@taylorandfrancis.com
Taylor & Francis Verlag GmbH, Kaufingerstraße 24, 80331 München, Germany